Romans

ROMANS

R. C. Sproul

Christian Focus Publications

© 1994 R. C. Sproul
ISBN1-85792-077-5

Published by
Christian Focus Publications Ltd
Geanies House, Fearn, Ross-shire,
IV20 1TW, Scotland, Great Britain.

Printed by Guernsey Press Company Ltd.,

Cover design by Donna Macleod

Contents

Preface

As a young seminary student I looked forward to one of my first courses, entitled 'Introduction to the New Testament'.

What stands out in my memory is the morning we were to begin our study of the book of Romans. The professor stood before the class and said, 'Gentlemen, most theologians get excited about the Epistle to the Romans, but I don't. I will say this about the book, that if the apostle Paul wrote any of the books that are attributed to him, he certainly wrote Romans. This was Paul's attempt at a brief, systematic theology. Now, on to Galatians.'

I sat there in the classroom in stunned disbelief. I couldn't take in the fact of a New Testament professor dismissing the book of Romans in about two minutes flat! Thankfully, most theologians do indeed get excited about the book of Romans, and I certainly do. For in Romans we have the nearest thing to a systematic theology to be found anywhere in the New Testament. Undoubtedly, Romans is the apostle Paul's most comprehensive study of doctrine.

No book in history has been so instrumental in changing lives as the Bible. We sometimes forget, however, that the Bible is really a library rather than a single book, being in fact a compilation of sixty-six books, each book making its own special contribution to the sum total of God's written revelation. Having said that, I really do believe that if there is any one individual book, out of the sixty-six, which God has used to change lives more than any other, it is the book of Romans.

Romans has had a profound impact on several of the great saints of church history. Think of Saint Augustine, who, as a young man living in the fourth century, had distinguished himself by his brilliant mind and his academic ability. He was not, however, persuaded of the truth of Christianity. His mother, Monica, was a devout believer and prayed for the conversion of her son every day, but she saw no evidence of her prayers being answered. She would visit Ambrose, the Bishop of Milan, and speak to him of her agony over her wayward son. In comforting her, Ambrose would say that perhaps some day God would convert Augustine and make use of his gifts for his own kingdom. So Monica persevered in prayer.

In the meantime, Augustine, living an immoral and licentious life, had given himself to the exposition of pagan philosophy. But one day, when he was particularly depressed and downcast, he strolled through a garden where some little children were playing. They were playing a child's game which had a Latin refrain, 'Tolla lege, tolla lege, tolla lege' which means, 'Pick up and read, pick up and read, pick up and read'. As Augustine, preoccupied with his own inner thoughts, ambled through the garden, this refrain penetrated his reverie and his eyes fell upon a copy of the New Testament. Picking it up and opening it at random, he read the portion of Romans in which Paul wrote: '... **not in orgies and drunkenness, not in sexual immorality and debauchery, not in dissension and jealousy. Rather, clothe yourselves with the Lord Jesus Christ, and do not think about how to gratify the desires of the sinful nature.**' Augustine was seized with a sense of conviction for his sin, as the Holy Spirit used these words from Romans to pierce his heart. This was the conversion experience of Augustine, who became what many regard as the greatest saint in the first thousand years of the Christian church.

Over one thousand years later we discover another young man who was very tormented in his soul. He had no peace concerning his life or his faith, and he was determined to find the truth about religion. He had become a monk in the first place, not out of a sense of devotion to God, but out of a fear of divine punishment. The story goes that the young man, the son of a German coalminer, was riding on horseback one afternoon when an electrical storm came up and a bolt of lightning struck so close to where he was riding that it knocked him from his horse. As he hit the ground, in his utter terror, he cried to God, 'Save me, and I will become a monk.' And he kept his promise by joining a monastery.

Even there, as he sought to find peace with God, young Martin Luther was besieged by doubts and filled with despair. Luther describes his days in the monastery as a time when he went through rigorous acts of penance, self-sacrifice and self-flagellation, 'If you had asked me, did I love God, I would say, Love God? Sometimes I hated him. I saw Christ as a terrifying judge, who had the sword of judgement above my head, and I had no peace.' A study in depth of the life of this tormented young monk provides a most fascinating portrait.

Luther developed great gifts as a scholar and, having become a Doctor of Holy Scripture, he went to Wittenberg University where he was appointed Professor and began to lecture in biblical studies. On one occasion he was preparing a series of lectures on the book of Romans. As he pored over manuscripts and read commentaries in his private cell in the monastery, he came to chapter 1:17: **For in the gospel a righteousness from God is revealed, a righteousness that is by faith from first to last, just as it is written: 'The righteous will live by faith.'**

He later recorded the effects of Paul's words: 'When I read those words, suddenly it dawned on me that the righteousness of God, of which Paul was speaking, was not that righteousness by which God himself is righteous, that righteousness that makes God so excellent and virtuous and transcendent in his holiness that makes me terrified of him, but rather Paul is expounding another theme, not only the righteousness of God by which God himself is righteous but that righteousness that God makes available to us who are not righteous; that righteousness of God that is granted to us as a gift in faith; that righteousness that is given to us through the righteousness of Christ, an alien righteousness, a foreign righteousness, that is granted to us for our own possession.' Luther went on, 'When I understood that, and when the concept of justification by faith alone burst through into my mind, suddenly it was like the doors of paradise swung open and I walked through.'

We can think too of a young Anglican clergyman in England during the 18th century who, though he had been trained in the seminary and had been ordained by the church, was cold of heart and not even a believer. One day he was standing in a crowd of people listening to a fervent preacher in Aldersgate, London. Although he wasn't really all that interested in the sermon, somehow he seemed drawn by the words he was hearing in a sermon taken from the book of Romans. And the young man, John Wesley, said, 'Suddenly, my heart was strangely warmed.' As the word of God from the book of Romans fell upon John Wesley, he was converted and later became one of the most forcible, religious reformers the world has ever known.

The list of those whose lives have been changed through Paul's letter to the Romans goes on down into our own day and includes a young Swiss theologian who was steeped in liberal theology and had been carried away by the unbelief and the anti-supernaturalism of 19th century theology. This young theologian wrote a book on the letter to the Romans, and called the church back to a Bible-centred theology. It was said by Karl Adam, the Roman Catholic theologian and historian, that in 1918 when Karl Barth's commentary on Romans was published it fell like a bombshell on the playground of the theologians, as the church was reawakened once more to the centrality of the sovereignty of God.

I too have a sense of identification with Augustine, Luther, Wesley and Barth because no book has had such a powerful impact on my life as the book of Romans.

Summary of Romans

Paul begins his letter to the Romans as he begins most of his epistles with the identification of his own person and of his calling as an apostle. In the first chapter the apostle discusses at length the concept of general revelation. This is the background to the announcement of the gospel, the fact that all men, everywhere, have a knowledge of God which is revealed to them in nature. What this knowledge does is to render every human being inexcusable before the judgment seat of God. However, all men distort and corrupt this revelation that God gives of himself, and exchange the truth of God for a lie, giving themselves over to idolatry.

In the second chapter, Paul goes on to indicate that not only do pagans and Gentiles distort the general revelation of God, but that the Jews who had the privilege of possessing the very oracles of God, the Scriptures, have gone astray. Paul summarises and says there is no partiality with God, for there will be tribulation and distress for every soul of man who does evil, the Jew first and also the Greek. Important also to the second chapter of Romans is Paul's declaration that not only is God revealed externally through nature, but also there is an inward knowledge of God that we all have, insofar as God has written his law upon the heart of every human being.

In the third chapter of Romans, Paul pulls it together and shows that both Jew and Gentile are under the judgment of God. It is here he gives his statement that there is none righteous, no not one. And then comes the conclusion that all have sinned and fallen short of the glory of God. The aim of the first three chapters is to bring every human being before the tribunal of God and show that every human being, if judged by his works, would fall short of what God requires. Therefore, the only hope that anybody has for salvation is to be justified by faith. And Paul introduces that concept at the end of Romans 3, where he says in verse 28: 'for we maintain that a man is justified by faith apart from observing the law'.

Chapter 4 contains an extended illustration of the principle of

13

justification by faith, in which Paul points to the Old Testament patriarch, Abraham, and shows that Abraham was justified by faith. He indicates that Abraham was justified before he ever did any works. He was justified, according to Genesis 15, when he believed the promise that God made to him, and it was counted to him as righteousness.

In chapter 5, Paul spells out for us in brief, the great fruits of justification. He points out that being justified by faith we have peace with God, we have access to God and we have a hope of the glory of God which makes it possible for us to endure tribulations and trials. And then, in referring to the free gift of Christ and his willingness to die for us while we were still sinners, he grounds our need for a redeemer in the fall of Adam. He makes a comparison between Adam and Christ and points out that death entered the world through Adam, but that life comes through Christ.

In chapter 6, Paul moves from justification to sanctification. Sanctification calls believers to a new kind of living, for the old man is to be put to death and the new man is to be fed, nurtured and brought into conformity to Jesus Christ. The fact that our salvation is gratuitous, based upon the mercy of God and the merit of Christ alone, does not give us a licence for sin.

Chapter 7 outlines the continued struggle that a Christian has as he seeks to grow in grace. Paul speaks of his own struggle between those things that he didn't want to do yet does, and the things that he wants to do that he leaves undone. He explains that the Christian still struggles with sin even though he has been freed from the curse and the bondage to the law. He is to live in the power of Christ, who sets us free from the bondage of our fallen nature.

In chapter 8, Paul continues his discussion of the warfare that goes on in the Christian life between the old nature and the new nature that has been made alive through Christ. He calls attention to the fact that the outcome of this warfare between the Spirit and the flesh is not in doubt in the life of a true Christian. For God has promised the final victory. Even the whole creation looks forward to the consummation of God's plan of salvation. Until then, the Holy Spirit is within believers helping them with their weaknesses, with their prayer life, searching their hearts, teaching them the good will of God.

In the latter part of Romans 8, Paul introduces the grand concept of the gracious election of God. He explains that God is for his people from before the beginning of time, going back to God's eternal decrees. No one can undo the election that God has brought to pass in the life of the believer. The Christian's assurance of perseverance is based on the promise of the God who has made their salvation gracious from beginning to end.

In chapters 9-11, Paul speaks about his burden for the Jews, his kinsmen according to the flesh. He shows how today in his plan of salvation, God has retained for himself a portion of the Jewish people, through his sovereign election. Paul makes the analogy in chapter 9 between Jacob and Esau, in which Jacob receives the blessing of election. Jacob is chosen and Esau is passed over. Paul explains that there is no injustice in God in this redemptive plan, and reminds his readers that God always reserves the right to have mercy upon whom he will have mercy.

In chapter 10, although he continues the expression of his burden and desire for the salvation of his race, he refers to the call to preach the gospel, and points out that anyone who believes in Christ will be saved. But no one can believe who has not heard, and no one can hear without a preacher, and he talks about how beautiful it is to have those committed to the cause of evangelism. Chapter 10 describes the way in which God brings his elect people to himself; the means of salvation comes through the preaching of the gospel.

Then in chapter 11, he raises the difficult question of the future status of the Jewish people. His comments have resulted in much controversy concerning the question, Does God have more in store for Israel? Paul describes the Gentiles as wild olive branches that are grafted onto the root and the tree which is Israel. His basic thesis is that if God was pleased to be merciful to the Gentiles, who are the wild olive branches, how much more merciful will he be to the original tree. So there will be a time when the deliverance of Israel will take place, with great blessing to the rest of the world. In the meantime

God will continue, for Abraham's sake, to work in the lives of people who are descendants of Abraham. Paul ends chapter 11 with a magnificent doxology.

So the first eleven chapters give an exposition of the way of salvation, the doctrines of grace, beginning with an exposition of our radical sinfulness and corruption which make it impossible for a man to justify himself through his own efforts. Then Paul spells out the doctrine of justification by faith alone, through Christ who alone has the ability and the merit necessary to justify those who are unjust. From justification, Paul moves to sanctification, the process of our working out salvation, of growing in grace, of putting to death the old man, and strengthening the inward man within us. He explains the fruit of justification that is seen in the new relationship of adoption as sons into the family of God, with its attendant blessings. Finally, Paul gives an exposition of God's sovereign election and of his work in history, using the Jewish nation, and reaching out to the Gentiles, and the promise for future actions with the Jewish people.

In chapter 12, there is a decided shift from theological exposition to practical application, in which Paul tells his readers that the appropriate response to so great a salvation is to present themselves as living sacrifices to God. They are to be transformed people, and that transformation comes through renewed minds.

Then, Paul speaks about the diversity that is found within the body of Christ. It is one body with many members and each one is called to a different service, each has different gifts according to the grace given to him. Each person is to exercise that gift which God has given him, and in exercising their individual gifts, Christians are called to live together in love and cheerfulness. They are to be devoted to one another. Paul gives us a series of virtues that believers are to practice: diligence, fervency in spirit, contributing to the needs of the saints, hospitality, rejoicing with those who rejoice and weeping with those who weep. He gives his indictment against pride and haughtiness and shows how destructive those characteristics are. Lastly, he forbids Christians from seeking vengeance.

In chapter 13, Paul spells out the responsibilities of Christians to obey the civil magistrates. He gives us the most thorough statements about his view of the existence of governments and of the state, and shows that government has been established by God. Government is a means of grace to keep unbridled spirits in check, to restrain evil, and Christians ought to keep a good conscience with respect to government, doing their duty as it is understood under God. And then he spells out what love means in the life of the Christian.

In chapter 14, Paul explains Christian liberty and the responsibility that goes with it. Though we have been freed from moralistic rules that are not a part of the real law of God, we are to exercise that freedom with a spirit of charity and consideration for weaker brothers who may not have the same understanding of the things of God that the more mature Christian does.

In chapter 15, he continues along these lines, explaining to us that we are to bear the weaknesses of those who differ from us, and that we are to be people who are people of peace, people of patience and people of hope. Towards the end of chapter 15 Paul reveals his intention to come personally to visit his friends in Rome and of his desire to go on to Spain.

Finally, in the last chapter, there is a long list of greetings and commendations to men and women who had served with Paul in his missionary journeys and in his ministries in the local churches, which give an insight into Paul as a person, a pastor, and a friend.

COMMENTARY

1
INTRODUCTION AND GREETINGS
(1:1-16)

Paul begins very briefly and succinctly with these words: **Paul, a servant of Christ Jesus, called to be an apostle and set apart for the gospel of God.**

PAUL, A SERVANT OF CHRIST JESUS (verse 1)

In seminary, I saw a manuscript written by Marcus Barth, the son of Karl Barth, of some 168 pages on these words, *Paul, a servant of Jesus Christ...*

In the Greek text, the word that the apostle uses is *doulos* which is not properly translated 'servant'. A servant in the ancient world was a hired employee, a person who could come and go at will, who could resign from one job and seek employment elsewhere if so inclined. But a *doulos* was a slave owned by a *kyrios*, a master or a lord. Frequently in the New Testament this type of imagery is used to portray the relationship between Christ and his people: 'You are not your own; you were bought at a price.' Christians are those who belong to Christ. He is our Lord, he is our *kyrios*, he is our Master.

Paul will explain in the book of Romans that man, out of Christ, is in bondage to sin and a slave to his own evil impulses, inclinations and desires. This is man's natural condition in the fallen state. Yet Paul wrote elsewhere that where the Spirit of the Lord is, where the Spirit of the *kyrios* is, where the Spirit of the Master is, there is liberty (2 Cor. 3:17). How are these truths to be reconciled?

Paul had learned that man is only free when he becomes a slave to Christ. Outwith Christ, he is a slave to sin; but when enslaved to Christ, he knows the royal liberation that only Christ can bring. Paul, in citing his own credentials, regards as his highest virtue that he is a slave of Jesus Christ.

CALLED TO BE AN APOSTLE (verse 1)

Paul, after identifying himself as a slave of Jesus Christ, writes, *called to be an apostle*. The idea of 'calling' and the verb 'to call' is used in many different ways in the Bible, just as we use it in various ways in our own vocabulary today. For example, the verb 'to call' can refer simply to someone shouting. There are, of course, a number of more weighty and important meanings of the verb 'to call' in the New Testament, three in particular.

First, there is God's call to sinners to repent. There is a sense in which this call of God is contained in the gospel itself, for in the gospel God calls men to repentance. This understanding of 'call' suggests a divine command, for their response to which men will be held accountable by God. When the gospel is proclaimed a call goes out that all men, everywhere, should repent and come to Christ.

There is, however, a degree of confusion on this matter in the Christian church today. Evangelists regularly conclude an address by calling for a response from the audience, and this call to commitment is often described as an invitation. But the idea of an invitation carries with it the moral right to accept the invitation or to reject it. If someone invites me to do something, it is not the same as being commanded to do it.

Such an invitation is emphatically not the call of the gospel. God does not *invite* people to repent, he *commands* them (Acts 17:30). This use of the word 'invitation' has always puzzled me. Perhaps it is used in order to soften the blow of the gospel to modern man, to assuage some of the hostility engendered when people are told that they are sinners in need of repentance, that they are morally obliged to change their lives and commit themselves to Christ.

This 'external' call, where God commands people to come to Christ in faith and repentance, is crucial to our understanding of the New Testament. In fact, the Greek word for 'church' in the New Testament is *ecclesia*, which means 'called out'. The church, then, is literally, 'those who are called out': those who are called out from the world to join the kingdom of God. To be a member of the church is to have responded to this external call of the gospel.

Secondly, there is in the New Testament an even more dramatic sense of the 'call' of God. This is termed the 'internal' or 'effectual' call of God. We even have a doctrine in theology called the doctrine of effectual calling. What is meant by the effectual call of God is that, when he calls, he calls sovereignly and effectively by an inward call which goes beyond the ears into the soul and into the heart. What we are speaking about is regeneration. Only God can do that and he does so by the power of his Spirit through the Word.

Thirdly, there is yet another way in which the Bible speaks of the call of God, a call illustrated by the next phrase: *set apart for the gospel of God*. This is what we call 'vocation', a concept which was popular when the Christian Faith had more influence in forming the outlook of our culture. It is a realisation that every human life is to be lived under the authority of God. This means that the career I pursue, the job I take, is to be in conformity with the will of God. In other words, my life is to be dedicated to God whether I am a minister, a farmer, a carpenter or a physician. Each one of us has a 'vocation', a calling from God that we are to carry out to his glory and for the benefit of his kingdom.

In the Bible there were certain specific callings which carried particular authority. These were prophets and apostles, who were of special importance for the people of God. It was really the same office - prophet in the Old Testament and apostle in the New Testament.

An apostle means literally 'one who is sent', someone who is commissioned with the authority of the one who sent him. Paul's claim that he was called to be an apostle was a dramatic and radical announcement, because if you read the book of Acts you will discover that there were three stipulations necessary to qualify for the apostolic office. First, the person had to be a disciple of Jesus during his earthly ministry; secondly, he had to be an eye-witness of Jesus' resurrection; and thirdly, he had to have his call from Christ himself.

One of the early controversies in the church arose when Paul became an apostle. Paul was not a disciple of Jesus during his earthly ministry, indeed he did not even know Jesus. Paul didn't encounter Jesus at the resurrection, but only after he had ascended into heaven.

So how could Paul be an apostle? Three times in the book of Acts, Paul bears witness to the call he received from Jesus. The risen Christ appeared to Paul and called him to be an apostle. By far the most important credential of an apostle was to have an immediate and direct call, which Paul clearly had on the road to Damascus.

What if somebody today claimed the same thing? If somebody came in from the desert and said that he had just seen Jesus who had called him to be an apostle, what would we say? If such a person started writing books and wanted to have them added to the New Testament, what would be our response? Couldn't a person make that kind of claim? Joseph Smith did and started Mormonism.

Notice that even Paul, in his extraordinary situation, could not begin to function as an apostle until he had been endorsed by the rest of the Twelve, whose credentials were not in question. Although it is theoretically possible that God could call a person directly today, it is impossible for that person to have his claim confirmed by other apostles whose apostleship is not in doubt. They have all passed from the historical scene.

That is why the church attributes special importance to apostles. They were agents of revelation, just as the prophets were in the Old Testament. The New Testament records the call of Paul to be an apostle, set apart for the gospel of God. It is that gospel which the apostle sets before us now in this magnificent epistle.

THE GOSPEL OF GOD (1:1c-6)

The whole book of Romans sets before us the gospel of God. I used to think when I read this text that the gospel of God meant a message about God. But that is not what Paul is saying here. By using the genitive of possession, he shows that the gospel belongs to God. Paul is saying that the gospel he is about to describe is not a message which he invented by means of his own brilliant and creative imagination. Rather the message he is setting forth here is the announcement of good news from God himself. It is God's gospel. God owns it, God originated it, God designed it, and now God is simply using the apostle Paul to communicate it to us. In other words, Romans is not at all the result of the theological insight of Paul, one of the most educated Jews in first century Palestine, but it is a message that comes from the mind of God, with the power to change lives.

Paul continues in verse 2 to elaborate on what he means by the 'gospel of God'. He says, parenthetically: **the gospel he promised beforehand through his prophets in the Holy Scriptures.** The first feature of the gospel is that it is not entirely new. That may seem strange because the word 'gospel' (*evangelion*) means literally 'good news' and we think of news as being that which is fresh and up-to-the-minute. But even though there is a new element in the proclamation, the basic theme of the gospel (albeit in a very brief and summary form) was preached by Adam, by Abel, by Abraham, by Moses and by the prophets.

In saying this, Paul relates the New Testament to the Old Testament. The focal point of the gospel is spelled out in verses 3 and 4: **regarding his Son, who as to his human nature was a descendant of David, and who through the Spirit of holiness was declared with power to be the Son of God, by his resurrection from the dead: Jesus Christ our Lord.** This gospel concerns Jesus who is called the 'Son of God', the 'Christ' and 'Lord'.

When we read through the New Testament we find that there is an abundance of titles ascribed to Jesus. The most frequent title is 'Christ'. So often is that title linked to the name of Jesus, that many think it is his proper name. But Jesus' name would have been Jesus bar Joseph or Jesus of Nazareth. His title is *Christos* or Christ, meaning literally 'Messiah'. Paul is affirming that in the Old Testament, God, through the prophets, spoke about the coming of the Messiah from the line of David, and that Jesus was this Messiah.

The second most frequently used title for Jesus in the New Testament is the title 'Lord', a title of enormous significance because it is the one ascribed to God in the Old Testament. It is the title *kyrios*, which is the Greek form of the Hebrew *Adonai*, meaning 'the sovereign one', the one who reigns over us. This title, which in Old Testament days was reserved for God, is now ascribed to Jesus. This is the name above every name about which Paul speaks in Philippians, when he says that every tongue will confess Jesus to be 'Lord' (Phil. 2:9-11).

Now Paul draws a strange contrast here. Although Jesus was the son of David, there is obviously a certain sense in which he is not the son of David. According to his human nature, Jesus was a descendant of David. But not only does he come from David, he also comes from God. He is the Son of God. At this point the apostle is declaring something about Jesus that is expounded throughout the New Testament: Jesus is not a mere man. In addition to his humanity which comes from David, Jesus is also declared to be uniquely the Son of God.

Verse 4 says that Jesus is declared to be the Son of God, *with power*, a declaration that God himself makes. Notice, it is not that Christ is declared to be the Son of God *with* power, but that the declaration of his sonship is made in a powerful way. When God declares the unique sonship of Jesus, he does not drop subtle hints here and there or offer esoteric suggestions that only the most brilliant of theologians can figure out. The evidence that God gave to confirm the claim of Jesus to be the Son of God is the resurrection.

The resurrection of Jesus is qualified by the phrase, **through the Spirit of holiness**. Just as Jesus was made of the seed of David according to the flesh, so also he is declared to be the Son of God through the Spirit of holiness. The reference is not to Jesus' human spirit but to the Holy Spirit. It was the Holy Spirit who raised Jesus from the dead when he brought the human flesh of Jesus back to life to bear witness to the trustworthiness of his claim to be the only-begotten Son of God. So the gospel involves Paul's affirmation of both the human nature of Jesus, which comes from the line of David, and the divine nature of Jesus, which comes from God.

In verses 5 and 6 Paul describes the result of preaching the gospel. **Through him and for his name's sake, we received grace and apostleship to call people from among all the Gentiles to the obedience that comes from faith. And you also are among those who are called to belong to Jesus Christ.** The role of an apostle was to lead people from all over the world to obedience to the faith. When

Paul was made an apostle, he was given a specific title: to be the apostle to the Gentiles. Paul was the first great missionary of the early Church.

The book of Acts follows the outline of the great commission, where Jesus instructed his followers to declare his gospel first in Jerusalem, then in Judea, then in Samaria and then to the ends of the earth (Acts 1:8). In thinking about this commission it is helpful to try and conceive of it as a series of concentric circles. In the centre of the circle is the focal point, the starting place of the expansion of the early church, Jerusalem. On the outskirts of Jerusalem we find the province of Judea, north of Judea is Samaria, and then beyond is the whole world of the Gentile nations. Paul, in reminding his readers that he has been commissioned to be an apostle to the nations, goes on to explain why he is so interested in them.

HIS READERS (1:7-8)
To all in Rome who are loved by God and called to be saints: Grace and peace to you from God our Father and from the Lord Jesus Christ (verse 7). Here we have a very typical salutation from the pen of the apostle. He states the destination of his letter, *to all in Rome*, and then in a very warm and personal way, he addresses his readers as *those who are loved by God*. That is a very pregnant, descriptive term because in the first instance and pre-eminently, it is Jesus Christ who is called 'the beloved', the special object of God's affection (Matt. 3:17; 17:5). In God's economy of grace, however, his love does not stop with his only-begotten Son, but pours out to those who are within his family, to those who are the adopted brothers and sisters of Jesus.

He further describes them as *called to be saints*.

There is a dual way in which the word 'saint' functions in Christian history. In Roman Catholic tradition, the term 'saint' refers to special Christians who have done extraordinary deeds of valour, or made extraordinary contributions to the life of the church. A few such people the church has canonised, elevating them to a status of heroic proportions so that they are called 'saints'. But there is a broader sense in which the term 'saint' is used (in fact the customary way in which it is used in the New Testament). It refers to the rank-and-file Christian, to anyone who is truly in Christ, to anyone who has within him the Holy Spirit.

In the New Testament, the word translated as 'saints' is *hagioi* meaning the holy ones. They are not holy in and of themselves; not holy because they have reached an unthinkable level of virtue or righteousness. Rather, they are those who have been made holy by the fact of having been set apart by God and consecrated to him. There is a very close link between the idea of God calling people and God sanctifying people (the word 'sanctify' literally means 'set apart' or 'saintly'). The church is both the *ecclesia* (those called out) and the *hagioi* (the saints).

One of the great designations of the church is the 'communion of saints', a phrase that dates back to *The Apostles' Creed*. Christians experience a mystical communion that is rooted and grounded in Jesus. It means that I am in fellowship with every living Christian in this world, no matter what national background or ethnic heritage, and that I am also in fellowship (in a mystical way) with all the Christians of all time. I belong to the same church as Augustine, Francis, Latimer, Luther, Edwards, Knox, and all of the saints through the ages. Paul was keenly aware of this fellowship when he wrote to those Christians in Rome.

His apostolic salutation *Grace and peace to you* comes from the pen of the apostle again and again (1 Cor. 1:3; Eph. 1:2; 1 Tim. 1:2). There is a sense in which nothing higher could be wished for the saints in the church than that they might know the fullness of the grace of God, and the peace that was the legacy of Christ, the *shalom* of God. This grace and peace is being sent, not merely from the apostle but *from God our Father and from the Lord Jesus Christ*.

WHY PAUL WANTED TO VISIT THE CHURCH IN ROME (1:8-17)

Paul informs his readers how happy he is to have knowledge of the church in Rome. **First, I thank my God through Jesus Christ for all of you, because your faith is being reported all over the world.**

Paul, presumably, had not yet visited the congregation of Christians that was in Rome, but their faith was known to him and he prayed regularly and consistently for them. In verse 9, Paul stresses how important mutual prayer is when he uses language that approximates an oath: **God, whom I serve with my whole heart in preaching the gospel of his Son, is my witness how constantly I remember you in my prayers at all times**.

Paul wants them to know that his relationship to them is not just based upon his authority as an apostle, but is also a pastoral relationship in which he regularly prayed for them.

What else does he pray about? **and I pray that now at last by God's will the way may be opened for me to come to you**. You can feel the heartbeat of the apostle here. He says in effect, 'I long to come to you. I want to meet you face-to-face. I want to be with you personally, in your midst.' That's what the apostle dreamed of, he wanted to go to Rome.

It is somewhat ironic, is it not, that Paul had such a fierce desire to go to Rome? Especially considering that when he arrived in Rome a few years later, he arrived in chains, and tradition has it that he was beheaded there. This city that he had a passionate desire to visit was the city of his death. We don't know exactly when this epistle was written, but the best estimates are somewhere between the years 54 and 56 AD, which means that Paul wrote this epistle nine or ten years before his death as a martyr in the city of Rome in 65 AD.

Why did he long to see them? **That I may impart to you some spiritual gift** (verse 11). Paul had been empowered with the ability to dispense the grace of God in miraculous healing and in all kind of powers and wonders, but he kept it in perspective, realising this was given not for his own benefit, but for the benefit of the whole church. Now he is saying, 'I just long to come to see you so that I can impart some spiritual gift to you.'

For what purpose? **to make you strong**. If any institution in the year 55 AD was tenuous, humanly speaking, it was the small Christian church. Insignificant, impoverished, unstable, living in the shadow of the strength and might of the most powerful government in the world, in the city of Rome, the church needed above all to be more firmly established, to be strengthened. This Christian community was just emerging, in its infancy, with very little strength. Paul intended to give to them spiritual gifts so that they would be firm and steadfast, and not blown to-and-fro with every wind of doctrine.

He adds to his prayer the further request: **that is, that you and I may be mutually encouraged by each other's faith** (verse 12). The apostle Paul was not a tyrant and he was never an isolated prima donna. Although he was an extraordinary theologian there is a very real sense in which the most conspicuous characteristic of his personality was his pastoral heart, and he was keenly aware of his own humanness. Despite his exalted position of authority as the apostle to the Gentiles, he expresses to the rank-and-file people of the church at Rome his longing to visit them in order to benefit from their ministry. That is the way in which the church of Christ is supposed to function, each member of the body being comforted and ministered to by the others.

Paul continues in verses 13-15: **I do not want you to be unaware, brothers, that I planned many times to come to you (but have been prevented from doing so until now) in order that I might have a harvest among you, just as I have had among the other Gentiles. I am bound both to Greeks and non-Greeks, both to the wise and the foolish. That is why I am so eager to preach the gospel also to you who are at Rome.**

Paul informs the Roman Christians that the reason for his failure to visit Rome is not because he did not want to come, but rather because, having made plans to come, he had been prevented. He now wanted to come so that he could have fruit among them, even as among other Gentiles.

Perhaps there was some ill-feeling in that infant congregation in Rome. They had heard of the mighty works of Paul and knew of his travels round the Mediterranean. The reports of his ministry had filtered back to the imperial city and yet this leading apostle of the church had never visited them. Humanly speaking, I am sure some of them were feeling that Paul didn't care. You can almost imagine them saying, 'He lets us work and minister here in the shadow of the Roman senate, while he is safely running round Asia Minor.' They didn't know of all the difficulties that Paul was getting into. But that's human nature, isn't it? Paul anticipates these things because he understands human nature, and so he reassures the people in the Roman congregation.

In verse 14 he makes this strong statement: **I am bound both to Greeks and non-Greeks, both to the wise and the foolish.**

What a strange statement to make! I am bound or I am a debtor. What does he owe the Greeks? What does Paul owe the non-Greeks? What does he owe to the wise? What does he owe to the foolish? Surely the obligation was on their side, to show honour and obedience to Paul? Surely they should be rushing across the plains of Asia Minor to sign up for courses in the school of the apostle Paul.

Paul understood that he was an apostle simply by the grace of God and that it was an unspeakable privilege for him to have that office. He realised that once Christ had commissioned him to carry the gospel throughout the world, to the Greeks, to the non-Greeks, to the wise, to the foolish, to the lettered and the unlettered, to the great and the small, he was under obligation to fulfil his calling. Love of Christ constrained him to carry out his commission.

Obviously his debt was to Christ, but since Christ assigned him to the Greeks and the non-Greeks, Paul now owes it to those people to bring them the gospel, which is why he writes: **That is why I am so eager to preach the gospel also to you who are at Rome.** Paul was consumed with his passion to preach the gospel. How do we explain this? Why was preaching the gospel not a laborious task, one that scared him because of all the criticism and flak that it might bring his way, but rather a delight?

Paul understood what it is like for a person to live in a culture where the gospel is despised. Like all human beings, he wanted to be loved and accepted by his peers. Nobody wants to be laughed at; nobody wants to be rejected or be an outcast. But he was willing for all of that to happen, because the gospel was so valuable and so important. Why? **Because it is the power of God for the salvation** of everyone who believes: **first for the Jew, then for the Gentile.**

I am not ashamed, says the apostle, because I do not have a message that is simply information. I have a message that is accompanied by the power of almighty God. I am not ashamed to preach because it is by preaching that God has chosen to save the world. It is a method which God has empowered from on high, and it contains within itself the power of God. For what? For salvation.

2
ALL MEN ARE SINNERS
(1:17-3:20)

The seventeenth verse of chapter 1 states the theme of the entire letter: **For in the gospel a righteousness from God is revealed, a righteousness that is by faith from first to last, just as it is written: "The righteous will live by faith."** It is the revelation of the righteousness of God, a righteousness that enables sinners to stand under the scrutiny and under the judgment of God. Paul is quoting an Old Testament statement from the book of the minor prophet, Habakkuk (2:4). Three times the New Testament quotes that Old Testament passage. Here in the book of Romans, once in Galatians 3:11, and once in Hebrews 10:38.

PAGANS ARE GUILTY (1:18-32)
How do we receive righteousness by faith, rather than by meritorious works? Paul expands on this theme, beginning in verse 18: **The wrath of God is being revealed from heaven against all the godlessness and wickedness of men who suppress the truth by their wickedness.** This verse seems 'abrupt' because Paul has just spoken of the gospel which is the good news. Why then does he suddenly shift his attention away from the good news to an announcement of the revelation of the wrath of God? Because until we understand the prior revelation of the wrath of God, we will never get excited about the revelation of the grace of God.

THE WRATH OF GOD (verse 18)
The word translated 'wrath' is *orge*, the word from which the English word 'orgy' comes. We usually think of an orgy as a sexual party of great debauchery and licentiousness, but in the ancient world there was a connection between orgies and religious feasts. Participants would get drunk to the point of stupor and out of that drunkenness and uninhibited behaviour came the sexual dimensions which were often

33

set forth in overtones of religious devotion. The idea was that through drunkenness and sexual expression, people were able to break through the normal, sobering, restricting categories of reason and rationality. The wine left them uninhibited, and many thought that this was a religious experience of ecstasy.

Because *orge* is used here with respect to the wrath of God, it has led some to the conclusion that God's wrath is an uncontrolled emotional outburst, a sort of divine temper tantrum. Nothing could be further from the mind of the apostle Paul at this point. He is not saying that God's wrath is irrational or capricious, but rather that his wrath is intense. God is very angry, but it is a holy wrath. The text sets forth for us the reason why God is so angry. In fact, the very context of this chapter should stop the mouths of those who suggest that God's wrath is irrational, because God defines for us here why he is so angry.

Two things are mentioned that provoke God to this intense anger: godlessness and wickedness. *Godlessness* has to do with our attitudes toward God. *Wickedness* has to do with how we behave towards our fellow men. Some commentators say that there are two distinct things that God is angry about: one is a general attitude of irreverence that men reveal towards God and the other has to do with moral acts of disobedience. Other commentators, and I agree with those who take this position, see the text as what we call a 'hendiadys', a peculiar literary form where one particular thing is included in two aspects of it. If we look at the text this way, we see that God's anger is directed against one specific thing which is both ungodly and unethical.

Before we begin to specify what the act is which incurs the wrath of God to such an intense degree, it is important to note that both ungodliness and unrighteousness are very general terms. There are all kinds of specific acts that can be called ungodly: irreverence, blasphemy, failure to be involved in proper religious devotion, and so on. Certainly the list of deeds that can be placed under the category of unrighteousness is innumerable. So the two terms are vague because of their generality.

But Paul doesn't leave us in the realm of the general; he gets specific.

He starts with the general and moves to the particular: **who suppress the truth by their wickedness** (verse 18). The apostle is saying that there is truth that God has made known about himself to mankind that mankind is suppressing, an action that provokes God to fury.

The Greek word *katakein* means to press down with force against something that is exercising a counterforce. The image that comes into my mind would be a giant steel spring, which would take the full weight of a human being to press down. Because of the tension, if the person lets go for a second, the spring will shoot right up. The word is used in a negative sense where people are thrown into prison and are held in prison against their will. They are, in a word, incarcerated.

Paul is saying that the truth of God is, in some way, pushed down, repressed, hindered, stifled. It almost sounds like a textbook in psychology, because modern psychologists note that this is exactly what we do with memories of painful and traumatic experiences. We push them out of the painful areas of our conscious minds and push them into the deepest recesses and chambers of our minds.

GENERAL KNOWLEDGE OF GOD (1:19-20)

Every person knows that there is a God: **Since what may be known about God is plain to them, because God has made it plain to them** (verse 19). It is one thing to say that it is possible for all men to acquire knowledge of God, but that is quite different from saying that all men already do possess a knowledge of God, as Paul says here.

God has made it plain to them. Theologians call this 'general revelation' as distinguished from 'special revelation'. Special revelation is found only in the Bible, which only a particular group of people have in their possession. People who have never had access to the written revelation of Scripture, have never received what we call 'special revelation'. This is not to suggest that they are without any knowledge of God. There is, in addition to this revelation of Scripture, the revelation that God gives to all men.

There is a dispute between commentators as to whether or not the general revelation of God gets through to man. Some say it does, while others say it does not because man is so hostile in his attitude towards God. A famous analogy is that man walks through this earth as if he were walking through a glorious theatre where the evidence for God surrounds him in the creation. But man is blindfolded. The idea behind the analogy is that no matter how much light there is, it never gets in because his eyes are covered and he is blinded.

However, Paul makes it abundantly clear that not only is there a revelation that proceeds from God, but that it penetrates human minds so that they have a real knowledge of God: **God has made it plain to them**. The revelation that God makes available to all men does not spell out in detail the Trinity or the work of Christ. For that information we need the written documents of Scripture. Rather the revelation is of a general sort, the content of which Paul spells out later in the chapter.

Verse 20 is pivotal to any understanding of how God reveals himself to all men in nature: **For since the creation of the world God's invisible qualities - his eternal power and divine nature - have been clearly seen, being understood from what has been made, so that men are without excuse**.

Immanuel Kant, perhaps the greatest philosopher in the history of Western civilisation, established a watershed in modern intellectual attempts to know God, by saying that it is impossible to use the traditional arguments for the existence of God, whereby men reason from this world back to a Creator. They look at the world around themselves and say, Something had to make this world. Kant said that it is not possible for us to move from visible things to an invisible God.

On that point we have an absolute collision between the best of secular philosophy and the assertion here of the apostle Paul. Paul is stating as clearly as he could possibly have stated, exactly what Immanuel Kant says is fundamentally impossible. He is saying that the invisible qualities of God are clearly seen in the created order. Just as we can look at a painting and know that there was a painter, so we can look at this universe and know that there is a Creator. Something of the nature of that Creator can be discerned from the visible things of his creation.

This revelation has being going on since the creation of the world.

Certainly Paul does not give us any hint that the only man to be found guilty of repudiating divine revelation is the first man, Adam. Rather, as we see in chapters 1-3, Paul is bringing the whole human race under the indictment of God's wrath for rejecting general revelation.

To what degree does this knowledge get through? Elsewhere in Scripture Paul states that unregenerate man does not know God (1 Thessalonians 1:8). The verb 'to know' is used in a wide assortment of ways. One frequent meaning is the knowledge of intimacy. Jesus warns of the last day when people will come before him, saying, 'Lord, Lord, didn't we do this, and didn't we do that in your Name?' Jesus will say, 'Depart from me, I never knew you' (Matthew 7:22,23). Does that mean he had no intellectual awareness of them? Certainly not. It means that they never had established a saving, personal, intimate relationship.

The revelation of God in nature does not provide us with intimate saving knowledge. But it does give a real knowledge, an intellectual awareness, what we call a 'cognitive' knowledge of reality.

The indictment comes to a crescendo: **so that men are without excuse**. The excuse that Paul has in view here is the excuse of ignorance. In all ages, there have been atheists and agnostics. There is a difference in attitude between the atheist and the agnostic. The atheist comes right out and says there is no God, but the agnostic says simply, I don't know. The reason the agnostic gives is 'insufficient knowledge'. The dreadful fear I have about agnosticism is that the agnostic adds insult to injury. He blames God for not producing enough evidence.

MAN'S REFUSAL TO ACKNOWLEDGE GOD (1:21-22)

For although they knew God, they neither glorified him as God nor gave thanks to him, but their thinking became futile and their foolish hearts were darkened (verse 21). What a sad commentary on man!

Ignorance is not the sin, but a recalcitrant refusal to give God the honour and glory that is appropriate and fitting to the Creator. To my mind, the ugliest word in the English language is the word 'futile', for it grates my soul that any labour is judged to be of no significance.

Philosophers throughout history have disagreed as to the existence of God. Why? Paul gives an answer to the question: **their
thinking became futile**. Now when does this futility of intellectual
search enter into the picture? According to the apostle it is after the
preliminary refusal of man to give honour to God. What Paul means
is that the issue of the existence of God, in the final analysis is not
an intellectual question, so much as it is a moral question. Man's
speculations end in darkness because they proceed from a denial at the
beginning of what they know to be true. Let me state it another way.
The problem with man is not so much a lack of knowledge of God,
as it is a refusal to acknowledge God, which at the bottom line is a
question of moral honesty and integrity. Paul is saying that man
begins his intellectual quest by refusing to acknowledge what he
knows to be true. That's what provokes God to anger.

This is the primordial sin of mankind, from which no human being
is exempt. No matter how brilliant the intellect, no matter how cogent
the argumentation, we all are thinking and reasoning and investigat-
ing within the context of our fallen nature. That is to say, we think
from a perspective of moral bias. It is not that man refuses to know
what God has made plain, but rather that he refuses to acknowledge
what he already knows to be true.

It should not surprise us that brilliant thinkers compose very
intricate, complex systems of philosophical thought that rise up in
opposition against the character of God. In fact, if a person is logically
consistent, there is a certain sense in which the more brilliant he is,
the further he will remove himself from the conclusion of the
existence of God.

Theologians have a concept which they call the 'noetic' effects of
sin. It comes from the Biblical word *nous* and in its adjectival form
comes across into English as 'noetic', which simply means 'mental',
or 'pertaining to the mind'. So when we speak about the noetic effects
of sin, we are speaking about the impact and influence that our sinful
nature has upon our minds, upon our thinking.

In the academic world, there is a negative word, a pejorative term, that is thrown about frequently: 'obscurantism'. An obscurantist is a person who refuses to deal with knowledge that is available to them, who will not examine data that might run contrary to his own conclusions. Liberals accuse conservatives of never really reading liberals, and of preferring to dwell in the darkness of conservatism, and therefore they are called obscurantists. By the same token, conservatives charge liberals with never reading conservative material, of just talking to themselves and among themselves, and being obscurantist about real, honest, open investigation of the data.

An obscurantist is one who chooses to remain in darkness. It carries with it a moral connotation, a question of one's intellectual honesty and integrity. Paul says that our moral darkness carries over to the mind, and leads us to obscurantism, a refusal to observe the light. Not only is the intellect involved but **their foolish hearts were darkened**. It is interesting that Paul uses the word 'heart' rather than the more specific word for mind. That's why God is angry. He is responding not to an intellectual weakness in the human race, not to a matter of mere ignorance, but rather to a moral problem. Man sets his heart steadfastly against God.

Out of this darkness, out of this refusal to acknowledge God, comes a growth and increase in human arrogance: **Although they claimed to be wise, they became fools** (verse 22). This is the grand paradox, the awful tragedy of human intellectual thought that man, at the very moment when he is acting in foolishness, brags about his wisdom.

The Bible declares that the beginning of wisdom is the fear of the Lord (Psalm 111:10). Authentic wisdom begins when the heart is disposed to adore and to revere God. So what happens to the person who refuses to give honour to God? He professes wisdom, but he possesses foolishness. There is no fool so tragic as the fool who thinks he is wise. Biblically, the description of the fool does not consist in an evaluation of his intellectual power, but rather in a moral and spiritual judgment about the state of his soul. It is the fool, said the Psalmist, who says in his heart, There is no God (Psalm 14:1). So atheism and agnosticism are not merely defective theories that need to be corrected by further study and more information. They are sin for which men are called to repent because God has made himself known to them.

There are, however, some who allege that men believe in God out of some deep-rooted psychological need. Part of the effect of the Enlightenment was that the existence of God is no longer held to be necessary in order to explain man and his world. So what followed was a series of studies into the question: If there is no God, why is it that so many people persist in believing in him?

The suggested answer was that religion arises out of a deep-rooted human need for comfort and stability. Men are afraid of nature, they are afraid of death, they are afraid of economic exploitation. So they seek some basis for hope in the midst of a hostile and indifferent universe. Man, therefore, created God in his own image to satisfy this deep psychological need for comfort and security. In other words, men believe in God simply because they need to believe in God.

There is a very important insight in this suggestion. I admit that I have a profound psychological need to believe in God. I can't stand to think that this universe is vacant; that in the final analysis, I am a meaningless blob of protoplasm; that my origin comes from nothing and that my destiny is annihilation, a return to nothingness. I need to know that my life is not an exercise in futility. The only thing that satisfies my mind as well as my heart, is the clear affirmation of the existence of God. I agree with Albert Camus: if there is no God, then the only question left for man to consider seriously is the question of suicide. I would be engulfed with darkness if I had to abandon my conviction of the reality of God.

But at the same time I recognise that it is possible for us to create, in the imagination, ideas that do not correspond to reality; ideas of hope that are very fragile indeed when subjected to critical evaluation. It is possible for man to invent a God even if there were no God. But we must not overlook the fact that it is also possible for people, out of psychological needs, to deny the existence of God. In fact, there are powerful and compelling reasons for denying the existence of the

God of the Bible. Why? Because the God of the Bible is the most threatening Being man can face. As the author of Hebrews says: 'It is a dreadful thing to fall into the hands of the living God' (10:31).

Scripture uniformly relates, time after time after time, that when men encounter the living God they are reduced to trembling and fear. Isaiah said, 'Woe to me. I am ruined. For I am a man of unclean lips' (6:5), when he encountered the holiness of God. Isaiah experiences the psychological process of disintegration. Habakkuk, when he saw the living God, said, 'I heard and my heart pounded, my lips quivered at the sound; decay crept into my bones, and my legs trembled' (3:16). Job saw God and said, 'I am unworthy – how can I reply to you? I put my hand over my mouth' (40:4). Again and again, when God manifests himself in his holiness, men are terrified, far more terrified than the fear engendered by the force of tornado, or of disease. In a word, the holiness of God is a trauma to a sinful man.

Peter and the disciples came in from a night of fishing with their boats empty. As they approached the shore, Jesus said, 'Cast your nets over the side of the boat.' Peter was obviously annoyed with Jesus, after all Peter was an expert fisherman. But as soon as they put in their nets, they caught so much fish that the boats began to sink. What would your rational expectation be of Peter's response? If I were Peter I would have whipped out a contract with Jesus for full partnership in my fishing business. That's not what Peter did. He looked at Jesus and said, 'Depart from me for I am a sinful man' (Luke 5:8). Isn't that a strange reaction? Peter is saying, 'Jesus, please leave! You make me uncomfortable, you threaten me, you stir up my psychology. I want you out of here, please go!'

The natural inclination of man, according to the Scriptures, is to flee from the presence of God. Our innate psychological disposition or bias is to run from God, not to God.

IDOLATRY (1:23)

They **exchanged the glory of the immortal God for images made to look like mortal man and birds and animals and reptiles** (verse 23).

What happens to those who have never heard of Christ? As a

teacher of theology, I would say that I have heard that question raised by students more often than any other. Sometimes it is put like this: What happens to the poor innocent native in Africa who has never heard of Christ? The answer can be given quickly: nothing happens to such a person. The poor innocent native in Africa doesn't need to hear of Jesus Christ. The poor innocent person in Russia doesn't need the gospel. The poor innocent person in America doesn't need the gospel. No one who is innocent needs to hear the gospel of Christ. The gospel of Christ is a proclamation that is to be announced to people who are guilty, who are already under the indictment of God.

The questioner is really asking the wrong question. He should be asking, What happens to the poor guilty native in Africa who has never heard of Jesus Christ? We could restate the question like this: Are there any innocent natives in Africa or in Asia, or in Australia, or anywhere else in the world? Paul is saying in Romans 1, what he certainly drives to a conclusion in Romans 3, that there are no innocent people anywhere. All men are brought before the tribunal of God and found wanting. All men are infected and corrupted by sin, both original sin and actual sin.

The problem is made more complicated by the fact that, in the New Testament, those who do hear the gospel of Christ are placed in a situation of double jeopardy. Once they hear the gospel, God holds them accountable for their response to the gospel. Therefore, some may reason this way: 'Wouldn't it be better for us to leave the people in remote areas of the world alone and never tell them anything about the gospel, because as soon as we do, we accentuate and accelerate their liability before God?' There have been many such objections raised against the whole process of world mission.

Such statements are based on sentiment and naivety, for the apostle is telling us that the native in Africa, or elsewhere, needs the gospel of Jesus Christ, because all men are exposed to the wrath of God as a result of their rejection of the general revelation of God.

The question can be stated in another way: Will God punish a person for not believing in Jesus if he never heard of Jesus? The answer to that question is straightforward. God will not punish any for rejecting what they have never heard, or had no opportunity to hear. If a person has gone through his life without ever hearing the name of Jesus Christ, God is not going to punish that person for rejecting Jesus Christ. How do we know that? Because God is righteous and just.

The problem with this whole question concerns a very important element that is often overlooked. Even Christians tend to think that the only sin heinous enough for God to punish by everlasting punishment is the sin of rejecting Jesus Christ. But where did they ever get that idea? Remember that God's wrath is being poured out, not against those who have rejected Jesus, but against those who have rejected God. Jesus came into a world to redeem people who were already estranged from God. The whole point of Romans 1 is that it is what mankind does with the revelation that they have from God which makes it necessary for them to be justified in the first place. It makes the coming of Christ all the more imperative.

An objection that we often hear from those who are critical of world missions is, 'Look, let's leave the native alone. He is already religious; he doesn't need the formal intrusions of the Christian Church, for he is worshipping God in the best way that he knows how.'

In addition, we have the assumptions of those sociologists and cultural anthropologists who are committed to an idea of the process of religious evolution. The theory goes like this: religion, as well as other aspects of life, is part of the evolutionary process, and the normal movement of evolution is from the simple to the complex. So religion has evolved from a very simple and primitive form, to a more highly complex form.

As the theory goes, religion begins in a primitive stage of what we call 'animism'. Animism is a superstitious belief concerning spirits inhabiting inanimate things like rocks, trees and animals. Simplistic, primitive religion began when men worshipped the spirits that dwell in the trees. But then as men progressed intellectually and historically, they moved into more sophisticated and complex forms of polytheism. Then, it developed into henotheism, which is the belief that each nation or each group has one god that is sovereign over the geographical boundaries of that particular group: a god for the Philistines, a god for the Amorites, a god for the Jewish people and so on. Finally, in the evolutionary scale of development, a sophisticated and complex variety of monotheism is reached.

This theory, assumed by many scholars around the world, is on a collision course with what Paul writes in Romans 1. Paul is not teaching an evolution of religion, but a devolution of religion; not a progress, but a regress. He is saying that monotheism is not something that appears late as a result of human striving, growing and achievement. Rather man begins with monotheism, with a clear understanding of the God of heaven and earth. It is because of man's sinful reaction to this one God, that religion deteriorates into idolatry.

From Paul's perspective, the fact that the so-called native in Africa is religious, does not minimise his guilt before God. Instead, it intensifies his guilt, because God does not simply command man to be religious, but to worship him properly. The fundamental prohibition of the Biblical God is the prohibition against idolatry. Not only have men refused to worship God as God, but they have insulted the majesty of God by replacing him with a creature.

This was a tremendous point of conflict in the Old Testament world. The prophets thundered again and again against those who practised idolatry. The essence of idolatry is that it substitutes the majesty of God for the corruption of this world. The glory of God is traded in for the glory of a snake or a crocodile or a block of wood.

But idolatry is something that takes place at every level of life in every human culture. We can even turn Christianity into an idolatrous religion by substituting the glory of God for something else and stripping him of his holiness. We make God in our own image, rather than responding to the God who is. This brings the judgment of God, for God will not tolerate idolatry.

JUDGMENT ON IDOLATRY (1:24-27)

How does God respond to idolatry? **Therefore God gave them over in the sinful desires of their hearts to sexual impurity for the degrading of their bodies with one another** (verse 24). God's judgment in sacred Scripture involves a poetic justice. He punishes in kind; there is a kind of symmetry between the type of sin and its punishment. The sin here is dishonouring God; the punishment is that men are given over to their own evil. God gives them over to sexual impurity.

What is the effect? **the degrading of their bodies with one another.** When men refuse to honour God, they begin to dishonour themselves. Wherever the glory of God is attacked, sooner or later the dignity of man suffers. Since man is created in the image of God, there is a very real sense in which if God goes, so goes man. If we corrupt and denude and denigrate God, then the image of God suffers accordingly.

They exchanged the truth of God for a lie, and worshipped and served created things rather than the Creator - who is forever praised. Amen. Here in verse 25, Paul reaches the climax of this portion of the letter. He concludes that men are guilty of trading in truth, and embracing in exchange for the truth, a lie. It is the wilful choice of man to embrace a lie rather than the truth. Notice that Paul cannot even mention the Creator without breaking spontaneously into doxology. As soon as he even mentions the Creator, he has to cry out, 'who is for ever praised. Amen.' There is passion in the apostle's writing. He is saying, How can men take truth and suppress it and in its place enthrone a lie? The human race reaches such an abysmal level that it actually worships and serves creatures rather than the blessed Creator.

Because of this, God gave them over to shameful lusts. Even their women exchanged natural relations for unnatural ones. In the same way the men also abandoned natural relations with women and were inflamed with lust for one another. Men committed indecent acts with other men, and received in themselves the due penalty for their perversion (verses 26,27). This passage has become exceedingly controversial in recent years because of the movement for gay rights.

Paul does not set forth a detailed prohibition against certain homosexual acts, but rather he isolates homosexual behaviour as the supreme example of the loss of human dignity. When the knowledge of God is suppressed, the nature of man suffers, and it manifests itself in gross, unnatural acts. Homosexual behaviour is here extrapolated in the text as an example of an unnatural human relationship that brings dishonour and a loss of dignity to the human race.

Because of this, God gave them over to shameful lusts. The Greek for 'shameful' is *atimias* which means, 'without honour'. When men refuse to honour God, God gives them over to lusts that are without honour.

What are those dishonourable passions? **Even their women exchanged natural relations for unnatural ones. In the same way the men also abandoned natural relations with women and were inflamed with lust for one another. Men committed indecent acts with other men, and received in themselves the due penalty for their perversion.** These passions which are 'without honour' are also contrary to or against 'nature'.

I have seen all kinds of attempts at exegesis to show that the Bible does not prohibit or in any way exclude the possibility of bona fide homosexual relationships. I don't see how the apostle could make it any clearer than he does here. For men to be involved sexually with men is dishonourable. It involves the committing of indecent acts and is receiving punishment. The very existence of it calls attention to man's fall under the wrath of God. So one could say that the expansion, proliferation and explosion of homosexuality in a culture is in a certain sense a reflection of a demeaning of man in general and an expression of the wrath of God upon that society.

Furthermore, since they did not think it worth while to retain the knowledge of God, he gave them over to a depraved mind, to do what ought not to be done (verse 28). God gives men up to the darkness that they choose for themselves in the first place.

Part of the sinfulness of sin is seen when people begin to call the truth a lie, or call a lie the truth. They begin to call good, evil, and evil, good. There is virtually no sin known to the human race for which somebody hasn't put forth a learned and sophisticated ethical defence to show that it is in fact really good.

We have seen it with the homosexual problem in the last two decades. Learned articles and books not only justify homosexual behaviour, but actually extol it as virtuous. People can present very persuasive arguments to support homosexual behaviour. They argue that people can't help being the way they are; they can't help the feelings they have. Why should these people be robbed of having a sexual expression to their humanity? What could possibly be wrong if two consenting adults agree to indulge themselves in homosexual behaviour? Who are they hurting? Others say that Paul was only attacking bi-sexuality here, not homosexuality. In other words, he is not attacking those who were born with this particular proclivity, but those who, despite a natural inclination towards the opposite sex, choose to cross the line to homosexuality.

Yet, we must distinguish between homosexual orientation and homosexual practice. If a homosexual has an orientation towards men, that is one thing. If that homosexual exercises his orientation by involving himself in practices forbidden by God, that is sin. It can only happen in a world where men have chosen first to dishonour God, so that then they lose any sense of honour and dignity among themselves and within themselves.

Paul has just described the nadir of human corruption and dishonour in the activity of homosexual behaviour. Now he goes on to expand the list of vices of which men are capable. But notice again, the reason for this outbreak of evil is that **they did not think it worth while to retain the knowledge of God**. Remember that the judgment of God comes upon men who know that God is, but refuse to acknowledge that he is. In the original text, the Greek word for knowledge has a prefix that intensifies it. It could translate this way, 'men did not think it worth while to seek after a *full knowledge* of God'. They did not see any purpose in pursuing a knowledge of God in any kind of depth or even maintaining with any serious depth the knowledge that they already had.

Let me ask you: How excited are you about mastering theology? The word 'theology' is often repugnant to people's ears. They say, 'I am not interested in theology', for they associate it with speculative or purely academic research into the things of God. But, at its simplest, theology means 'a knowledge of God'.

Paul moves immediately from 'he gave them over to a depraved mind' to 'to do what ought not to be done'. He is stressing that behaviour and action follow thought, that practice follows theory. I can talk about what my theories are, but my life reveals what my real theories are because I always behave according to what I really think is right and proper.

What things are not proper? **They have become filled with every kind of wickedness, evil, greed and depravity. They are full of envy, murder, strife, deceit and malice. They are gossips, slanderers, God-haters, insolent, arrogant and boastful; they invent ways of doing evil; they disobey their parents; they are senseless, faithless, heartless, ruthless** (verses 29-31). The apostle is saying that when a man's thoughts are devoid of God, his life is characterised by not just a touch of unrighteousness but a fullness of unrighteousness that touches every part of his life.

He mentions, first of all, *greed* or covetousness. The greedy person is self-centred, seeking to amass for himself things that he would rob from other people. Such a person has a hostile attitude to his fellow man, for he will stop at nothing for his own private gain. The greedy man's thoughts are void of God. When we take God out of the mind, there is nothing to restrain the human heart and the human spirit in their lust for power and for greed.

And then he uses the term, *depravity*. An often maligned word in today's theological parlance, depravity refers to our morally corrupt nature. Not only liberals, but many evangelicals refrain from using this term because it has pronounced implications with respect to our sin nature, our will, consciences, heart and mind. Pertaining to all aspects of our personality, we are totally depraved. This should not, however, be confused with utter depravity, because there is always room for depravement. Being totally depraved we are slaves of sin (John 8:34), exploiting every opportunity to sin in every area of our being, in thought, word and deed; by commission and omission. This rightful acknowledgement of our sinfulness, however, becomes the occasion for multiplying our indebtedness to the graciousness of God's saving grace.

Full of envy is the next vice the apostle mentions. Where men look at somebody else's property, status and position, they begin to envy them. This attitude leads to attempts at undermining the other person's position or possessions and gaining them for ourselves. Think for a moment of the human capacity for envy, especially when a person is filled with 'blind ambition'. What happens to the quality of life in your community, in your office, in your church, in your family, when just one member is filled with envy. How it tears apart any possible cohesive power of human relationships. How much misery and suffering it brings upon the quality of our lives.

We move from envy to *murder*. God regards the malicious murder of a human being as an assault on his own dignity. The first command about capital punishment is found very early in the book of Genesis. What is the reason given? Because man is the image-bearer of God (Gen. 9:6). His life is so sacred, so dignified, so valuable, that to destroy it by murder is to do violence against one who carries in his body the image of God. If we don't have much regard for God, can we really have much regard for man?

Out of this rejection of the knowledge of God, flows *strife* or contentiousness, an embattled spirit, being argumentative. The next is *deceit* or dishonesty and lying.

Then *malice* which flows out of the mind that has no regard for the things of God. God links together the command to love him and the command to love our neighbour (Matt. 22:36-40). We cannot hate God and love our neighbour. Man's interpersonal relationship, man's co-humanity, is rooted and grounded ultimately in man's commitment to God. If that vertical relationship is disturbed or destroyed, then it has radical repercussions on the horizontal level of human relationships.

They are *gossips*. How do you feel when someone tells a lie about you? How do you feel when people spend time gossiping maliciously, spreading rumours or even telling people unnecessary things that are true? *They invent ways of doing evil*. It is not enough that men do the normal kind of sins, but they are so sophisticated in learning new ways to sin. *They disobey their parents*. God regards obedience to parents as important enough to be mentioned in the ten commandments. When we see a breakdown of respect for parents, we see a culture that is no longer in pursuit of the knowledge of God. Then he gives some negative examples. Men become: *senseless, faithless, heartless, ruthless*.

Although they know God's righteous decree that those who do such things deserve death, they not only continue to do these very things, but also approve of those who practise them (verse 32). Charles Hodge comments that 'to take pleasure in those who do good, makes us better; to delight in those who do evil is the surest way to become even more degraded than they are themselves.' It is fair to say that it shows a greater depravity to encourage others' sin than to commit the sin yourself. Remember, Paul first says that such people know God's righteous decree. They sin against knowledge; they are not ignorant of the demands of God's righteous law. This, too, only serves to intensify their guilt and shame.

JEWS ARE GUILTY (2:1-5)

In chapter 1, the apostle has presented a severe indictment of paganism, bringing all pagans before the tribunal of God and finding them guilty for having rejected general revelation, that knowledge of himself which God makes available to all men.

Now, in chapter 2, the apostle shifts his attention away from the pagans and draws attention to the Jewish community. He begins: **You, therefore, have no excuse, you who pass judgment on someone else, for at whatever point you judge the other, you are condemning yourself, because you who pass judgment do the same things**. The apostle is speaking to his own people, the Jewish nation. He says that to do the very things that they condemned in the pagans was to condemn themselves.

He continues in verse 2: **Now we know that God's judgment against those who do such things is based on truth**. The apostle says that men are aware of the fact that when God condemns sin, he condemns it justly. The judgment of God is not simply righteous, but it is according to truth. God makes no mistakes when he hears a case, when he brings us before him on trial. There's no possibility of an error in the proceedings or an error in judgment. There is no possibility of a biased judge who will overlook some salient point of the evidence.

And the apostle says: **So when you, a mere man, pass judgment on them and yet do the same things, do you think you will escape God's judgment?** (verse 3). Scholars are almost in unanimous agreement that Paul is directing his comments here specifically to Israel, because it was commonplace in the first century, among the Pharisees particularly, to assume that God would excuse certain behavioural patterns in Jewish people that he would condemn among the pagans. Why did they think that God would excuse in them, what he would condemn in others? Because of their conviction that there existed a privileged relationship between God and the children of Abraham. God had made a covenant promise to Abraham and to his seed: a promise of blessing, and a promise of incorporation into the kingdom of God. So there were many who came to the conclusion that redemption on the last day would not come on the basis of individual performance, so much as on the basis of membership within a privileged group, or within a privileged class. Those who were part of the covenant community of Israel had nothing to fear for they were children of Abraham automatically.

That may seem outrageous to us, but many people do think that because they are members of a church, or some special group, their membership will get them into the kingdom of God. Paul is warning people who think that their membership in a particular human group will guarantee their exclusion from the judgment God has appointed at the end of the age.

No matter how many groups we are members of, there is one thing we must keep before our eyes constantly: in the final analysis, when we stand before Almighty God, we stand alone. I cannot appeal to the righteousness of my father, or to the righteousness of my mother, or to the righteousness of my sister, or to the greatness of the church to which I belong. I have to answer for my life by myself before the throne of God.

So this fond hope of the Pharisees that they were going to escape the judgment has been dashed into pieces by the apostle at this point.

Paul continues in verse 4: **Or do you show contempt for the riches of his kindness, tolerance and patience, not realizing that God's kindness leads you towards repentance?** To despise the riches of God is to neglect them, to consider them unimportant and insignificant. How much time have we given to a consideration of the mercy of God towards us? In Jonathan Edwards' famous sermon, *Sinners in the Hands of an Angry God*, he reminded his people of this. He said, 'O sinner, can you give any reason why since you have risen from your bed this morning God has not stricken you dead?' What Edwards was getting at was this: if you consider honestly the rebelliousness that you have practised since you got out of your bed this morning, can you give a rational explanation for why God has withheld judgment from you? If you are thinking that the reason is because God is kind and merciful, you would be correct. But some people are perpetually angry with God, feeling that God has not treated them fairly. What is it that God owes us?

To show contempt for the riches of God is not to hate the mercy of God, it is to think lightly of it. For the most part we take God's kindness for granted and therein lies the danger. Notice, it is not just a bankrupt kindness, or a stingy kindness, but the *riches* of kindness that is being bestowed upon us by God. Paul uses a term that calls attention to the abundance that we receive from God, not only of kindness, but of tolerance and patience.

The purpose of God's kindness, tolerance and patience is to bring us to a proper state of repentance before him, but just the opposite effect takes place. Instead of our taking advantage of God's kindness, by coming to him in repentance and faith and expressing our gratitude for his patience, we assume that it really doesn't matter to God that we are disobeying his law.

It is possible, as the apostle here indicates, that God can lead us in certain directions in which we refuse to go. So God leads to repentance, but we don't follow. So what is the result of that? In verse 5, we have one of the most terrifying verses in all the apostolic writings: **But because of your stubbornness and your unrepentant heart, you are storing up wrath against yourself for the day of God's wrath, when his righteous judgment will be revealed**. This deals with another dreadful error which people often make, namely, that if we sin once, we might as well sin ten times because it really doesn't matter to God whether we since once or whether we sin ten times.

Sometimes we think it is ludicrous when somebody who is involved in mass murder is convicted on eight counts of first degree murder, and sentenced to eight consecutive life sentences. How foolish that sentence seems, for a person only has one life, so how can he serve eight sentences? In this world it is impossible, but in God's eternity it is not impossible. The point is that God's judgment will be perfect and every sin that we commit will be punished to the degree of severity the sin deserves.

When we refuse to repent and take proper advantage of God's kindness and longsuffering, we build up a negative balance in the bank account with God. When Paul talks about 'storing up wrath', the allusion is to the secular culture where a person builds a treasure by investing a little bit at a time. As long as stubbornness persists, men are adding grievous insults to God, so that when they come to the end of their lives, they have this huge negative balance of sin for which they will be judged.

WILL GOD JUDGE US ACCORDING TO OUR WORKS? (2:6-11)

The vast majority of Christians will answer, 'No, of course not. We won't be judged according to our works, our justification is by faith, and no-one will ever be justified by works.'

It reminds me of an examination that I once gave to my theology class. The students were in their senior year and just completing their seminary preparations, having taken the courses in systematic theology. I gave a true/false question test to the class of graduating seniors and one of the true/false questions was this: True or false - we are justified by faith but our rewards in heaven will be distributed according to our works? Every single person in that class answered the question by saying, 'That's false.'

Yet, according to classical Protestant theology, we are justified by faith but our reward in heaven will be distributed according to our works. Those who are justified by faith will have imputed to them the work of Jesus, by which they are justified. But the primary basis of God's eternal judgment on mankind will be works. That point is made on no less than twenty occasions in the New Testament and it is made very clearly here in verse 6: God **will give to each person according to what he has done**. The ground of God's judgment is not our ceremonies, our church affiliations or our family relationships, but our deeds. And that is true for everyone. Each individual's performance will be evaluated by Almighty God.

I can hear Christians protesting, 'Doesn't the Bible say that as Christians we have passed from judgment to life, that there's no condemnation for us?' Yes, the Bible does teach so for those who are in Christ. But even the Christian must face the judgment of the evaluation of his life. All will stand before God, and we will be evaluated according to our deeds.

Paul goes on to explain the judgment which will follow: **To those who by persistence in doing good seek glory, honour and immortality, he will give eternal life** (verse 7). There is a problem of sentence structure here. It could be that Paul is saying those who persevere in doing good will receive glory, honour, immortality and eternal life. Or we could read it that all those who by persevering in doing good, search for glory, honour and immortality, they will be rewarded with eternal life.

Another question that I often stumped the seminary students with is, How many ways are there to get into heaven? They will respond, There is only one way to get into heaven and that is by faith in Jesus Christ. I reply, That's true, realistically speaking. But theoretically, there is another way to get into heaven–by leading a good life. If a person lives a life that is in perfect obedience to the law of God, they don't need Jesus Christ. Jesus Christ came to save people who do not live perfect lives. The tragedy is that there are actually people who believe that their lives are good enough to get them into heaven.

But for those who are self-seeking and who reject the truth and follow evil, there will be wrath and anger (verse 8). The apostle is saying that in the judgment God is going to distribute two possibilities: eternal life on the one hand, and wrath and anger on the other. Who will receive eternal life? Those who persist and endure in doing good. Who will receive the wrath and anger of God? Those who are selfishly ambitious and do not obey the truth but follow evil.

Paul gives us a future prophecy, a graphic view of what will happen at the last judgment: **There will be trouble and distress for every human being who does evil: first for the Jew, then for the Gentile; but glory, honour and peace for everyone who does good: first for the Jew, then for the Gentile** (verses 9,10).

The word 'Gentile' refers to anyone who is not a Jew. But a person's nationality does not affect whether he will receive reward or punishment. **For God does not show favouritism** (verse 11). Again the idea of ethnic identification that was held so strongly by the Pharisees is smashed by the apostolic teaching. God is no respecter of persons. All will stand or fall on the basis of their goodness or the absence of goodness. Pedigree, social status, ecclesiastical affiliation and ethnic background will count for nothing at the judgment seat of God.

THE GENTILES AND THE LAW OF GOD (2:12-16)

All who sin apart from the law will also perish apart from the law, and all who sin under the law will be judged by the law (verse 12). Paul has in view here that great point of demarcation between the Jew and the Gentile. The Jew possessed the law of God while the Gentile did not.

In verse 13 he elaborates: **For it is not those who hear the law who are righteous in God's sight, but it is those who obey the law who will be declared righteous**. The Jewish people heard the law recited on all kinds of sacred occasions. The scrolls of the Old Testament were presented in the synagogue and read verbally and audibly. Most concluded that because they possessed these documents, which were part of the covenant God had made with them, there was a guarantee of entrance into the kingdom of God. Paul states what should be obvious. It is not the hearers of the law who will be declared righteous before God, but the doers of the law.

Verses 14 and 15 are more difficult: **(Indeed, when Gentiles, who do not have the law, do by nature things required by the law, they are a law for themselves, even though they do not have the law, since they show that the requirements of the law are written on their hearts...** Some have wrongly interpreted this passage to mean that whereas the Jews had the law but did not keep it, the Gentiles, although not having the law, kept it. The idea is that nonreligious people can live a good enough life to get them into the kingdom of God.

Paul chooses his words carefully here. He isn't saying that the Gentiles, who do not have the law, in fact keep the law. He is saying that they do the things required by the law. That is quite different from saying they keep the law perfectly. Paul has already made it abundantly clear in the first chapter that all pagans are under the judgment of God and he will make it even more clear in the third chapter.

But pagans, who have never heard of the Old Testament, do display what is called 'civil acts of virtue' or civic righteousness. We find pagans with enough human morality to take care of their children and to refrain from stealing. They don't obey the whole of the law, for they don't love God with all their hearts and all their minds and all their souls. But this partial obedience reveals that there is a certain sense in which the law is written in their hearts.

Here we have the classical location in the New Testament for the apostolic teaching of some sort of natural law. Every human being has some moral sense, some light of nature, by which he is able to distinguish right and wrong. Even the secular philosopher, Immanuel Kant, went to great pains to prove this point, that there is a sense of rightness in the breast of every human being. Human behavioural patterns, no matter how primitive the culture, bear witness to the fact that man is born with some sense of moral awareness. We all have some built-in understanding of what is right and what is wrong. God gives us that innate or inward knowledge of morality.

Paul goes on, **their consciences also bearing witness, and their thoughts now accusing, now even defending them.**) Paul is not saying that conscience is this built-in moral sense of what is right and what is wrong. Conscience is not the same thing as natural law. Rather, conscience is another dimension that bears witness to the presence of a built-in moral awareness.

The fact that we have conscience bears witness to the fact that we are aware of things being right or wrong. Even in pagan nations, that have never heard of the Bible, we see the manifestation and the practice of conscience.

Some have argued against the apostolic teaching here by saying, 'We find in every society that we examine, some moral sense. Moral values may vary from culture to culture, but we've never found any primitive society that does not exhibit some moral sense in their culture. This indicates that morality is culturally derived, and their sense of right and wrong is imposed upon them by their culture.'

Similarly, we are told that our scruples about sexual morality are simply the result of the Victorian era's influence, or the Puritanical ethic of New England. Now that we are becoming liberated we realise that all these moral persuasions are simply the result of societal or cultural taboos.

But that is a naive explanation for this universal sense of moral oneness. How did society ever universally get to the place where it had such sanctions to impose upon the consciences of its members, if it were not for the fact that the individuals concerned already had some sense of moral responsibility?

The apostle is saying here that it doesn't matter whether or not you know the Old Testament law, you are not excusable. Whether or not you have read the ten commandments, you are exposed to the law of God in some sense. Therefore, the law of God will be the basis of our judgment. This does not deny what the Bible says elsewhere that God will judge all men according to the light that they have. The more light one has, the greater the responsibilities that go with it.

In verse 16 he says, **This will take place on the day when God will judge men's secrets through Jesus Christ, as my gospel declares.** The apostle is introducing a new element to the discussion. Not only will there be a last judgment and not only will that judgment be on the basis of the justice of God, but the judgment will be through Jesus Christ. This fact, that Jesus will serve as the Judge of all men, is in keeping with the Old Testament portrait of the Son of Man, who is established by God to be the Judge of all the earth.

The apostle speaks of that day when God will judge the secrets of men. There are skeletons in every man's closet. We all have secrets that we seek to preserve and conceal from the scrutiny of other people. But the point of this text is that those very things which we seek to keep secret will come before the throne of God.

JEWS AND THE LAW OF GOD (2:17-29)

Paul turns his attention again to those who are taking the luxury of false confidence, resting on their identity as Jews to escape the judgment of God. He speaks to them directly in verse 17: **Now you, if you call yourself a Jew.** For many people today, the name 'Jew' is an ugly name. Think of the Holocaust, the ignominious suffering that was imposed upon the Jews and the wide pockets that still exist of anti-Semitism. But in terms of Old Testament history and the perspective from which Paul is writing, to be called a Jew was to be called something very honourable. Paul was proud of his own Jewishness, and rightly so, because the heritage of the Jewish nation was magnificent and it was out of the Jewish nation that Christ himself came.

> ... **if you rely on the law and brag about your relationship to God; if you know his will and approve of what is superior because you are instructed by the law; if you are convinced that you are a guide for the blind, a light for those who are in the dark, an instructor of the foolish, a teacher of infants, because you have in the law the embodiment of knowledge and truth - you, then, who teach others, do you not teach**

yourself? You who preach against stealing, do you steal? You who say that people should not commit adultery, do you commit adultery? You who abhor idols, do you rob temples? You who brag about the law, do you dishonour God by breaking the law? (verses 17-23).

Paul is zeroing in on the problem of hypocrisy whereby we condemn in others the very things that we do ourselves. That is the way the apostle began this chapter: 'You, therefore, have no excuse, you who pass judgment on someone else, for at whatever point you judge the other, you are condemning yourself, because you who pass judgment do the same things.'

Paul was directing his comments specifically to the Jewish nation, because they did pride themselves in being correctors of the foolish, teachers of the immature, and they were confident they were a guide to the blind and a light to those in darkness. Why did they have such confidence that theirs was a unique position of maturity? Paul answers the question in verse 20: **because you have in the law the embodiment of knowledge and truth**. The Jews did possess the truth, they did have the law of God, and what they had was a possession so rich, so magnificent, that it transcended the greatest insights and wisdom of even the highest period of classical Greek culture. Moses had more wisdom than Plato. Jeremiah knew more truth than Aristotle. Amos understood righteousness far better than Socrates. This was not because these men had better minds or were by nature more acute thinkers. It was because, by the grace of God, they had received revealed truth, God himself had written on those tablets of stone and revealed from heaven what authentic wisdom was.

The very word 'philosophy' that was so important to the ancient Greek means the 'love of wisdom'. The Wisdom Literature of the Old Testament was named because it contains consummate wisdom, wisdom that came from the very mind of God. That is what Paul is saying: the Jews had the deposits of truth, the mind of God written down for them. They had transcendent, infinite wisdom in their possession. No wonder they felt confident enough to be guides to the blind, lights for those in darkness, teachers and instructors for the immature.

But how is it possible that, possessing riches of transcendent wisdom, they failed to teach themselves?

A very painful statement is made by the apostle Paul, one that should cause every Christian to hang his head: **As it is written: "God's name is blasphemed among the Gentiles because of you"** (verse 24).

I remember when I was doing some seminars on the value of the person in labour and management. The vast majority of people who came to the seminars were not members of any Christian church. I had the opportunity to speak with many of them, and I would ask them the same question, Were you ever a member of a church? Almost all of them said that they had been. And I would ask them why they stopped going to church. In almost every instance, the answer was basically the same: they had been hurt or offended by someone in the church. There was bitterness because the church is filled with hypocrites.

Now often that judgment is false and sometimes slanderous. People expect church members to be perfect when the one absolute prerequisite for joining the church is the admission that one is not perfect. The only organisation I know which demands that you be a sinner in order to join it, is the Christian church. So it shouldn't surprise anybody to see Christians sin. But there is a specific sin of hypocrisy.

Paul had already condemned the Gentiles for blaspheming God on the basis of the revelation that God gave to them. But that blasphemy is increased by the sin of hypocrisy among Jews.

The apostle, in verse 25, mentions circumcision. **Circumcision has value if you observe the law, but if you break the law, you have become as though you had not been circumcised.**

There developed in the history of Israel a belief that circumcision, the sacred rite which was the sign of the Old Testament covenant, was all it took to be saved. We have a similar confusion in the Christian church today where some people believe that baptism automatically guarantees salvation. One rabbinic tradition says, 'Circumcision saves from hell'. The same rabbi wrote that Abraham himself sits before the gates of hell and does not allow any circumcised Israelite to enter there.

Paul says that circumcision is of value if you practise the law. In fact, it is the sign of your promise to practise the law. But if you are a transgressor of the law, your circumcision has become uncircumcision. Paul is coming at this same point again and again, from a slightly different angle each time. He is saying that the only thing which counts on the judgment day is real righteousness. If you don't keep the law your circumcision has become uncircumcision and in the sight of God you are as a pagan.

If those who are not circumcised keep the law's requirements, will they not be regarded as though they were circumcised? (verse 26). He is saying the same thing he said earlier. If those who are Gentiles do the things of the law by nature, God will honour that.

The one who is not circumcised physically and yet obeys the law will condemn you who, even though you have the written code and circumcision, are a lawbreaker (verse 27). If the uncircumcised person is more righteous than those who are circumcised then that is going to double the guilt, because they have done more with less.

Then he comes to the conclusion in verses 28 and 29: **A man is not a Jew if he is only one outwardly, nor is circumcision merely outward and physical. No, a man is a Jew if he is one inwardly; and circumcision is circumcision of the heart, by the Spirit, not by the written code. Such a man's praise is not from men, but from God.** Jewish opponents of Paul were continuing to build their hopes for eternity on the mere fact that they were biologically descendant from Abraham. Earlier these same people had rejected John the Baptist for similar reasons (Matt. 3:9; John 8:33,39).

In the physical act of circumcision something was cut away and removed. Inward circumcision by the Spirit is accomplished when our hardness of heart is removed, and a new birth (regeneration) causes our heart to come alive to the things of God.

Isn't this a fitting climax to the argument in chapter 2? What Paul has been driving at all along is this: God is going to look at the heart. We can come adorned with all kinds of externals, but if there is no circumcision of the heart, it will be to no avail. He is a Jew who is one inwardly, and real circumcision is of the heart, by the Spirit - that is by the Holy Spirit - not by the letter.

ADVANTAGES OF THE JEW (3:1-8)

Chapter 3 begins with a question: **What advantage, then, is there in being a Jew, or what value is there in circumcision?** This is a natural question for Paul to raise because he has just spelled out the fact that being a Jew was no guarantee of entrance into the kingdom of God, and even the covenant sign of circumcision was no guarantee of getting into heaven. Therefore, he asks these two questions: What advantage is there in being a Jew? What is the value of circumcision? We would expect him, in the light of his previous argument, to say that there is no advantage in being a Jew and no real benefit from circumcision. But that's not what he says. In fact, he says just the opposite: **Much in every way!**

First of all, they have been entrusted with the very words of God (verse 2). The singular advantage that Israel enjoyed over all other nations was of having in their possession the Old Testament Scriptures. Every Jew had proximity to the word of God, he was not left to learn of the things of God merely by an examination of nature.

Is there any advantage in being a church member if you are not a sincere church member? Now, of course, the church does not extend membership to those who profess to be unbelievers; the church only has on its roll those who make professions of faith, those who claim to be believers. But we know that not everyone who professes to believe in Christ really does believe.

This is one of the reasons why theologians have made the distinction between the visible church and the invisible church. The visible church is an institution composed and comprised of all the members listed on its rolls. The invisible church refers to all those members within the visible church who really do believe in Christ.

It is called 'invisible' not because people are invisible, but because their hearts are invisible to us. If a man says that he believes, I have no right to deny that profession of faith. Only God knows if it is real.

What advantage does a person who is not a true believer have in being a member of the visible church? We can use the illustration of three concentric circles. The outer, larger circle represents every human being. The middle circle represents all those who are members of the visible church. The inner circle represents all true believers.

To use the language of both the Old and New Testaments, those in that second circle (who are not also in the inner circle) are members of the covenant community. They have made their profession, they have gone through the rites of entrance into the community. In the Old Testament they would have been circumcised Jews who were not true believers, and in the New Testament be baptised Christians who were not true believers in Christ.

Now the question is, Is there any advantage to being in that second circle? Certainly there is nothing which could be compared to the inner circle of true believers who have the advantage of redemption. But yet in that second circle we do have the means of God's grace. What are the means of grace? This is a classical term that has reference to the benefits and instruments given to the church which God uses to bring about people's salvation: the preaching of the word, the sacraments of baptism and the Lord's Supper, prayer and so on. They are by no means restricted to the visible church, but they are concentrated there.

There was a great advantage, then, in being a Jew, because they were entrusted with the word of God.

Paul continues by raising another question: **What if some did not have faith? Will their lack of faith nullify God's faithfulness?** (verse 3). Paul here is calling attention to a difference between God and man. As human beings, we are by nature covenant breakers. We do not always tell the truth. We do not always keep our promises. Does that mean that we should project on the character of God our own sinfulness and suggest that he might from time to time break his promises? To ask such a question is to answer it. No wonder the emphatic tone of Paul's writing at this point: **Not at all! Let God be true, and every man a liar.** It is utterly unthinkable that God would ever break a promise.

As it is written: "So that you may be proved right when you speak and prevail when you judge". The point the apostle is making is that God is always righteous, both in his judgments and when he speaks. David wrote a majestic psalm of penitence, perhaps the most lucid example of genuine repentance that has ever been written by human hand (Psalm 51:4). In it he begs God to deal with him, not according to justice, but according to mercy and lovingkindness. But in so doing, David acknowledges, 'O God, "you are proved right when you speak and justified when you judge".' That's the point David is making in the psalm. He is acknowledging the fact that God had every right to condemn him.

But again, another objection is brought forth. As the Jews reply, **But if our unrighteousness brings out God's righteousness more clearly, what shall we say? That God is unjust in bringing his wrath on us? (I am using a human argument.)** What is behind this very difficult question?

There were those who argued that God is absolutely perfect, and when we sin, our sin, in a certain sense, bears witness to the greatness of God, for the more we sin, the more righteous God appears by contrast. So there is a certain sense in which by sinning we are exhibiting the righteousness of God. Our unrighteousness demonstrates the righteousness of God. And if God shows his righteousness by exposing our unrighteousness, are we not - and here's the distortion - doing God a favour by continuing in unrighteousness? Are we not adding to Divine glory by sinning?

Again, to ask such a question is to answer it, and how does Paul answer it? **Certainly not! If that were so, how could God judge the world?** (verse 6). If our unrighteousness were justified on the grounds that it makes all the more clear and vivid the righteousness of God, then God would have no reason to judge us. Instead he should reward us, compliment us.

But again, **Someone might argue, "If my falsehood enhances**

God's truthfulness and so increases his glory, why am I still condemned as a sinner?" Why not say - as we are being slanderously reported and as some claim that we say - "Let us do evil that good may result"? (verses 7-8). There is a clear teaching in Scripture that God has a remarkable ability to bring good out of our evil. For example, he brought the redemption of the world through the treacherous act of Judas. Can Judas stand at the judgment seat and say, 'God, give to me a great reward because no one has ever done a greater kindness to the human race than I. I delivered Jesus to be crucified and if it wasn't for me there would have been no atonement'?

Paul concludes this brief section by simply saying: **Their condemnation is deserved**. Judas has no basis upon which to claim a reward from God. His act was altogether wicked. His condemnation at the hands of God is perfectly just, in spite of the fact that God was able to overcome his evil. It is an irrational distortion of truth to conclude that, because God's righteousness is enhanced indirectly by our unrighteousness, we are to continue doing evil that good may come.

THE DOCTRINE OF TOTAL DEPRAVITY (3:9-12)

Orthodox theologians teach that man is so corrupt he is said to be totally depraved. Usually that doctrine of Total Depravity is linked to the names of the sixteenth century Protestant Reformer, John Calvin and the fourth century Church Father, St Augustine. As one who stands in the Reformation tradition, I hold to the doctrine of the total depravity of mankind, though very much aware of the misunderstandings and caricatures of that doctrine which abound. There is a distinction which I have found to be helpful: total depravity does not mean utter depravity. Utter depravity would mean that every human being is as wicked as it is possible to be, and we know that this is not the case. As much as we sin, we can always contemplate sinning more often, or more grievously than we presently do.

Also, the term 'total depravity' sounds as if there is absolutely nothing of any value left in the human race. I am involved in a ministry called *The Value of the Person* and it might be asked how anybody who believed in the total depravity of man could speak of the value of human beings? It sounds paradoxical and ironic, but I have lectured on many occasions saying that the Christian faith in general, and Calvinism in particular, has the highest, most exalted view of man of any anthropology. The very fact that Calvinists take sin so seriously is because they take the value of human beings so seriously. It is because man was made in the image of God, called to mirror and reflect God's holiness, that we have the distinction of being the image-bearers of God.

But what does 'total depravity' mean? Total depravity means simply this: that sin affects every aspect of our human existence: our minds, our wills and our bodies are affected by sin. Every dimension of our personality suffers at some point from the weight of sin that has infected the human race.

This is what the apostle is expounding in verse 9: **What shall we conclude then? Are we any better?** Of course he is referring to Jews and Gentiles. Are Jews better than the Gentiles? Not at all. What shall we conclude then? Are we any better? **Not at all!**

In chapter 1, Paul gave his attention primarily to the sinfulness of the Gentile, the pagan who is outside the camp of Israel. In chapter 2 he turned his attention to the sinfulness that is present within the community of Israel, and so the conclusion follows inevitably: **We have already made the charge that Jews and Gentiles alike are all under sin**.

Notice, he doesn't say that both Jews and Greeks are all sinners. He has already said that manifestly. He says here that Jews and Greeks are all *under* sin. Does this mean under the judgment of sin, under the weight of sin or under the power of sin?

We speak this way, somewhat metaphorically. When we get behind in our work, or behind in our payments, or whatever, when we have lost that sense of being on top of things, we say we are underneath it all. Being 'under' suggests the metaphor of being weighted down by a terrible burden, a heavy obstacle that seeks to crush us. We think, for example, of John Bunyan's imagery of the pilgrim, Christian, who goes through life stumbling underneath the dreadful weight of sin that is crushing him. It is only when he comes to the foot of the cross and meets the Saviour that the burden rolls off his back and he is able to stand upright, free, once again. Paul is saying that everybody, Jew and Gentile, is under sin.

Then follows this lengthy citation from the Old Testament to corroborate his statement that all men are under the weight of sin: **As it is written: "There is no-one righteous, not even one; there is no-one who understands, no-one who seeks for God. All have turned away, they have together become worthless. There is no-one who does good, not even one."'**

This is one of the most radical and extensive indictments of the corruption of man ever to appear in print. Let's look at it carefully so that we can catch the full flavour and the full force of the apostolic indictment.

He begins with what we call, in terms of propositional analysis, a universal negative: **There is no one righteous, not even one.** How are we to understand that? The apostle is saying that no human being who has ever lived (apart from Jesus of Nazareth), when judged by the standard of the law of God, can rightfully be called 'righteous'.

Then he says: **there is no one who understands.** Understands what? Obviously, though it is not stated, he means that there is no-one who really understands what righteousness involves. The righteousness of God is the theme of this epistle. There is a sense in which these statements flow sequentially out of each other. If there is none righteous, no one understands. Or, to reverse it, if no one understands, no one can be righteous.

Our lack of righteousness affects our understanding, because if we are not righteous, we don't have the capacity to understand the fullness of what righteousness is. Our very minds are infected by unrighteousness.

Now if we do not understand true righteousness, what would be the consequence of that? **no one who seeks God.** This statement has been a source of much controversy and confusion. How many times have you heard it said of somebody who does not claim to be a Christian, 'Well, that person is not a Christian, but he is seeking, he is searching for God.' In fact, there are people who claim to be seeking after God, but are having profound difficulty in finding him. If they are right, Paul must be wrong, because the apostle Paul says that no one in his natural condition seeks God.

Doesn't the Bible appeal to people to search after God? Why did Jesus say, Seek first the kingdom of God (Matt. 6:33), or, Seek and you will find (Matt. 7:7)? Keep in mind that when Jesus gave those instructions and admonitions he was giving them to believers. He was speaking to his disciples, to those who had already embraced him. Those who are believers have the capacity to seek God, but outside of faith, outside of belief, nobody seeks God. So it is improper for us to speak of the pagan seeking after God.

But why does it seem to us that people do search after God? The great Roman Catholic theologian, St Thomas Aquinas, wrestled with this particular question. He gave us this insight: when we see people searching for such things as truth, peace of mind, eternal life or happiness, they are searching for relief from their guilt. These are things that Christians know only God can give them. So we leap to the conclusion that since they are searching diligently for those things which only God can give them, they must therefore be searching for God. But it is precisely this in which man's sinfulness consists, says Aquinas, that man seeks for the benefits of God, while fleeing from the Person of God.

Do we really believe in a God who plays hide-and-seek, a God who hides himself from those who would search after him? Is it our task to find God, or is it God who is searching after us? The whole of Scripture, from the Garden of Eden in Genesis to the conclusion of the book of Revelation, describes the great God who is searching for and seeking to save that which is lost. God is pursuing us, while we are the fugitives fleeing from him.

Look at this quotation in descending order again: if there is nobody righteous, then certainly nobody understands. And if nobody understands, certainly no one ever really seeks for God. On the other hand, look at it in ascending order: if no one seeks for God, it is obvious they will never understand who God is, and if they never understand who God is, they will never come to a real understanding of righteousness.

So Paul can then say: **All have turned away, they have together become worthless** (verse 12). If we are fleeing from God the first thing we want to do is to get our feet off the path that would lead us to God, so we all turn aside. This image is found repeatedly in Scripture, that, like sheep, we have turned aside (cf. Isaiah 53:6). No one follows the straight and narrow path that leads to God, rather we are moving helter-skelter all over the place as we seek to flee from the presence of God. All have turned aside and together we have become worthless. That is, with respect to righteousness, we have become useless.

Then Paul brings the first portion of this lengthy citation to a conclusion: **There is no one who does good, not even one.** Think about the extent of this indictment. Paul is not merely saying that there are none who are perfect, none who are righteous. Yet didn't he earlier say that the pagan does by nature the things of the law? Yes, but Paul was very careful there in his choice of words. He did not say that they did the law, he nowhere ascribes to the unbeliever the performance of a single good deed. How is that possible? Is Paul saying here that unless a person is a believer in Christ, he will not ever do a good deed? That is precisely what it means. It may seem outrageous, but nobody ever does a single thing that is good, we are so corrupt that our sin infects even the best of our deeds.

When God examines an action, he considers it both in terms of its external action and its internal motive. For example, the law requires that we don't steal. If I refrain from stealing, I have done half the good deed, the external part. But the Bible teaches that a truly good deed is motivated by a heart that seeks to honour God, by a heart that is loving God. That's the internal dimension of the good deed. Though my outward acts may in fact conform to the external demands of the law, if they do not spring from a heart that loves God, then they are motivated by selfish desire. It is in that high sense of goodness that nobody outside of Christ ever does a good deed.

What's the point? Not just to have an abstract theological

discussion of goodness, but something very practical. Paul is speaking to those who really believe that they can stand before God at the last day and depend upon their good deeds to get them into the kingdom of heaven.

John the Baptist called the Pharisees a 'brood of vipers' (Luke 3:7). He likened them to poisonous snakes. It sounds like harsh language, but there is a sense in which the apostle Paul applies the same kind of description to all of us.

The apostle gathers quotations from the Old Testament in such a way as to build a picture of the organs of the human body which God designed to be used for righteousness but in fact have become tools of wickedness. **"Their throats are open graves; their tongues practise deceit." "The poison of vipers is on their lips." "Their mouths are full of cursing and bitterness." "Their feet are swift to shed blood; ruin and misery mark their ways, and the way of peace they do not know." "There is no fear of God before their eyes."**

There is mention of the throat, the tongue, the lips, the mouth, the feet and the eyes. The body that God has given them, is used by sinful people for purposes of evil.

Paul starts with the description of the throat, and says that the throat is an 'open grave'. Doesn't that remind you of Jesus' rebuke of the Pharisees, when he said that the Pharisees were like 'white-washed tombs' (Matt. 23:27)? Very carefully painted and white-washed on the outside to give a picture of placid tranquillity, of purity and cleanliness. But they cover up the decay and deterioration, said Jesus, of dead men's bones.

Keep in mind how strict the Jews were with respect to dealing with corpses. Not having the advanced means of disposing of dead bodies that is customary in the modern world, there were quite stringent restrictions about coming in contact with a corpse, lest one become defiled. The biological danger was also great, as disease was easily transferred from the corpse to a live person. Therefore, it was a matter of health regulations in the ancient world, that burial sites be heavily covered.

Paul says that the throat of fallen man is like an unsealed and uncovered grave. The throat is the tunnel, as it were, that leads to our hearts, to the inside of man. Jesus said it is out of the heart, out of the inner core of man's being, that we are corrupted.

Their tongues practise deceit. The tongue comes in for quite a lot of discussion in the New Testament. James gives almost an entire chapter to the tongue, and its capacity for destruction (James 3). He says that the tongue is a little member that boasts of great things. The tongue is likened to the rudder of a ship, the very small piece that determines the course of the large vessel. How difficult is the tongue to control. It is like a spark, with the capacity to set forests ablaze. So many sins that the New Testament speaks of are sins of the tongue. Think how we wound other people with unkind remarks, with slander, insult and unnecessary criticism; how we use the tongue to blaspheme God, to tell lies and desecrate the sanctity of truth. This is the specific use of the tongue to which Paul calls attention here. Fallen man has revealed the deadly corruption of his heart by use of the tongue for lies. Satan is the Father of Lies, one who was a liar from the beginning (John 8:44). The fracturing of truth is characteristic of fallen man and sets man apart from God who speaks no lie.

Paul moves from the tongue to the lips: **The poison of vipers is on their lips** (verse 13). The lips are compared to poison that can kill. The power of a poisonous snake to kill is well known to people who live in India and Africa. The metaphor is a strong one and is emphasising the fact that we can inflict unbelievable pain and destruction and wounds upon people by the words that we speak.

He then says: **Their mouths are full of cursing and bitterness** (verse 14). Cursing is usually perceived in our culture as a sign of masculinity. It is as if by filling our speech with cursing, with caustic cynicism and bitterness, that somehow we will bring a degree of respect to ourselves as strong or mature. But Biblically the cursing mouth, the bitter mouth, is a sign of human fallenness. The mouth was made to be an instrument of blessing, to be an instrument of healing, to be a vehicle for words of kindness and of truth.

Picture a person whose tongue is full of lies, whose lips are poisonous and whose mouth is filled with cursing and bitterness -

what kind of a person is that? In a word, he is 'hostile'. This describes the hostility that fallen man has against God, and not only against God, but against his fellow man and even against himself.

It is only after men are filled with bitterness that **Their feet are swift to shed blood** (verse 15). The hostile person is in a hurry for violence. He enjoys inflicting violence and even sometimes just seeing violence, the sight of it, the thrill of it. The book of Genesis (6:13) tells us that when God destroyed the earth by the flood, one of the reasons for that judgment was because the world was filled with violence. A mark of the fallen man is that he is quick to engage in violence.

Ruin and misery mark their ways (verse 16). What else could be the consequence of a humanity accustomed to deceit, to poisoning each other, to bitterness and to violence? We have been able to conquer all kinds of obstacles to the lifespan of mankind: diseases, safety factors and so on, but it is as true today, as it was in the first century, that destruction and misery are in the pathway of humanity.

And the way of peace they do not know (verse 17). It is not simply that they have not followed the pathway of peace, they haven't ever really understood it. Peace was the ultimate hope and desire of the ancient Jew. So deeply embedded in his consciousness was this desire for peace, that instead of saying Hello and Goodbye when he met a friend on the way, he would say Shalom! (Peace). This is the desire of the child of God, to know peace, because the world is not a peaceful place.

Finally, he concludes, **There is no fear of God before their eyes** (verse 18). We talk about that which is before our eyes as that which comes into our field of vision. A more abstract word for 'before their eyes' may be 'perspective'. Each one of us has a perspective on life, how we look at things.

Paul, in describing fallen man, says, There is no fear of God before their eyes. How does a person look at things who has no fear of God? We can take that word 'fear' in two ways. Sometimes we think of fear as that which frightens us, hence Paul is saying that nobody is afraid of God any more. There is a certain sense in which that is still true. We live as if there were no God; we live as if we never had to stand before God; we live as if God couldn't possibly hurt us or do anything to cause us grief if he wanted to.

But of course, the deeper meaning of the fear of God in Scripture is not a servile fear that causes us to tremble in fright in the presence of God, but rather a fear born of honour. It is 'filial' fear, fear to offend one whom we love, adore and respect. Paul is saying that the human race is an irreverent race; that humanity has no profound respect for God.

Paul summarises in verse 19: **Now we know that whatever the law says, it says to those who are under the law.** Sometimes when the New Testament writers speak of the Law, they are referring to the books of Moses, sometimes specifically to the book of Exodus, sometimes to the ten commandments and sometimes to the many laws that we find throughout the Pentateuch.

Who are those who are under the law? Look back to verse 9, where Paul says, 'We have already made the charge that Jews and Gentiles alike are all under sin'. They couldn't be under the judgment of sin unless first they were under the pronouncement of the law because, as the apostle labours in this book, where there is no law, there is no sin. The point he is making is that every human being is under the law of God to some degree, **so that every mouth may be silenced and the whole world held accountable to God.**

Paul is drawing a courtroom scene, and God is sitting on the bench. The indictment is being read to the defendant - fallen man. Can you imagine being brought into a courtroom, having an indictment read and then having the judge say to you, How do you plead? As you start to give a defence, suddenly the judge cuts you off in mid sentence and says, You may not speak! There is a certain sense in which the judgement scene of the human race will happen like that.

In Psalm 46, the Psalmist says, Be still, and know that I am God. That passage is often cited as if it were an invitation to enter in to a quiet and tranquil mood of peacefulness, in which one can contemplate the wonders and majesty of God. But that's not the force of this psalm. The Psalmist is using, in Hebrew, very strong language. What he is having God say, literally, is, Shut up! Be quiet! Stop it! and know that I am God.

On numerous occasions in the teachings of Jesus we are told (or it is hinted) that at the final judgment there will be a profound silence. Why is that? When we stand before the judgment seat of God, the indictment against us will be so clear and the evidence so overwhelming that it would be futile, foolhardy, to even protest our innocence. The time for excuse-rendering, for explanation and rationalisations, will be over.

God never offers false charges against people. It is foolishness to speak against the indictment of Almighty God. The only appropriate response to his judgment is either silence or the wailing, piercing cry for mercy. To debate one's guilt, to deny one's sin, is futile. The best lawyer in the world would be a waste of money for that particular hearing. The law of God says to those who are under the law that every mouth may be stopped for all the world is guilty before God. That's the verdict at the ultimate tribunal. Each of us is guilty before God.

Why does Paul labour this point of the universality of human guilt? Is he one of those preachers who seems to enjoy wallowing in the corruption of the human race, giving us a bad self-image, paralysing us with guilt feelings? That is not his intent at all. But it is impossible to really hear the gospel, until one has first heard the gavel crash and the verdict sounded unequivocally - Guilty! As long as we delude ourselves by attempts at self-justification, or try to make light of, deny, or shift to somebody else's responsibility or blame, the sin that is a reality in our lives, we can never really hear the gospel. Unless we understand the justice of God, how can we possibly know anything of his mercy or his grace. Grace and mercy depend for their very meaning on the background of the reality of justice.

Therefore no one will be declared righteous in his sight by observing the law. If we were to apply the rules of logic to this text, we would recognise immediately the presence of what is called a 'universal negative'. This is a negative that encompasses every individual. God says that no-one shall be justified by observing the law.

This is what the Protestant Reformation was all about. Anyone who is trusting in his own merit is committing the ultimate folly.

What does Paul mean by the word 'justified'? It is very simple. The problem of mankind is this: God is just, fallen human beings are not just. How can those of us who are unjust ever be justified? Excuses for real sin never justify the sin. If I sin once, I cannot undo the transgression. I may try to compensate for it, make retribution for it, apologise for it; I can do all of those things, but I cannot undo it. I cannot make the imperfect, perfect.

The 'universal negative' of the preceding verse is counterbalanced by this significant positive assertion of what the law can do: **rather, through the law we become conscious of sin**. While the law cannot save, it does serve to spotlight how far short of God's standard of perfection we all fall. As this manifestation of God's standard it points us to Christ, who alone saves.

The knowledge it brings is at least intellectual cognition, and more. The law has the capacity to bring inward conviction, dread, guilt and shame. Its power is linked to its sure ability to persuade in a convincing manner that trusting in one's own righteousness will only lead to condemnation; as such the law functions as a forerunner of Christ, preparing for the reception of the good news of the gospel.

3
JUSTIFICATION AND ITS FRUITS
(3:21-8:39)

WHAT IS JUSTIFICATION? (3:21-31)
Paul in this section will describe the righteousness that solves the dilemma between our injustice and God's perfect justice. **But now a righteousness from God, apart from law, has been made known, to which the Law and the Prophets testify** (verse 21).

Because of the word *now* in this text, some have concluded that the people in the Old Testament couldn't solve the dilemma of justification and it is only now, in the New Testament period, that the righteousness of God is made available to us by faith. That's not the apostle's point. He is saying that a righteousness from God has been *made known*, that is, made clear. It was what Abraham looked for but only perceived in shadowy form. He could see it at a distance but it was vague and veiled, through distant promises. But now that promise has been fulfilled, for the atonement of Jesus Christ has been offered.

To which the Law and the Prophets testify. It is not a brand new novelty, unheard of in the Old Testament. This doctrine that is now crystal clear in the work of Jesus Christ, is the same way of salvation that God proclaimed to Abraham, to Moses, to David, to Jeremiah and to Isaiah. The just shall live by faith. Justification is by faith alone. That was the cardinal principle enunciated by Martin Luther in the sixteenth century and has become the central foundation upon which all Protestant theology is established.

This righteousness from God comes through faith in Jesus Christ to all who believe (verse 22). Here Paul is getting to the core of his message, to the heart of his theme.

Before we go on, it is necessary to explain some terms. The slogan of the Reformation is *justification by faith alone*. The word 'by' refers to the means by which something is accomplished, the instrument that links us to Christ. Some think that the very act of believing is so meritorious that it earns for us a place in the kingdom, rather than doing other works of the law. But that's not what the apostle means by justification by faith. Rather faith is the instrument that links us to Christ.

Perhaps a more accurate way to state the doctrine of justification by faith alone is to say: justification is by Christ alone. It is his righteousness that justifies us. It is his merit that provides a place for us in the kingdom of God. Faith links us to him, so that we participate in his righteousness in the sight of God. This righteousness is given to every person that trusts in Christ.

What is justifying faith?

When Luther announced this concept in the sixteenth century, it provoked a hue and cry of opposition that split the Christian Church asunder. Many people were afraid that what Luther was teaching was the idea that all one had to do was to have a casual, cavalier belief in Jesus, and could live any kind of life of wickedness they then desired. Such a doctrine would cut the rug out from under earnest attempts at striving after godliness among Christian people. So Luther was forced to ask the question, What is saving faith? He described saving faith as *fides viva*, a living faith, a vital faith, a faith that was beating with a heart pulsating after God.

Some people think that Protestants trust in Christ for their redemption whereas Roman Catholics trust completely in themselves and in their own good deeds. That's simply not true. The Roman Catholic church does not teach and has never taught that people are justified on the basis of their own good works without any need of the redemptive activity of Christ. What Rome objects to, however, is the concept of faith 'alone'.

Let us sketch the difference. It starts in an understanding of the first step in justification. Protestantism teaches that the instrument by which we are brought into a justified relationship with Jesus Christ is faith.

Rome deals with the problem of justification in two different ways. In the first instance, justification occurs through the instrument of baptism, when the grace of justification is infused into the soul of the child. The child is then regarded as being in a state of grace for as long as he keeps himself pure from mortal sin, a sin so grievous that it has the ability to destroy the grace of justification. If a person commits a mortal sin, however, there is a second manner by which that person can be justified. The Roman Catholic Council of Trent in the sixteenth century described the sacrament of penance as the second way of justification for those who had made shipwreck of their souls. In this sacrament of penance there are different parts or aspects. First, a penitent person must make a confession of his sins to the priest. Then the priest pronounces absolution. But the issue in the sixteenth century was not confession or even priestly absolution.

The real issue was the next dimension of justification which taught that in penance the penitent sinner was required to do works of satisfaction. These works were defined by the Roman Catholic church as bestowing upon the penitent merits of congruity, merits that were fitting or congruous for God to justify that person again. The penitent must have faith in Jesus Christ, but he also must produce real righteousness within himself in order to be justified. It would be fair to simplify the Roman Catholic view like this: justification happens as a result of a combination of faith plus works.

Protestantism says that we cannot add anything to the merit of Jesus Christ, the only merit that avails for our justification. Protestantism believes, however, that the true believer will then show a manifest change of life and bring forth works worthy of repentance, works of obedience. But those works of obedience are not the basis for their salvation. For Rome, faith plus works equals justification. For Protestantism, faith equals justification; but that faith produces good works.

Why must justification rest on faith alone? Why can our works not serve as a basis for it? In verse 20 Paul has excluded any possibility of our being justified by the deeds of the law. Our justification is by faith in Jesus Christ. Why? **for all have sinned and fall short of the glory of God** (verse 23). Paul turns again to the theme that he has been expounding throughout this epistle, that all men are guilty before the judgment seat of God. We may think that we are more righteous than other people but compared to the ultimate standard of God, we fall short, abysmally short, miserably short.

Paul continues: **and are justified freely by his grace through the redemption that came by Christ Jesus** (verse 24). Here he uses the word 'freely' to modify *justify*. Justification is something that God bestows as a gift. That which is a gift can never be imposed by obligation; nor can it be earned or deserved. He emphasises this by saying further that we are justified freely 'by his grace'. That is the real heart of the issue: merit or grace.

What is *redemption*? In New Testament times the noun 'redemption' or the verb 'to redeem' meant primarily to pay a ransom, to purchase back something that was being held in captivity or in bondage. Its original meaning was to buy back out of slavery, out of indebtedness or out of captivity. This is precisely how the New Testament describes the work of Jesus on our behalf. Jesus is our Redeemer. He is the One who paid a ransom for our souls.

We have to be careful here, for there are all kinds of theories about what Jesus did. One that has been very famous in the history of the church is that Jesus paid a ransom to the devil, in order to buy us back from Satan's possession. But that's an utterly unbiblical concept. The ransom or the purchase price is not paid to Satan. It is paid to God, for it is to God that we are in debt.

The question is, Who will pay the price that God's law requires from us? The meaning of justification by faith alone is that we are justified freely by the unmerited favour of God, through a redemption that is in Christ Jesus. Some people object to that because they say it sounds like a drama going on within the Godhead itself: God the Father has set out to destroy us, but God the Son satisfies his wrath in such a way as to bring us redemption. But that, of course, would come perilously close to blaspheming the righteousness of God.

God presented him as a sacrifice of atonement, through faith in his blood (verse 25). It is God the Father who sends the Son into the world. It is God the Father who by his grace freely justifies us through the merit of Jesus Christ. It is God who sets forth his only-begotten Son to be a propitiation. So there is agreement within the Godhead. God himself initiates and sets into motion this grand plan of redemption, whereby he reveals a way to satisfy the demands of his own righteousness. In doing this God does not compromise himself, nor does he take lightly the transgressions against his holiness. God deals with his own justice by requiring the price of sin at the hands of his only-begotten Son.

God's intent in sending Jesus into the world was to placate his wrath. His sacrifice was made to fulfil all of the demands that God had imposed as sanctions upon the committing of sins. God never pronounces guilty people innocent. The atonement does pay the penalty for the one who is judged guilty. The sinner is not cleared or exonerated, the sinner is declared guilty. It is not at the point of judgment that he is redeemed, but at the point of sentence.

Not only does Christ offer the sacrifice to reconcile the sinner to God by paying the ransom that is required, but a double transfer takes place. Not only is the sinner's guilt transferred to Christ, but in God's sight, his merit is given to the sinner. After the transfer takes place, God looks at the sinner and declares him to be justified. Not because he has been cleared of his sin, but because he has been redeemed from his sin.

When Luther defined the doctrine of justification in the sixteenth century, he used a Latin phrase *simul justus et peccator*, which means 'At the same time, just and sinner'. This gets to the heart of justification by faith alone. Though in and of myself I am a sinner, once I have received the benefit of Christ's propitiation, I am just in the sight of God. Just, by virtue of Christ's righteousness; sinner, by virtue of my own performance.

Through faith in his blood. When the Bible speaks of the blood of Jesus, some people attribute almost a mystical character to what flowed through the veins of Jesus of Nazareth. An Episcopalian priest once raised this question with me. He said, 'R C, if Jesus had scratched his finger on a nail, would that have done the atonement?' He was not trying to be blasphemous, but was asking a serious theological question. What lay behind the question was this: if Jesus scratched his finger on a nail and drew blood, wouldn't that be enough since salvation comes through the blood of Christ? No. Jesus didn't simply have to bleed, he had to die, because the penalty that God imposes upon sin is death. So when the Bible says 'through faith in his blood', it literally means through faith in his death.

He did this to demonstrate his justice, because in his forbearance he had left the sins committed beforehand unpunished. God's forbearance refers to his longsuffering, not his indulgence. Sometimes we wonder why God doesn't punish sin immediately. God is not winking at our sins, but he is forbearing so that we may avail ourselves of the righteousness of Jesus Christ.

He did it to demonstrate his justice at the present time. The cross of Jesus Christ not only redeems us, it also vindicates God. It makes it perfectly clear that God takes sin very seriously. How many times have you heard people say: The God of the Old Testament is a God of wrath, the God of the New Testament is a God of grace, mercy and love.

Where do we find in Scripture the fullest expression of the love of God? In the cross. Where do we find the most awful manifestation of the wrath of God? Is it not also in the cross, where he pours out wrath upon his own Son? That same act shows that God judges sin, and yet is a loving and merciful God.

God did this to vindicate his own righteousness, **so as to be just and the one who justifies those who have faith in Jesus** (verse 26). When God spares me and gives me the gift of his kingdom and access into heaven, he does not compromise his own integrity to do it. His righteousness is preserved and maintained throughout.

Paul asks in verse 27: **Where, then, is boasting?** It is almost as if he is looking through an empty room and is saying with puzzled astonishment, 'Where's boasting? Where is it? I can't find it.' He answers his own question: **It is excluded**. Why? He asks another question: **On what principle? On that of observing the law? No, but on that of faith**.

Paul is saying that the doctrine of salvation, which comes to us graciously through the work of Christ, banishes boasting from the

Christian life. If our justification was even in part based upon good works, we would have something to boast about. It is the concept of justification by faith alone that crushes the voice of human arrogance and human pride.

For we maintain that a man is justified by faith apart from observing the law (verse 28). It is this verse more than any other single verse in Scripture which most clearly articulates the doctrine of justification by faith alone. But does not James contradict that in the second chapter of his book: 'You see that a person is justified by what he does and not by faith alone.' Can you imagine the consternation that this has caused to people in the church for hundreds of years?

Some people say this is a clear example of the Bible flatly contradicting itself. Or is it possible that James means something quite different from what Paul means? The question that James is addressing is a quite different question. He is facing this problem: What good is it if a man says he has faith, but has no works? James is dealing with people who say they believe. Anybody can say they believe, so he said, Show me your faith by your works. And then he goes on to say that faith without works is dead. Can that kind of faith save anybody? Of course the conclusion is 'No', and Paul would certainly agree. The only way you will ever know that my faith is real, is if you see it in my behaviour.

Is God the God of Jews only? Is he not the God of Gentiles too? Yes, of Gentiles too, since there is only one God, who will justify the circumcised by faith and the uncircumcised through that same faith (verses 29,30). Christianity is a faith that transcends all national, cultural, and racial distinctions. Neither is it time bound to a particular period of history. Rather, Paul boldly professes that it is a universal faith. This may not strike us today as a particularly profound truth, but to the ears of a first-century Jew this would have been shocking.

Charles Hodge comments on Paul's words by saying: 'We Gentiles may now look up to heaven, and confidently say, "Thou art our Father, though Abraham be ignorant of us, and though Israel acknowledge us not".'

In verse 31, Paul ends this chapter with a strong reaffirmation of both the law and faith: **Do we, then, nullify the law by this faith? Not at all! Rather, we uphold the law.** Some might wrongly conclude that since the advent of the gospel and the Pauline development of justification by faith alone, the law is abrogated. However, one does not invalidate the other, but rather each was given by God for particular purposes. Functions such as the law's revelatory character and moral instruction remain valid, even though its ceremonial and theocratic role has been fulfilled. The tragedy of the contemporary evangelical church is its failure to know and establish the law of God.

ABRAHAM WAS JUSTIFIED BY FAITH (4:1-22)

Chapter 4 represents a lengthy illustration of the truth proclaimed in chapter 3. The principal character of the illustration is Abraham, the Old Testament patriarch, who is called, in the New Testament, the 'father of the faithful'. Paul points to him as his exhibit A, his principal model of one who is justified by faith.

What then shall we say that Abraham, our forefather, discovered in this matter? (verse 1). Paul is reminding his readers that he, himself, is a Jew when Abraham is called 'our forefather'. He says in verse 2, **If, in fact, Abraham was justified by works, he had something to boast about - but not before God.** Paul introduces here what we call a 'condition contrary to fact'. He doesn't say that Abraham 'was' justified by works, but rather if Abraham were justified by works. The language here indicates that Abraham was not justified by works. Paul is envisaging a hypothetical situation that is, in fact, not the case.

What does the Scripture say? Paul asks another question - what does the word of God say? Not what does that council, or this synod, or that theologian say? For Paul, the supreme authority is nothing less than sacred Scripture. He appeals to the teaching of the Old Testament to underscore his using Abraham as a model for justification by faith. He answers his own question, citing Genesis 15:6, **Abraham believed God, and it was credited to him as righteousness** (verse

3). This verse is crucial for understanding the historic Protestant doctrine of justification by faith alone.

First of all, the verse that Paul cites says that Abraham believed God. It is one thing for us to believe that God exists, it is another thing for us to believe what God says, to trust God, to put our confidence in him. That is what saving or justifying faith is: not merely believing in God, but trusting God for our redemption.

Paul's intention is to answer a parenthetical question: If the New Testament teaches justification by faith, how were people justified in the Old Testament? The point Paul is making is that people were justified in the Old Testament in precisely the same way as in the New Testament. They were justified by faith. The instrument by which they were brought into a state of justification was faith. Now, you say, how could they have justifying faith by believing in Christ in the Old Testament when Christ hadn't even appeared to make atonement for sin? The answer is that the Old Testament saints believed in the future Redeemer who was to come, whose work was typified by the sacrificial system in Old Testament worship. The people in the Old Testament looked forward to the future, trusting in that which was to come. We, in the New Testament age, look backward to that which has already been accomplished. But it is believing the word of God that is crucial in both Testaments.

It is the second part of verse 3, however, that is so crucial to the historic debate: **"Abraham believed God, and it was credited to him as righteousness."** It is not that God looked down upon Abraham, and said, 'There is a righteous man; I will justify him on the basis of his obvious righteousness.' Rather, because Abraham believed, God counted him as righteous. If we had to wait until we were perfectly righteous before we could be justified, none of us would make it. All of us have some degree of sin clinging to us as long as we live in this world. If God were to judge us on a strict standard of absolute righteousness, none of us would be able to stand. The same was true of Abraham. But Abraham believed God and his faith was counted by God as righteousness.

This concept is called by Protestant theology 'forensic justification' or 'synthetic justification'. These are technical, theological terms, and they may be strange and foreign to those who are not in a theological seminary. Let's consider for a moment what is meant by the term 'forensic justification'. Where do we hear the word 'forensic' in our common language? The concept of forensics has to do with legal declarations, and so when we talk about forensic justification we are referring to the fact that God makes a legal declaration about those who believe. When a person believes, God legally declares that person just.

It's precisely at this point that Roman Catholic theologians have protested. One of the reasons why the Protestant doctrine has been rejected by Rome, historically, is that Rome understands this idea of forensic justification to be 'a legal fiction', arguing that it would make a liar out of God. How could God call people just or righteous, when in fact they are not righteous? Well, if God, arbitrarily and gratuitously, declared unrighteous people righteous, we would certainly understand these protests. It would indeed be a legal fiction and would cast a shadow on the integrity of God.

But when a person believes in Christ and the righteousness of Christ is imputed to him, the argument of Protestantism is that the transfer of the merit of Jesus Christ to the account of the believer is a real transfer. It is, therefore, real merit, Christ's merit transferred to the believer. So when God looks at that person who has trusted in Christ, he sees the unrighteous person covered with the righteousness of Christ.

Synthetic justification means that something is added to the sinner, in his standing before God. When we say that justification is synthetic, we mean simply that when God looks at the believer, he sees him as having the merits of Christ added to him.

The Roman Catholic view is called *analytical justification* which means that when God analyses the sinner, unless he finds true righteousness within the sinner, he cannot be justified. So, in a certain sense, before a Roman Catholic can be justified, he must first be sanctified. Protestantism teaches just the reverse: before a person can even begin to be sanctified, he must first be justified.

Another distinction is also crucial: the debate between Rome and Protestantism often hinges on two words: 'imputed' and 'infused'. To impute something is to transfer to someone's account. To infuse is to pour in. Now both Rome and Protestantism believe that there is no justification apart from the work of Christ. The debate is this: how does the righteousness of Christ become ours? How is the objective work of Christ subjectively appropriated? That is the issue.

Protestantism teaches that the righteousness of Christ is imputed to any believer by a Divine declaration, so that God counts us righteous. The Roman Catholic view is that, in baptism, the grace of justification is infused into the soul. It is not a clear cut statement - but the tendency is to think of grace in quantitative terms, something that can be added to or lost, augmented or diminished. They speak of 'losing grace' or 'adding grace' or 'increasing grace' to the soul. As that added measure of grace is infused into the soul, there is a greater opportunity, a greater strength, a greater power, to actually become righteous. This is why the Roman Catholic Church believes that the commission of mortal sin destroys salvation, and a person must start over again, as it were, through the sacrament of penance.

There is a strange incongruity here. The Roman Catholic Church objects in principle to a doctrine of justification by imputation, and insists upon infusion, rather than imputation. Yet, the doctrine of the 'treasury of merits' which emerged in the Middle Ages and is still held by the Roman Catholic Church, teaches that the power of the keys of the kingdom of God is held by the church; and the church has the ability to transfer excess merits, stored up in the treasury, to those who are in purgatory and who need certain amounts of merits, in order to proceed from purgatory to heaven. This was the theological basis for the 'indulgences' that were so controversial in the sixteenth century.

Now what makes up the 'treasury of merits'? According to the Roman Catholic Church, the great saints of the ages, like Augustine, or Thomas Aquinas, or Teresa, lived lives which were so virtuous, so meritorious, that they accrued to their own account more merit than they themselves needed in order to get into heaven. They have done what the church describes as 'works of supererogation': works which are above and beyond the call of duty, producing excess merits. This extra merit is then deposited in the treasury of merits and the church may transfer excess merits from the treasury to those who do not have enough merits of their own to move out of purgatory and into heaven. Here is the grand irony: the Roman Catholic Church repudiates the concept of the imputation of the merit of Christ, but builds a whole doctrine upon the imputation of the righteousness of the saints, through the treasury of merits. A point that is crucial to the controversy.

Back to the text. Paul declares that Abraham believed God and it was credited to him as righteousness. Abraham didn't possess that righteousness in and of himself, and this is the point that the apostle is going to develop throughout the rest of chapter 4.

Now when a man works, his wages are not credited to him as a gift, but as an obligation (verse 4). Again, we see the clear distinction between merit and grace. If I am truly virtuous, then a just and holy God need not exercise grace to redeem me. If I am truly righteous, he must let me enter into the kingdom of God on the basis of pure justice, because my virtue requires reward.

However, to the man who does not work but trusts God who justifies the wicked, his faith is credited as righteousness (verse 5). Paul is saying that our justification is on the basis of grace. He brings in David in verse 6: **David says the same thing when he speaks of the blessedness of the man to whom God credits righteousness apart from works.** Here is one who receives the blessing of God: God transfers righteousness to his account apart from works.

David rejoiced in this: **Blessed are they whose transgressions are forgiven, whose sins are covered** for they could not atone for their own sins. But they had the blessing that their iniquities had been forgiven and their sins covered. Therein is justification. We are blessed because our iniquities are forgiven in Jesus Christ and our sins are covered by his righteousness. Paul stresses this in verse 8: **Blessed is the man whose sin the Lord will never count against him.**

Paul now asks some further important questions: **Is this blessed-**

ness only for the circumcised, or also for the uncircumcised? (verse 9). Is this gift of God, this gracious redemption, given exclusively to the Jew? Is only a circumcised person able to be justified? Or is this something that comes also to those who are not circumcised?

We have been saying that Abraham's faith was credited to him as righteousness. Under what circumstances was it credited? Was it after he was circumcised, or before? He answers this question at the end of verse 10: It was not after, but before! Abraham, the father of Judaism, was justified before he was circumcised.

Circumcision, among other things, was a sign of the very faith and justification that Abraham already possessed before he was circumcised: **And he received the sign of circumcision, a seal of the righteousness that he had by faith while he was still uncircumcised.**

So then, he is the father of all who believe but have not been circumcised, in order that righteousness might be credited to them (verse 11). Abraham is not only the father of the Jew, he is the father of the Gentile Christian as well. He is the father of all who are justified by faith: **And he is also the father of the circumcised who not only are circumcised but who also walk in the footsteps of the faith that our father Abraham had before he was circumcised** (verse 12). The point being made is that Abraham was justified before he ever did any of the works of the law.

It was not through law that Abraham and his offspring received the promise that he would be heir of the world, but through the righteousness that comes by faith (verse 13). In other words, the promise that God made to Abraham was a promise that was carried on, not through the law, but through faith.

For if those who live by law are heirs, faith has no value and the promise is worthless, because law brings wrath. And where there is no law there is no transgression (verses 14, 15). If it is only through the law that we become heirs of the kingdom of God, faith becomes empty and useless, and the promise of God has no effect. Why? Remember what he said earlier: 'Therefore no-one will be declared righteous in his sight by observing the law' (3:20). If justification is through the law, then we have no hope because nobody, apart from Jesus, has kept the law.

Paul states the effect of the law in verse 15: **because law brings wrath. And where there is no law there is no transgression.** What the law does is expose our guilt and reveal our unrighteousness; it can't possibly be a means of justification, only a means of condemnation. And, Paul presses his point to say that where there is no law, there can be no sin, because the very concept of sin is the lack of conformity to a standard. Therefore, where there is no standard there can be no lack of conformity.

He continues: **Therefore, the promise comes by faith, so that it may be by grace and may be guaranteed to all Abraham's offspring - not only to those who are of the law but also to those who are of the faith of Abraham. He is the father of us all** (verse 16). It 'comes by faith, so that it may be by grace' - not by merit, but by grace. God doesn't analyse us and then, under that analysis, pronounce us righteous because he has found pure righteousness in us. No, God graciously gives us the gift of justification when we believe, by imputing the righteousness of Jesus to us.

As it is written: "I have made you a father of many nations." He is our father in the sight of God, in whom he believed. The apostle is referring to the promise made to Abraham in Genesis 15 that he would be the father, not only of the Jewish nation, but of many nations. The promises of God are not limited to Israel. Whoever you are, wherever you live, whatever land is your homeland, whatever your racial or ethnic background, if you place your trust for your standing before God in the work of Jesus Christ, Abraham is your father. You too are numbered among those who believe and are justified by faith.

The apostle breaks into a brief parenthesis of doxology: **the God who gives life to the dead and calls things that are not as though they were** (verse 17). He calls attention to the greatness of God, in that only God can bring life out of death. Only God can call those things which are not as though they were. Only God can bring something into being from nothing. In the book of Hosea, God said,

'I will say to those called "Not my people", "you are my people".'
I am unrighteous, but in Jesus Christ I am adopted into the family of
God. I am a Gentile - what God called 'no people', and yet he has
called me in Christ to be of his people.

Paul returns to Abraham and speaks of the strength, tenacity and
authenticity of his faith: **Against all hope, Abraham in hope
believed and so became the father of many nations, just as it had
been said to him, "So shall your offspring be"** (verse 18). Saving
faith is not an empty faith, a mere profession of faith, it is real faith,
real trust. God told Abraham, when he was an old man and his wife
was barren, that he was going to be the father of a great nation, that
his descendants would be as the stars of the sky and the sands of the
sea. How could a man even begin to entertain the possibility that such
a promise would come to pass when he is an old man physically
incapable of physical reproduction and his wife no longer biologically
capable of bearing children?

But Abraham believed God. **Without weakening in his faith, he
faced the fact that his body was as good as dead - since he was about
a hundred years old - and that Sarah's womb was also dead. Yet
he did not waver through unbelief regarding the promise of God,
but was strengthened in his faith and gave glory to God, being fully
persuaded that God had power to do what he had promised. This
is why "it was credited to him as righteousness"** (verses 19-22). In
these verses Paul reviews the nature of Abraham's faith, and points
out several key factors that we should note.

First, Abraham's faith clung to the promises of God to save, not
to his own subjective faith. He believed only in the spoken Word of
God, just as our faith must be solely in the promises of the written
Word.

Second, Abraham believed in the promises in the face of evidence
to the contrary. He and Sarah were as good as dead - the outward
earthly perspective was more than bleak.

Third, the level of Abraham's assurance is notable. He did not
waver in unbelief (the negative) but was strengthened in his faith and
was fully persuaded (the positive).

Finally, his faith was not inert, but rather was active. As we have said, authentic faith is a faith that acts. In the face of overwhelmingly discouraging circumstances, Abraham gave glory to God.

So we see that faith based not on ourselves, but on God's promises, that has full assurance despite the earthly evidence, is a faith that is credited as righteousness and which necessarily results in the act of giving glory to God.

BENEFITS OF JUSTIFICATION (4:23-5:11)

Paul makes it clear that the reason why the Old Testament record preserves the narrative of Abraham's justification, was not simply for Abraham's edification, but for ours: **The words "it was credited to him" were written not for him alone, but also for us, to whom God will credit righteousness.** The apostle is saying that this was not an isolated incident in history, but that Abraham was the prototype, the father of the faithful. All are justified in precisely the same way as Abraham, through the imputation of the righteousness of Christ to our account. But notice what Paul says in verse 24: **for us who believe in him who raised Jesus our Lord from the dead.** Thus the condition, the necessary prerequisite for our justification is that we trust God, that we believe in Christ.

He was delivered over to death for our sins and was raised to life for our justification (verse 25). Here we see something of a strange thought. Christ's death was an atonement for our sins. He was delivered for our offences. We understand that. But how does the resurrection fit in?

The Bible speaks often and in depth about the significance of the resurrection of Christ. We know that, on the one hand, the resurrection of Christ occurred because it was impossible for death to hold him. In and of himself Jesus was sinless, and if God had allowed sin to hold him eternally, this would have been an injustice against Jesus. And so, Christ is vindicated by the Divine act of resurrection. God demonstrates the innocence of Jesus by raising him from the dead.

But God did not do this as an isolated incident, for we are told repeatedly in the New Testament that Jesus is the first-born of those who are to be raised from the dead. We who are in Christ will participate in his resurrection.

Had Jesus died and not been raised from the dead, that would have indicated that his atonement was not acceptable to God. The fact that God raised him demonstrates to the world that God is satisfied with the perfect work of his Son. The resurrection of Jesus is the verdict of the Judge of heaven and earth, that the atonement has been made and all who trust in Christ will participate in the benefits of the righteousness of Christ.

Paul begins the fifth chapter: **Therefore, since we have been justified through faith, we have peace with God through our Lord Jesus Christ**. As we know, the chapter divisions and versifications that we find in the English Bible were not in the original epistle. It is always surprising to see a chapter in the New Testament begin with a word like 'therefore' as chapter 5 does. We should always pay close attention when a word like 'therefore' occurs in the text, for the word is introducing a conclusion based on what has gone before it. Paul has explained the meaning of justification and perhaps he is anticipating a reaction by his readers who may say, What does it all mean?

The primary effect of justification for us is peace with God. That is an astonishing conclusion, a fantastic announcement. But some may react, 'What's so good about having peace with God? I didn't know that we were at war.'

The New Testament declares that by nature we are fallen creatures, that we have a built-in hostility towards God and we are exposed to the wrath of God. This may sound utterly incredible, but the New Testament clearly teaches that deep down within us, our natural inclination is to hate God. But when we come to Christ, when we repent of our sins, the war is over. God signs a peace treaty.

What is this peace that God brings to us?

First of all, it transcends earthly dimensions of peace. I remember, during my childhood, the Berlin blockade, the Russian threat and the scary tactics of nuclear war. I remember going to grade school and having air raid drills in the event of an atomic attack. Yes, we had peace; the hostilities of World War 2 had ceased, but the hostilities were replaced by a Cold War. That Cold War then erupted into real heat in Korea, and then later in Vietnam. The peace that we experience in this world is always a fragile peace, a peace that comes with uncertainty, a peace that may not last.

But when God declares peace, when he declares us just, the war is over. And it is over for ever. To be sure, believers may incur his displeasure, they may cause him to respond with chastisement, but never again does God lift up the sword against his children. The war is over; the peace of God is ours. It is a transcendent peace, a peace that passes understanding. A peace so stable, so deep, so rich, that in its fullest dimension it remains incomprehensible to us. It is the peace of a healed, restored and reconciled relationship that once was broken.

Today, there is also talk about inner peace, peace of mind. People are troubled and, as Augustine said, Our hearts are restless until they find their rest in God. There are people all over this world, this very moment, who are desperately seeking peace of mind. They are seeking it in their vocation; they are seeking it in romance; they are seeking it in material possessions; they are seeking it in political upheaval; they are seeking it in a multitude of ways. We can find certain levels of peace in this world, and things to pacify our anxious souls. But there is a foundational anxiety that can never be quieted apart from our justification. A person cannot be fulfilled inwardly, no matter what he does, no matter what he has, if he is estranged from his Creator, if he is at war with God.

When the peace is established in the relationship, that peace penetrates our innermost being. So there is not only the outward peace of the actual relationship, but the inner peace where the unquietness and the troubledness of our souls is put to rest. Jesus, when he left his world, provided a legacy for his disciples: 'Peace I leave with you; my peace I give you. I do not give to you as the world gives' (John 14:27). The peace that characterised the innermost being of the soul of Jesus is bequeathed to his people. It is not a temporary peace, not what Luther called a 'carnal' peace that will be destroyed with the first rattling of a sound. It is not a peace without honour; it is not a peace by appeasement such as was attempted at Munich by Neville Chamberlain. It is a peace that is won by the honourable victory of Christ on the cross; a peace that is purchased by the precious cost of his own life; a peace that is guaranteed, signed and sealed by his vindication by resurrection. That is the first fruit of our justification.

Peace is not the only fruit, it is not the only benefit. Paul elaborates: **Through whom we have gained access by faith into this grace in which we now stand** (verse 2). What does Paul mean?

To understand this we must go back to the book of Genesis and read the narrative of the transgression of Adam and Eve and how God drove them out of the Garden of Eden. Man was no longer to have immediate access into the Presence of God. The Bible does teach us that God is omnipresent. There is also a sense in which, after God made a covenant with Abraham and renewed it with Moses at Mount Sinai, he promised to be in the midst of his people in the Tabernacle. Even then, however, it was only the High Priest who could enter God's immediate presence and then only once a year on the Day of Atonement; and he had to go through complex rites of purification and cleansing before he dared enter the Holy of Holies. People could draw near to God, but no one was allowed direct access into his presence, except the High Priest under the circumstances just described.

A massive curtain of several folds and layers, which was far more difficult to destroy than a huge wooden door, kept people out of the Holy of Holies. This veil was a reminder to the people that God was inaccessible. The veil hung there until the hour of the death of Christ, when it was torn in two as if a giant hand had reached down from heaven and ripped it like tissue paper (Matt. 27:51). Why? Because the barrier between God and man was removed. The sin of man was now atoned for, and those who are justified are now able to come into the presence of God. They have access by the grace of justification. Paul is emphasising the fact that for us to be in the presence of God is not a matter of merit, rather it is God's mercy and grace that make it possible for me to enter into fellowship with him.

When I believe in Jesus, his righteousness is imputed to me and I have access to God. It is a grace in which I *stand*. I have been elevated to a position of privilege, to stand in the presence of God by grace.

The first two fruits of our justification are peace with God and access into the presence of God. But that's not all: **And we rejoice in the hope of the glory of God.** We are given a new experience of joy and a new experience of hope, and the two are interrelated. The Biblical concept of hope is not to be confused with the secular notion of hope that permeates our society which is often only a desire, a wish, that is uncertain. The New Testament hope is certain because it is certified by the promise of God, who cannot lie. It is confirmed within us by the work of the Holy Spirit, and it becomes the anchor of our souls. It is stable, it is trustworthy, it is solid. And because we have this hope, which is really a certainty for the future, it is the occasion for joy. We rejoice in our hope of the glory of God.

We can't pass that phrase 'the glory of God' without a brief comment. The Greek word is *doxe*; its Hebrew equivalent, *karvode,* meant 'heaviness' or 'weightiness'. Glory has to do with the intrinsic significance, weightiness and dignity of God himself. Everyone is aware that one of the most crucial issues of the twentieth century is the issue of human dignity. We would have to be deaf to fail to hear the sighs, the screams and the cries of protest that bombard our ears from every corner of this world about human dignity. Many philosophers have abandoned hope of the dignity of man, saying the only significant question left for philosophers to examine is the question of suicide.

But the Christian declares that there is a real, substantial, eternal basis for the dignity of man. Our dignity is not rooted in our own humanity but is derived. It is assigned to us by the only one who has intrinsic, eternal, self-existent dignity - God himself. We rejoice in the hope of the glory of God, because he has promised that not only will he remain dignified, but he has made us dignified. In fact he promises us the ultimate completion of our justification, what the Bible calls 'glorification'.

I sometimes become very discouraged and disappointed by the fact that I do not always behave as I should. There are times when I am disgusted with my own nature and my own sinfulness. But part of me desires to be righteous, to be done with sin, to be done with evil, to be done with selfishness, to be done with pride, to be done with dishonesty, to be done with all those things that take away from the joy and the richness of human life. To be done with disputes with other people, to be done with broken relationships. God promises those of us who are in Christ that someday we will all be glorified. Sin will be totally removed from the community of heaven. So we rejoice because the glory of God is going to prevail. The Christian gets a taste of future glory. He receives the down payment of a transaction that God promises to pay in full.

But Paul is not finished. He goes on to say **Not only so, but we also rejoice in our sufferings**. We don't just tolerate tribulation with a stiff upper lip like the Stoics, who react to a bad situation by saying, 'Since there is nothing I can do about it, there is no sense in getting upset about it.' Paul is saying that if God is in control, then the most bitter human experiences we are called upon to endure (death, disease, the loss of loved ones, war, terror, all of these things that we dread in the depths of our beings) become not only tolerable, but we can actually glory in them because we know that God has promised to redeem every pain that we experience.

Why do we rejoice in sufferings? The apostle answers that question: **because we know that suffering produces perseverance** (verse 3). We immediately think of Job. In fact, when anybody talks about patience, the prototype of patience is mentioned, 'the patience of Job'. But the thing that is most characteristic of Job's life was not patience, but tribulation. He was a man who suffered, perhaps like no human being apart from Christ ever suffered. Yet it was out of that suffering and pain that the virtue, the character, the steel of his soul was fashioned into **perseverance**, and from perseverance, **character; and character, hope**.

Have you known Christians that seem to be unconquerable? No matter how many miseries, sufferings, trials and tribulations they endure, it seems only to strengthen their faith and confidence in the future. I know that all Christians don't manifest those traits, but I have known some who did.

What does the hope do? **And hope does not disappoint us**. I have been embarrassed at times when I have made frivolous predictions about the future, and had to eat my words and admit that I was wrong. That's the way earthly hope works. We hope that things happen, and when they don't turn out as we hoped, sometimes we are embarrassed and, almost always, painfully disappointed. Dealing with disappointment is one of the hardest disciplines that a human being can ever learn. But there is one hope that God has given to us that will never disappoint us and it is the future promise of the total victory of his kingdom and of his glory. No matter how many tribulations we endure in this life, there is another world, another chapter to human history that is still to be written.

Paul mentions another fruit of justification: **God has poured out his love into our hearts** (verse 5). The Bible distinguishes between three different kinds of love: *eros* - erotic love, *philao* - brotherly love, and *agape*, a special kind of love that is a gift of God to his people, a fruit not only of justification but of the Holy Spirit. It is *agape* love which Paul refers to here. An ability, a power and a capacity to love is actually implanted in the heart of those who are truly in Jesus Christ. Perhaps the biggest change in our personalities is the fact that the new capacity for love has been put there by a supernatural work of grace, by the work of the Holy Spirit. He sows it in the hearts of his people. Now it is true that some Christians have a greater capacity for love than others. This love has a capacity to swell and grow, to be nurtured, to be strengthened. Sometimes we wonder if there is any love at all in the hearts of some Christians, but if they are truly in Christ they must have some capacity for love that they never had before, because God plants this love in the heart of every believer.

Specifically, God gives us not simply a love for each other but a love for himself and a love for Jesus. The supreme test of whether or not a person is a Christian is whether or not he has an authentic love in his heart for Jesus Christ. He may make mistakes in his doctrine, he may not have his life entirely cleaned up, but the question is, Does he love Jesus at all? Without this work of grace, without this work of the Holy Spirit, people do not love Jesus. They may respect Jesus, they may admire Jesus, they may say good things about Jesus, but there is no love for Christ outside of justifying faith.

Love is a very important fruit of justification. But how is the love implanted within us? **by the Holy Spirit, whom he has given us.** The Holy Spirit indwells the believer. He takes up residence in the temple of a human being. Inside of every Christian lives the Holy Spirit, the presence of Christ. That is why people should be able to look at us, and somehow, see the presence of Christ.

You see, at just the right time, when we were still powerless, Christ died for the ungodly (verse 6). The whole emphasis in this text is that God does not wait for us to become righteous before he brings about our redemption. What does the apostle mean here by the phrase, 'at just the right time'? It could have one or two specific references. On the one hand, it could refer to the timeliness of God in providing a redemption for man when man could not possibly redeem himself. On the other hand, Christ's coming into the world was planned and purposed and foreordained by God. As the Scriptures elsewhere state, he was born in the fullness of time (Gal. 4:4).

The Swiss theologian, Oscar Cullmann, wrote a very important trilogy of books, the first of which was entitled simply, *Christ and Time*. Dr. Cullmann, in the book, examined the Biblical concepts of time and showed the difference between the Hebrew understanding of time and history and that of the ancient Greeks. Many of the ancient Greek philosophers had what we call a 'cyclical' view of time. They believed that there is no definitive beginning and no consummate point of ending to history. History goes round and round in a circle and in a cycle, where there is nothing new under the sun. In fact, the book of Ecclesiastes is thought by many to be written as a critique of that ancient world view, that cyclical view of history, where there is ultimately no progress.

Biblical time, however, operates on a more linear model. It begins with the statement: 'In the beginning', indicating that there is a beginning to world history. The Scriptures also speak of the 'end times' and of eternity welling up into the ages. So we have a progression, a flow, a chronology of time. Dr. Cullmann also pointed out that the Greek word *chronos* is used in the New Testament to call attention to that flow, that moment by moment passage of time, which we call history.

In addition to this chronological flow of second by second, minute by minute, hour by hour and year by year, there is also in Greek (*cheiros*) and in English the distinction between the historical and the historic. Not everything that happens in history is historic; everything that happens in history is historical, but not everything is historic in the sense of having pregnant meaning and radical significance for everything that went before and everything that comes afterwards.

The Bible has this concept of a pregnant moment in the midst of time that changes everything. There is a *cheiros*, an historic moment that God had planned from the beginning of the world, by which he sends his only-begotten Son into the world to die upon the cross in an historic, once-for-all event. It is an event that can never be repeated, duplicated, surpassed, or even augmented. This is one of the reasons why Protestantism has reacted so negatively to the Roman Catholic celebration of the Mass. For the Roman Catholic Church, the Mass is, in a very technically defined sense, a repetition of the death of Christ, a re-presentation of Christ to the Father. God certainly doesn't need to be reminded of it, because that atonement, made in the fullness of time, was so rich, so inexhaustible and of such infinite worth that it never needs to be repeated. Nor can we possibly add anything to it by way of merit or value.

Christ died for the ungodly. Many have died so that others could live. But Jesus did not extend our lives by 10, 20, 30 or 40 years, rather he died to extend our lives for ever, for eternity. Notice what Paul says, **Very rarely will anyone die for a righteous man, though for a good man someone might possibly dare to die** (verse 7). This is a difficult passage. Paul is saying that it is scarcely possible that somebody would die for a righteous man, yet maybe somebody would dare to die for a good man. There is a division among Biblical scholars and commentators about what Paul is saying here. Some say that Paul is simply repeating himself, using a change in words to bring emphasis, saying it is possible to conceive of somebody dying for someone who is righteous and good. So 'righteous' and 'good' are used interchangeably, as synonyms, just two ways of looking at the same thing.

Other commentators have pointed out a subtle difference between the words that may have some significance. In Biblical terms there is a slight difference between righteous (*dikaos*) and good (*agathos*). A righteous person is just, obeys the law, is straight and has integrity. The good person, in Biblical terms, is characterised by kindness, warmth and love. Now we can conceive of a person who is strictly obedient to the external laws and is just, but who is cold and not particularly warm or kindly to other people. As one theologian pointed out, what righteousness does in a person is to generate respect from other people, but goodness evokes affection.

If these commentators are correct, Paul is saying that it is scarcely conceivable that somebody would die for a righteous man, but more likely and more understandable that somebody would die for a good man, for whom there was genuine affection. Whichever view we take, however, the basic point of the text is unchanged.

The point is that Jesus did not die for people who are either righteous or good. Fallen man is not kindly disposed toward God, and the conclusion that Paul reaches in verse 8 is: **But God demonstrates his own love for us in this: While we were still sinners, Christ died for us**. A sinner is a transgressor of the law, and so we can say that while we were being actively disobedient to God, while we were in a state of rebellion against God, while we were hostile to God, while we were ignoring God, while we were refusing to submit to him, refusing to love him, refusing to worship him, at that time, while we were at enmity with God, Christ died for us.

Paul changes the emphasis in verse 9: **Since we have now been justified by his blood, how much more shall we be saved from God's wrath through him!** Here is a distinction between the present and the future, a distinction between justification and salvation. People say, 'I was saved the day I believed in Jesus Christ,' and they use the term *salvation* as if it were an exact equivalent to justification.

But that's not the case in the New Testament. Justification is one step in the process of salvation. The concept of salvation is used in a very complex way. It is used in the past tense, the imperfect tense, the present tense, the future tense, and so on. There is a sense in which we *are* saved, we *are being* saved and we *shall be* saved, because the full complex of salvation covers the whole of Christian experience. Justification occurs the moment I believe, and at that point I am brought into a state of salvation; but my salvation is still to be finalised, still to be consummated, still to be fully realised through my sanctification and my glorification. I don't receive my ultimate salvation until I am in heaven. If I am justified, I will certainly receive that ultimate salvation in heaven.

Elsewhere the apostle tells us that Christ saves us from the wrath which is to come (1 Thess. 1:10). God has promised that there will come a day when he will judge the world, and manifest and express his holy indignation, his righteous anger against sin. But those who are in Christ are not only presently justified, but they are assured that they will be saved from that wrath which is certain to come.

So he says, **For if, when we were God's enemies, we were reconciled to him through the death of his Son, how much more, having been reconciled, shall we be saved through his life!** (verse 10). Not only has Christ's death meant that we are justified at the present, but Christ's resurrection life, which is promised to us in the future, will save us from the wrath of God in judgment. We will be given eternal life by Jesus.

Not only is this so, but we also rejoice in God through our Lord Jesus Christ, through whom we have now received reconciliation (verse 11). Reconciliation is not something that is going to happen in the future. In the future, we will receive our glorification, and we will be made perfect. But in the meantime, we are still mortal, we are still imperfect, we are still weak, we will still fail from time to time. Nevertheless we have reconciliation, for we received it when we believed in Christ.

Yet there is a past, present, and future aspect to the work of God on our behalf; therefore our rejoicing is for what God has done, is doing, and will yet accomplish for us. But at this point Paul encourages us to rejoice not only in the work of God, but more so in the person of God. Praise and adoration are appropriate for who God is in his being - his wisdom, power, grace, love and so on. Even if we never knew or experienced the work of God on our behalf, praise for him would still be our appropriate response.

ORIGINAL SIN (5:12)

What is original sin? How does it affect us? How are we to understand it? What are the problems connected with it?

A widespread and common misconception about original sin is that it refers to the original transgression committed by Adam and Eve, namely the first sin. But, in fact, original sin refers to the result of the first sin, not the first sin itself. Original sin is not a specific sin, a particular act of disobedience; it has to do with the nature of mankind. The Bible tells us that our nature is fallen, that not only do we sin, but we are pervaded by sin, that is, our natures are corrupt. Jesus put it this way: a bad tree brings forth corrupt fruit. It is not that we are sinful because we sin, but rather that we sin because we are sinful. The activity of sin flows out of a sinful nature, a fallen nature, a heart that is out of sync with God. Man is fallen in the depths of his being, and he has a basic disposition towards sin rather than towards righteousness.

That raises all kinds of difficult theological problems. Since I am born with the sin nature, how could God possibly hold me responsible for committing actual sins?

The Bible makes it very clear that sin entered into the race through one man, by the fall of Adam. Adam was created with no disposition towards evil; yet in some mysterious way, Adam himself commits a sin. God didn't cause the fall of Adam, but once Adam chose to sin, God's punishment was to allow Adam to deteriorate into a fallen moral condition, which moral condition is then transmitted to all future descendants.

There are widely diverse theories of how original sin is implicated in our lives. Here are some of the most significant.

One view is called 'Realism' and is based partly on philosophical speculation and partly on inferences drawn from Biblical passages. The basic thesis of Realism is this: God is righteous and would never hold a person responsible for something that somebody else did. How can this square with the doctrine of original sin? The Realists agree that the Bible teaches that we all sinned in Adam, and that the Fall is a result of what took place in the Garden of Eden. So it would seem to the Realist, on the surface at least, that God does in fact perpetrate an injustice, that God does hold future generations responsible for something that Adam did. But the Realists' argument is this: the only way God could do that justly would be if somehow we were actually there, involved with Adam in his sin. In other words, this view involves a kind of spiritual pre-existence, whereby our souls were all present in Adam, and so we were really there. Hence, when we were born in this world, we were born with souls already tainted and corrupted centuries ago in the Garden of Eden.

The Biblical argument for this is drawn from the Book of Hebrews (chapter 7) where the author gives a lengthy discourse on the superiority of Christ's priesthood. He argues for the superiority of the priesthood of Melchizedec over the priesthood of Levi by saying that Levi paid tithes to Melchizedec while he was still in the loins of his father Abraham. Now how are we to understand that verse? The Realists do it the same way they treat the Fall: that Levi somehow pre-existed within Abraham, and when Abraham paid the tithe, Levi was paying it too. They say that just as you can have a real action of a future generation, as in Hebrews, so you can have it back in time, as in the Garden of Eden. The way to understand the Fall is to realise that we were there in the loins of Adam, just as Levi was in the loins of Abraham. We sinned with Adam, that is why we fell with Adam, and so there's no injustice on God's part.

Another view which has been very popular in modern days is that the whole story of the Fall in Genesis is only a parable illustrating the universal propensity of mankind to sin. To err is human and Adam simply did what we all do. Every individual is born basically neutral, but then inevitably manifests sinful behaviour by choosing the way

Adam did. That sounds good because it exonerates God from the charge of holding future generations responsible.

But it raises other problems, some Biblical and some philosophical. The Biblical problems are obvious: that's not what the Bible teaches. The Bible teaches that we in fact fell in Adam and that Adam was a real historical person.

But beyond that dispute about the historicity of Adam or whether we interpret the story of Adam and Eve as simply a parable of human actions, we have to ask the question that the great theologian, Jonathan Edwards, asked. He said, Let's suppose for a moment that everybody was born neutral, with no disposition either for sin or against sin. Certainly you would expect that a certain percentage, perhaps 50% of those born in the state of neutrality, would live their lives, make the right choices and not choose sin. You would expect 50% to sin and 50% not to sin. So you would expect half the human race to be sinless, while the other half might be fallen. But even if we don't want to push it to a percentage level of 50-50, certainly if every human being was born sinless, we would expect some people, at least 1% or half of one percent or 100 people, or whatever, who would make it through life without succumbing to the temptation of sin.

Some have answered that by saying, The reason why people are drawn to sin, and why sin is so popular, is because sin is imposed upon us by society. 'We live in a fallen society, in a fallen civilisation and the impact of that civilisation upon me as an individual is so overwhelming that it will overthrow that 50% chance not to sin.' But we have to ask the question, 'How did this civilisation get so universally corrupt in the first place.' We cannot account for it other than the fact that it is built in.

Some philosophers have argued that the reason why sin is universal, is that the failure to be perfect is something built in to our being finite. If that's the case, then sin is merely an expression of our finitude, and the fact that God made us finite would again raise the serious problem that God is holding man responsible for doing that which comes naturally. So it doesn't solve the problem.

The classical Protestant answer is usually defined by what is called 'federalism'. Adam was our representative, he was the federal head of mankind. God put him on probation and he was on probation not only for himself, but for the race. Now one might say, 'Wait a minute, that's not fair. Now you are going to say that I am held responsible for something that Adam did.'

There is only one time in all of human history when we have been perfectly, accurately represented, and we did not choose our own representative. God chose our representative for us. Adam was the perfect choice for you and for me. God holds me accountable for what Adam did, because Adam did in fact truly, perfectly and infallibly represent me. He was my candidate. I did not choose him; God did. But again, if we suppose that when God chose Adam to represent us, that his choice was malicious or foolish, fallible or inaccurate, what are we saying about God? When we make those kinds of complaints and registe those kinds of protests, we are proving how accurate the choice was, because when we assail the integrity of God in making the selection for us, we are revealing our own fallenness.

The Scriptures tell us that God appointed one man to represent us, that he perfectly represented us and hence we are held responsible. Notice that the way in which original sin comes upon me is through representation and through the imputation of Adam's guilt to me. There are Christians who object to that, and I want to speak to them.

If you are objecting on the grounds that the principles of representation and imputation are wrong in and of themselves, then you must realise that you have just taken away the ground basis for your salvation. It is only by representation that you are saved, and only by imputation that you are redeemed. If it is right for God to save a man on the basis of another man's work, it is also all right for God to punish us on the basis of another man's work.

Adam acted for me far more capably than any human being that I might select on my own. Because Adam sinned, we all suffer the consequences of sin. Because Adam sinned, sin came into the world, and with that sin came death. Because Adam died, I am under the death sentence of God. I will be executed in this world. Yes, I will live for ever, I will be raised from the dead, but I must pass through the vale of death because I am a child of Adam. It is because I am a child of Christ that the sting of that death will be removed and that I will be raised again to eternal life.

VICTORY OVER DEATH (5:12-21)

Paul introduces one of the consequences of Adam's fall in verse 12: **Therefore, just as sin entered the world through one man, and death through sin...**, that is, the instrumental means by which death was introduced into the world was sin. Death was a consequence of sin; it was not built into creation. It comes as a punishment upon the human race for the infection and pollution of sin that is passed on to us through Adam.

One of the problems we have in the Christian faith is the impact that Greek philosophy has made over the centuries on Christian theology. Many times you have heard the concept of the immortality of the soul. Well, in the Greek view of things, man is made of body and soul. There is a physical aspect to man and there is a spiritual aspect to man. But in Greek philosophy the soul is innately, intrinsically, irrevocably and immutably indestructible; the soul is the part of man that is eternal. It will never perish because it cannot perish, it is incapable of disintegration. So the Greeks believed in an immortal soul.

Doesn't the Christian faith believe in immortality too? Yes, but it is an acquired immortality. Let me explain that. The Bible tells us that we are born mortal. We are like a seed that is sown in mortality, but will be raised in immortality. In creation, God made man with the capacity for dying, body and soul. Man's nature was every moment dependent for its life on the sustaining power of God. The question of whether or not that human being (Adam) would continue to live indefinitely, or have his life terminated by death, was centred on the question of obedience. If he had passed the test of obedience he would have become immortal, as we shall be in heaven. But the punishment for sin was the curse of death, and that curse has come upon the whole world.

Remember that in the Garden of Eden the penalty for sin was death 'that day' (Genesis 2:17). Since Adam and Eve did not die a physical death on that very day, some have interpreted Scripture to mean that they experienced spiritual death. On this interpretation, punishment for sin is spiritual death, but physical death is a natural dimension to our humanity. But that is not what the Bible teaches. Indeed, God exercised his prerogative of mercy and grace by not imposing the full measure of the penalty for sin which was instantaneous death. He did instantly impose spiritual death and he also imposed the penalty of physical death, but that was delayed so that man was given a few years to live in this world before he had to suffer the punishment for his sin.

How do we know that every human being is a sinner? Well we know it because every human being eventually dies: **and in this way death came to all men, because all sinned - for before the law was given, sin was in the world. But sin is not taken into account when there is no law** (verses 12,13). When does the law begin? It is commonplace for many to assume that the law of God began on Mount Sinai, when God gave the tablets of stone to Moses. But Paul asks a very interesting and a very penetrating theological question: How could there be sin if there wasn't any law, because where there is no law there can be no transgression? Sin, by definition, is a violation of God's law. If there isn't any law, there can't be any sin. And if there can't be any sin, as the logical progression goes, there can't be any death. But death has reigned from Adam: **Nevertheless, death reigned from the time of Adam to the time of Moses, even over those who did not sin by breaking a command, as did Adam, who was a pattern of the one to come** (verse 14). The only rational explanation, if there was death all that time, is that there had to be sin from Adam to Moses. What else does it mean? It means there had to be law.

Paul has already expressed in the second chapter of Romans that, in addition to the special revelation of the written law of God at Sinai, God has written his law in the hearts of all men (2:14, 15). There is a natural law and every human being is, to some degree, aware of right and wrong. God has not left this planet in mute silence with respect to human moral responsibility. The consciousness and awareness of this can be distorted through cultural rules and regulations, but there is still a built-in sense of righteousness that every human being knows. Men didn't commit the same sin that Adam did, but if death reigned over them, it is clear that they were involved in sin.

Paul draws the very important contrast between the work of the first Adam and the work of the Second Adam in verse 15: **But the gift is not like the trespass.** There are parallels and there are differences.

For if the many died by the trespass of the one man. He is saying that because of the offence of one man, many are dead. In fact not just many, but all are exposed to death; **how much more did God's grace and the gift that came by the grace of the one man, Jesus Christ, overflow to the many!** Here we have the idea that there is a parallel of imputation and representation. Our salvation rests upon this. It is through the first Adam that we are plunged into the ruin, by representation and imputation; by the Second Adam we are redeemed through representation and imputation. Jesus Christ represented me on the cross. On that cross, Jesus Christ paid the penalty for my sin. And not only was my sin imputed to him, but his righteousness was imputed to me.

Although there is a parallel, Jesus and Adam were not equals. What Adam did was destructive; what Jesus does is redemptive. Not only that, the grace of God has overflowed to *many*. Jesus didn't just save a few, he saved many. He hasn't saved everybody, but the imputation of his righteousness has been given by grace to many people. Death is something we earned; salvation is something that we receive as a gift. You cannot earn it or buy it. Paul uses the word 'gift' in the next verse: **Again, the gift of God is not like the result of the one man's sin: The judgment followed one sin and brought condemnation, but the gift followed many trespasses and brought justification. For if, by the trespass of the one man, death reigned through that one man, how much more will those who receive God's abundant provision of grace and of the gift of righteousness reign in life through the one man, Jesus Christ** (verses 16,17). Paul is saying that the power and impact of the Second Adam is much greater than the impact of the first Adam. The impact of Adam has been awful, it has put men in misery, in ruin. But the solution is infinitely greater, because Christ has abounded in winning eternal life for men. We have to go through a travail of tears for our threescore and ten years on this planet and still have to go through the valley of the shadow of death. But what is that compared to the eternity of felicity and joy and happiness without pain, without sorrow, without tears, which Christ has won for us in his role as the Second Adam?

Through the work of Christ, through his obedience and his righteousness, we are made alive and are brought into eternal life. He repeats and summarises this in verses 18 and 19: **Consequently, just as the result of one trespass was condemnation for all men, so also the result of one act of righteousness was justification that brings life for all men. For just as through the disobedience of the one man the many were made sinners, so also through the obedience of the one man the many will be made righteous.** It sounds as if Paul is saying that through Adam's sin, the whole world comes under condemnation; and that through Christ's righteousness the whole world will be saved. But this has to be understood in the light of everything else the apostle Paul says in this epistle. Beforehand, he has made it very clear that not everybody experiences salvation.

The law was added so that the trespass might increase (verse 20). Paul is speaking of the law of Moses, and this is a difficult verse because it does seem to be saying that God's purpose in giving the law was to make sin worse. Paul elsewhere describes more than one purpose behind the law, but obviously what he is saying here is that sin, by the presence of law, is shown to be sin. Law doesn't, in and of itself, create sin; it is the evil disposition of our hearts that creates sin, not the law. What the law does is define and condemn it and reveal it for what it is - sin.

But where sin increased, grace increased all the more, so that, just as sin reigned in death, so also grace might reign through righteousness to bring eternal life through Jesus Christ our Lord (verses 20, 21). There is a greater measure of grace in this world than there is of sin and of evil. Think about the implications of that.

Suppose God removed his grace - what would happen? In fact, some understand Paul's teaching in 2 Thessalonians, when he talks about the emergence of the Antichrist and the end of the world, as referring to such a scenario. If things are bad now, just imagine what this world would be like if God's common grace were removed. We have no conception of the capacity for evil and wickedness that dwells in the human heart. I am not talking about hardened criminals in Death Row, I am talking about your heart and my heart. There is virtually no heinous act which I am intrinsically incapable of committing. And I am speaking as a Christian. What sin is there that Christians haven't committed, unless it be the sin against the Holy Spirit? Christians have committed murder, Christians have committed adultery, Christians steal, Christians lie, Christians start wars, Christians have abortions. They do all kinds of unspeakable wicked things. Even the presence of regeneration and the indwelling of the Holy Spirit does not totally remove sin. The righteousness of Christ is God's gracious way of bringing eternal life to all who believe in him as Lord

CHRISTIANS ARE DEAD TO SIN (6:1-23)

At the close of chapter 5, Paul seems to be saying that whenever men sin, God moves in with grace, and the more sin there is, the more grace there is. An evil person could jump on that statement and distort it as a licence to sin. He may say, 'If sin is an occasion for God to give a greater portion of grace, then the more I sin, the more God is going to send grace into the world to counteract it. Therefore, I am called of God to add to the sin in the world!'

Paul anticipates that kind of distortion at the beginning of chapter 6: **What shall we say, then? Shall we go on sinning, so that grace may increase?** How does he answer it? **By no means! We died to sin; how can we live in it any longer?** (verses 1,2). Such an idea is utterly unthinkable for anybody with a Christian heart and a Christian mind.

I would say that one of the greatest problems in evangelical Christianity today is the pervasive influence of what we call 'Antinomianism'. Antinomianism says, 'I am saved by faith, therefore I never have to be concerned in the slightest about obeying the law.'

Antinomianism says that the commandments of God have no binding influence on my conscience. That is not just a distortion of Christianity, it is a fundamental denial of Christianity. Yet this notion is commonplace in Christian circles.

Good works that follow from your conversion will not count for your justification, but if they are not there, it proves that faith is not there either. Your works don't give you salvation; the work of Jesus gives you salvation. But if you do not have works in your Christian life, you are not a Christian; you have never been redeemed; you have never trusted in Jesus Christ as Lord and Saviour. Antinomianism is the very thing Paul says is utterly unthinkable for a true believer: **By no means! We died to sin; how can we live in it any longer?**

When he says that we are dead to sin, does this mean that we don't sin at all? Of course not. He makes it clear in chapter 7 that the Christian is not free from the battle with sin. But the death sentence has been pronounced upon my old nature. I have been crucified with Jesus Christ, representatively. In God's sight my evil nature is dead. My sin was put to death on the cross of Jesus Christ and my sins were paid for. I was released from the bondage to sin.

Identification with Christ

Or don't you know that all of us who were baptised into Christ Jesus were baptised into his death? (verse 3). Here Paul speaks of baptism in a somewhat mysterious way. He says that if we were baptised, then whatever else baptism signified for us, one of the crucial elements of the symbolism of baptism is that it marks our identification with the death of Jesus.

Paul is not saying that the very act of baptism automatically gives us all the benefits of Christ's atonement. We know that, just as in the Old Testament many people were circumcised and never became believers, there are multitudes of people in this world today who were baptised but who have never been regenerated. Paul is not saying that baptism automatically conveys the benefits of the death of Christ.

Paul tells us to go back to the beginning of our Christian lives, to go back to the marks of our baptism, and to remind ourselves what baptism signifies. My baptism signifies my identification with Jesus' death on the cross, and that I am mystically crucified with Christ. I identify with that act; I put my personal trust in the act of Christ on the cross, and as Christ was taken down from the cross and buried in the ground, so I, in terms of my old nature, am put to death and buried.

We were therefore buried with him through baptism into death in order that, just as Christ was raised from the dead through the glory of the Father, we too may live a new life (verse 4). Paul extends the analogy. Jesus died, he was buried, he was raised again. Our old lives have been crucified with Christ, they have been put to death. When we embrace Christ in justifying faith, we put to death the old man, the old life, the old corrupt human nature. It is dead and buried. Just as Christ came out of the tomb with a new power of life, a resurrected life, so the Christian, once he is reborn and justified by faith, is to show evidence of new life, because a new power for life has been imparted to him by the indwelling Holy Spirit.

Again, Paul extends the image in verse 5: **If we have been united with him like this in his death, we will certainly also be united with him in his resurrection.** How can we as Christians identify with his death and not identify with his resurrection? How can we identify with Christ's death on the cross by faith and then continue to live as if nothing has happened, as if there is no new power, as if there is no resurrected life within our souls?

Paul says in verse 6: **For we know that our old self was crucified with him so that the body of sin might be done away with.** The old self, the old corrupt human nature, has been crucified with Christ. The purpose of redemption was that the old might be destroyed. Paul uses a phrase here - 'that the body of sin might be done away with' - that is very difficult to understand. We are not entirely sure what Paul had in mind when he spoke in this way. One interesting theory that scholars have suggested concerns punishments that were used occasionally in the ancient world for those who were guilty of murder. A somewhat barbaric form of this punishment was for the convicted murderer to be sentenced to have the rotting corpse of his victim tied to his own back, so wherever he went he was reminded of the loathsome act that he had committed. He walked around with a dead human body attached to his own back reminding him of his criminal transgression. Some have said that this is what Paul had in mind by the phrase 'body of sin'. We carry the foul-smelling, corrupt old man that is still clinging to us, but in our sanctification we are to be set free from the power of that corpse.

To what end? **that we should no longer be slaves to sin - because anyone who has died has been freed from sin** (verse 7). We have experienced the greatest exodus that is possible to human beings: we have been freed from sin.

Does this mean that the real test of being Christians is whether or not we ever sin again? In chapter 7 Paul makes it very clear that the old man still has a residual effect in our lives and Christians, in fact, continue to sin. How then can he say that we are dead to sin and that we are now freed from sin?

We are freed from the dominion of sin in our lives. We still sin, and we still sin wilfully but a Christian can never say that he had to sin. God has said that every time we face a temptation he has given us a way to escape (1 Cor. 10:13). We can't say, 'The Devil made me do it' or 'My fallen nature made me do it'. We may surrender to the lusts of our fallen nature, but we do have the power within us to resist.

However, as believers we face multitudes of opportunities and occasions for sin. Every waking moment we are deciding between righteousness and unrighteousness, between godliness and ungodliness. Given the strength of the power of sin that still resides within us, along with the astronomical number of opportunities that we have to sin, it is inevitable that sooner or later, and most often it is sooner, we do succumb to sin. But if we take each temptation in isolation from all of the rest, and consider them one at a time, we can never at any given moment look at a particular temptation and say, 'We didn't have the power or the grace to resist that sin.' The power is there; the grace is there. We may grow weary in welldoing and succumb to sin inevitably, but never by necessity.

Now if we died with Christ, we believe that we will also live with him (verse 8). We shall live for ever with him. But again, Paul is not so much concerned to give us assurance of our eternal life, as to speak about living with Christ in the present. Christ is raised; Christ is alive now; Christ's power of life is alive in us now. Since we identify with his cross in justification, then we must also identify with his life right now.

For we know that since Christ was raised from the dead, he cannot die again; death no longer has mastery over him (verse 9). Christ does not have to die any more. That is why Protestantism repudiated the idea of a re-creation of the death of Christ in the Mass. That is why Protestant crosses are empty; there is no crucified Jesus on them. Christ is alive.

Paul says we are to follow that example: **The death he died, he died to sin once for all; but the life he lives, he lives to God. In the same way, count yourselves dead to sin but alive to God in Christ Jesus** (verses 10, 11). Notice the word 'count', that is, think of yourselves in this way. Paul is making here a very simple deduction. If God reckons you dead in Jesus Christ, if God accounts your sins to be dead on the cross, then you also ought to reckon yourself to be dead. Paul is not asking us to do anything toward ourselves that God has not first done for us. We are to consider that our old life is dead. Put it away, it's over, it's done. It died once and for all. You can't go back.

Dedication to Christ

In verse 12, Paul comes to a preliminary conclusion mixed together with an apostolic mandate. This is a command which we are to receive as a command from Christ himself: **Therefore do not let sin reign in your mortal body so that you obey its evil desires.** Paul is using a structure of the Greek language, a literary form that communicates a command. A justified person can continue in sin, but he ought not to.

In our former lives, in the old man, we were under sin. Our corrupt natures ruled our souls. Sin was the monarch on the throne of the heart, and we did obeisance to it. But that is no longer the case for the

Christian. The Christian no longer has sin as the dominant principle in his life. Certainly the old sin-nature is still there, and still wants to capture us and rule over us. However, it is a usurper, it has no right to reign in our bodies, and it can only reign if we allow it to. Paul says this is exactly what we ought not to allow it to do.

Do not offer the parts of your body to sin, as instruments of wickedness (verse 13). He is not just talking about the body, but includes the mind, the heart, and everything else. Nothing of what makes up a human being is to be yielded as a tool or an instrument of sin.

Instead Paul says, **but rather offer yourselves to God**. We are to recognise that God is sovereign and surrender ourselves to him, **as those who have been brought from death to life**. Imagine God coming to a cemetery and raising people from their graves, and then the people walking out of the graves refusing to acknowledge him as God. That's what it would be like if a person who is justified, buried with Christ and then made alive, disregards the one who has raised him from the dead. No, we are to yield ourselves to God as those who are alive from the dead. Paul continues, **and offer the parts of your body to him as instruments of righteousness.** What does that mean? It means that as a Christian, you are to surrender your mind, your heart, your will, your arms, your legs, your eyes, your ears, your mouth, indeed every part of the complex make-up that constitutes you as a human being. Each part is to be surrendered and yielded to God, so that your mind is committed to righteousness, your heart is committed to righteousness, your ears are committed to righteousness, your legs are committed to righteousness. We cannot yield part of ourselves to righteousness and the rest to unrighteousness. We are called to yield our entire selves as instruments of righteousness to God. That's the response of a justified person; a person who commits his whole life to God.

For sin shall not be your master (verse 14). Here Paul is elaborating upon what he said earlier: believers have been freed from the dominion of sin, so sin shall not have dominion over them. That is, if you are truly in Christ you will not be under the rule and reign of sin **because you are not under law, but under grace.**

To be under sin means to be under the bondage of sin, under the pressing weight of sin and under the curse of the law. Previously, we were groaning under the weight of the law. But now, grace has come into our lives and has replaced the awful threatening judgment of the law. As Christians we live under grace. We began the Christian life in grace, we continue to live the Christian life in grace and the Christian life will be completed by grace. The grace of God is to rule our lives.

What then? Shall we sin because we are not under law but under grace? By no means! Don't you know that when you offer yourselves to someone to obey him as slaves, you are slaves to the one whom you obey (verses 15, 16a). Sometimes Paul has a marvellous way of stating the obvious. If I yield myself as a slave to God, then what am I? I am a slave of God. If I bow before God, that makes me a slave of God. If, on the other hand, I yield myself to sin, then that obviously makes me a slave of sin. Remember in the very first verse of this letter, how Paul identified himself: 'Paul, a slave of Jesus Christ'. The very first thing that Paul said about himself after he gave his name, was that he was a slave to Christ. The conclusion is clear: **whether you are slaves to sin, which leads to death, or to obedience, which leads to righteousness?** (verse 16b). 'Sin which leads to death' or 'obedience which leads to righteousness' are the only options: You either serve sin, and if you do you are doomed to death, or you serve obedience, in which case you will be moving towards righteousness.

But thanks be to God that, though you used to be slaves to sin, you wholeheartedly obeyed the form of teaching to which you were entrusted (verse 17). Paul doesn't know the name of every person to whom he is writing; he doesn't know the state of each person's soul. All he knows is that the people who will be receiving this letter have made a profession of faith in Jesus Christ. But Paul also knew what Jesus had said, that there would be people who would make a profession of faith, but who had no faith. Nevertheless, he exercises the judgment of charity, and so should we.

But Paul is also saying, 'If you are in Christ, you have obeyed from the heart that form of doctrine which was delivered to you.' Paul talks about doctrine not as an abstract science, but as resulting in obedience from the heart. Our doctrine leads to obedience, not simply to knowledge. Our doctrine is designed for action.

You have been set free from sin and have become slaves to righteousness (verse 18). Sanctification begins right away. Notice the tense here: 'You *have been* set free from sin and *have become* slaves to righteousness'. The moment you received Christ as your Saviour you also yielded to him as Lord and became a slave of righteousness. Now you are the slave of righteousness, you are called to have your life devoted to righteousness.

I put this in human terms because you are weak in your natural selves. Here he explains why he has given this lengthy figure of speech. Paul could understand doctrine at a heavier level, but he realised others were not so able.

Just as you used to offer the parts of your body in slavery to impurity and to ever-increasing wickedness, so now offer them in slavery to righteousness leading to holiness (verse 19). Notice that when a person surrenders himself to wickedness the result of that wickedness is more wickedness. Sin breeds sin, which breeds sin, which breeds sin. Sanctification is the goal of our Christian life, and the more we yield ourselves in obedience to righteousness, the more that righteousness brings about holiness.

When you were slaves to sin, you were free from the control of righteousness (verse 20). Notice the play on words here. If you are free from one thing, you are bound to another. No one is autonomous. Augustine said that a human being is like a horse, and the horse has one of two riders: either Satan or Christ is riding the horse. Before you were justified, Satan was riding the horse. Now that you are justified, Christ is riding the horse. When you were the servants of sin, you were free from righteousness.

What benefit did you reap at that time from the things you are now ashamed of? Those things result in death! (verse 21). Think back, O Christian, to your non-Christian days: what kind of fruit did you have? You didn't have any. Had you lived out your life, following the course that you were on, you were headed for death. You can only be ashamed of the style and character of your life when you were a servant to sin.

But now that you have been set free from sin and have become slaves to God, the benefit you reap leads to holiness, and the result is eternal life. Sanctification is the result of this new, and willing, slavery to God. Holiness. Being increasingly conformed to the image of God in Christ. Putting off the old, being adorned with the new. These concepts, these realities, should be the delight and goal of each believer. Nothing should suppress the longing for personal holiness that the Spirit has implanted in our hearts. The contrast between our new estate and our former shameful life (verse 21) should be a shining example to the church and the world of the free gift of eternal life.

For the wages of sin is death, but the gift of God is eternal life in Christ Jesus our Lord (verses 22,23). Servants of sin earn wages; they get what they deserve. But eternal life in Jesus Christ our Lord is a gift from God. A gift cannot be purchased, a gift cannot be earned, a gift cannot be merited. It is something that God gives freely.

THE CHRISTIAN AND THE LAW (7:1-8:1)

Paul is assuming certain things about his readers. **Do you not know, brothers - for I am speaking to men who know the law - that the law has authority over a man only as long as he lives?** This has caused some to think that Paul is writing to Jewish believers. But I don't think so. I think he is assuming that his general readers at the church at Rome, even those who have been converted from the Gentile world, would have some understanding of Old Testament law, because people who converted to Christ were instructed in Old Testament history.

In verse 2 Paul introduces an analogy for the purpose of simplifying something difficult. Unfortunately, this analogy which was designed to simplify, has been the occasion of much confusion and a great deal of stumbling over the centuries. **For example, by law a married woman is bound to her husband as long as he is alive, but** if her husband dies, she is released from the law of marriage. So then, if she marries another man while her husband is still alive, she is called an adulteress. But if her husband dies, she is released from that law and is not an adulteress, even though she marries another man (verses 2,3).

The analogy is very simple. If, while a woman is married, she marries another man, she has committed adultery. But if the husband dies and then the woman remarries, she is not guilty of adultery. Death breaks the obligation of the law for that woman to be faithful to her husband.

Now Paul applies the illustration to our relationship with the law. He says in verse 4, **So, my brothers, you also died to the law through the body of Christ, that you might belong to another, to him who was raised from the dead, in order that we might bear fruit to God**. Here is where confusion arises. Some people read in the text this idea: once we were bound to the law, but now the law is dead and so it is utterly irrelevant to the Christian life. This analogy becomes a proof-text to support the spirit of Antinomianism, the idea that the Christian is no longer related to the law of God in any way.

That is not what the apostle is saying. It is not the law that dies, but me! Because my old self is dead my relationship to the law is broken. Under the former style of life, while I was dead in my sins, I was in bondage to the law. I was under the curse of the law, and under the burdensome, crushing domination of the law. Paul says in verse 1, 'the law has authority over a man only as long as he lives'. Notice, not as long as the law lives, but as long as the man lives. The law doesn't die, the man dies.

So in what sense have we died to the law? We have died with Christ; our old selves have been put to death and the curse of the law has been taken in its fullness by Jesus Christ. The destructive fruit that the law elicited within us, inciting us to sin, has died. Nevertheless, although we have been made alive in our inward man, we do still have a relationship to the law, albeit radically different from the old relationship to the law.

Christians have been resurrected into a new life in Christ, so that they should now bear fruit to God. What the law failed to elicit from us, Christ wants to see born through our relationship to him. So justification by faith and living under grace is never a licence to sin. But we are to be encouraged by our new status, by the power of life that is within us, that righteousness is a possibility and that the fruit of Christ can be brought forth in us.

Paul is now going to set a contrast before us, looking from a slightly different angle at what it means to be alive in the flesh as opposed to being alive in the spirit. He says: **For when we were controlled by the sinful nature, the sinful passions aroused by the law were at work in our bodies, so that we bore fruit for death. But now, by dying to what once bound us ...** (verses 5, 6a). When we were in the flesh the desires of sin were activated by the very presence of the law. And these passions, worked out in our members, brought forth fruit for death. But now, we are delivered from the law. What the law did to us before, it no longer does.

What was God's purpose in delivering Christians from the law? Verse 6: **we have been released from the law so that we serve in the new way of the Spirit, and not in the old way of the written code.** We are still called to serve, we are still called to obedience but 'in the new way of the Spirit, and not in the old way of the written code'. Here is another passage which has been misconstrued over and over again. Whenever we talk about law, we make a distinction between the letter of the law and the spirit of the law. The letter of the law is the precise written requirement. The spirit of the law has to do with the deeper intent, or motive, behind the law. This was at the heart of the controversy, for example, between Jesus and the Pharisees. The letter of the law says: Thou shalt not kill. The Pharisees refrained from murder and, by keeping the letter of the law, thought they had done all that the law required. Jesus' Sermon on the Mount was a profound expansion of the full meaning of the law to the Pharisees.

Some assume that, in the verses we are considering, Paul is talking about the letter of the law and the spirit of the law in the terms I have just described. But that is not what he is talking about. When he talks about the new way of the Spirit, he is not talking about the law, he is talking about something that takes place in us. The new Spirit within me is what makes the difference, and the Spirit of which he is speaking is the Holy Spirit. We are called to obey the law, not out of a state of spiritual death, but as those who have been made alive by the Holy Spirit. Our whole response to the law, our whole attitude to the law is the attitude of those who have been empowered from within by the Holy Spirit.

Neither is Paul saying that what concerns God is keeping the spirit of the law and forgetting about the letter. Suppose Paul did mean that God wanted Christians to ignore the letter of the law. Look at the ten commandments - it's OK if you keep the spirit of the prohibition against adultery, but you can violate the letter. Could you have a good, sound, healthy, righteous motivation while committing adultery!? Or could you have a good spiritual attitude while committing murder or stealing or coveting? Jesus kept both the letter of the law and the spirit of the law. And the Christian, with the help of the indwelling Holy Spirit, is called to keep the letter of the law and the spirit of the law.

So far, Paul is talking about that old situation in such grim terms it almost sounds as if he is saying that the law is bad. But that's not what he is saying. The problem was not that the law was bad, but that we were bad, morally impotent and could not bring forth the intended fruit of righteousness, spelled out in the law. **What shall we say, then? Is the law sin? Certainly not! Indeed I would not have known what sin was except through the law. For I would not have known what coveting really was if the law had not said, "Do not covet"** (verse 7).

How shall we understand what sin is unless we have some standard of righteousness enabling us to differentiate between good and evil? Without law there is no sin; without commandments there can be no transgressions. We define sin as any want of conformity to, or transgression of, the law. Sin by definition depends on some kind of standard by which performance and behaviour is measured. So it is through the law that sin is made known. It is not that there would have been nothing evil without a law, but we would never have known what sin was.

Verse 8 is crucial: **But sin, seizing the opportunity afforded by the commandment, produced in me every kind of covetous desire. For apart from law, sin is dead.** Not only does the law identify sin for us, but it incites sin by functioning as an external stimulus to our own sins. That is, nothing is so attractive to us as the forbidden.

Now is that a fault in the law? No. All the law does is call attention to the wickedness that resides within our corrupt hearts. It is not that the law is evil, but that sometimes the more law we see, the more evil we become, because the prohibition incites us to sin. We want to be able to possess what we are not allowed to possess, and to do what we are not allowed to do. Deep within each of us there exists a rebellious spirit.

Once I was alive apart from law; but when the commandment came, sin sprang to life and I died (verse 9). Paul is speaking in terms of his own personal history. Does he mean that as a child he was born without original sin and there was a period in his life, before he understood the law, that was sinless? No. He is speaking comparatively here. There was a time - from his birth until he was a cognisant, knowledgeable creature - when he did not know actual sin. That is why we make distinctions like the age of accountability. We don't know when that age is but we have different requirements for four year olds than for forty year olds. We recognise that in the child there is a lack of understanding of what is commanded and what is prohibited.

The transition from childhood to adult is marked in the Jewish culture by the ceremony of Bar Mitzvah. It is a rite of passage from childhood to manhood, from immaturity to maturity. In Judaism, and particularly Old Testament Judaism, the Bar Mitzvah signified the age of accountability. Bar Mitzvah means 'son of commandment', indicating that the child was able, as he was instructed in the law, to have a clear moral sense of what was required by God. He became a son of the commandment, one who was instructed in the law and expected to serve and obey the law. I think those commentators are right who speculate at this point that Paul is thinking back to his own childhood and has specifically in mind his own Bar Mitzvah.

Paul is recalling that the more he learned about the law as a young man, the more sin was stirred up within him and revived: **I found that the very commandment that was intended to bring life actually brought death** (verse 10). The fault is not in the law, nor in the commandment. God's commandments are a guide to life, and the child of Judaism learned, memorised and studied the meaning of the law, not so that he would be enticed to sin and embrace death, but so that he would understand how to live. But Paul's personal testimony is, **For sin, seizing the opportunity afforded by the commandment, deceived me** - My own sinful disposition took the law of God and instead of using it as an instrument for life and righteousness, I distorted it. My sin deceived me **and through the commandment put me to death** (verse 11).

What was the means that my sin used to kill me? The commandment. It is like a sword. There is nothing evil about a sword. If I pick up a sword and kill somebody, it is not the sword that goes on trial, it is not the sword that is put in prison. So what he is saying is that sin deceives and kills, and the tool it uses is the commandment.

So then, the law[1] is holy, and the commandment is holy,

---

1. Elsewhere Paul speaks about the positive benefits of the law both for the unbeliever and the believer. Calvin, in book 2, chapter 7 of the *Institutes*, sets forth his famous three-fold use of the law as beneficial to us. The first beneficial use of the law that Calvin cites is what he calls the 'law being used as a kind of mirror'. What he means by this is that the law reveals to us what righteousness is, and if we hold up that standard of righteousness and look at it and compare ourselves with it, as if we were looking into a mirror, the law will tell us how hopelessly unrighteous we are. But what good is the law if it teaches very clearly that no one will ever attain perfection? Because it admonishes each one of us about our own unrighteousness and shows us the absolute necessity that we have for a Saviour. That is a benefit.

Secondly, the law is called by Calvin a 'means for restraint'. That seems to fly right in the face of everything that Paul has been saying

righteous and good (verse 12). How much more clearly can the apostle speak? It is not that grace is good and law is bad. It is that law is good and sin is bad. The law is holy; the commandment is holy, just and good. What I do with these things may bring death and destruction but that is my sin. Obedience to the law of God never killed anybody in the sense in which the apostle is talking about killing, namely, spiritually killing.

Did that which is good, then, become death to me? By no means! But in order that sin might be recognized as sin, it produced death in me through what was good, so that through the commandment sin might become utterly sinful (verse 13). There is an irony here. The more I see the commandment, the more I sin; the more I sin, the more I reveal how holy and righteous the commandment is, and how wicked and deceitful I am.

The second half of chapter 7 is one of the most difficult sections of this epistle and, on first reading, seems confusing. In fact it is so confusing that we may even be tempted to conclude that the apostle himself was confused when he was writing it. But of course we know that that is not the case.

We know that the law is spiritual; but I am unspiritual, sold as

---

about the law inciting people to deeper evil, because the more we see the law, the more we want to break the law. Well, it is true from one perspective, and to some degree. But there is another side to that coin. Laws do exist and do, to a certain degree, restrain the wicked, and protect the weak from the strong. This is a common grace benefit that all men enjoy by the fact that we don't live in a universe where there is no law.

But it is the third use of the law that is most significant in Calvin's writings, where he talks about the great importance of the law in the life of the Christian. The law is dead as far as its cursing power; the law cannot have dominion any more; the law is not the means to justify oneself before God. But the law has an extremely important value to the Christian, namely, its 'revelatory function'. The law of God reveals the character of God, and what is pleasing to God.

a slave to sin (verse 14). There is a distinction, common throughout evangelical Christianity, that there are three types of people: those who are not Christians; and then two kinds of Christians - spiritual Christians and carnal Christians. This has created quite a bit of confusion and, because of that confusion, we must examine carefully what Paul says, 'But I am unspiritual (carnal, KJV), sold as a slave to sin'. Remember that the apostle is writing after his conversion and yet he is using the present tense. So if we ever have any absolute authority to call someone a carnal Christian it would have to be the apostle Paul, because he declares under the inspiration of the Holy Spirit that he is (in the present tense) carnal.

The word translated 'unspiritual' is a form of the noun, *sarx*, which is usually translated by the English word 'flesh' in the New Testament. The difficulty is that there are times in the New Testament where the word *sarx* has specific reference to the physical dimension of our existence, that is, to our bodies. At times it can be used as a synonym for the Greek word *soma*, which is translated by the word 'body'. Other times the word *sarx* refers to the nature of the whole man in his fallen state prior to his conversion.

Since the word *sarx* is capable of two different renditions, how do we know which one it refers to when we meet it in the New Testament? The standard key is this: whenever the word *sarx* is set in contrast to the word *pneuma* (spirit), then it refers to the sinful nature. Here is one of those examples, because Paul in this particular passage is contrasting *sarx* with *pneuma*, flesh and spirit. He says that the law is spiritual. What does he mean by that? Not that it's mental, or that it's non-physical, rather that it comes to us from the Deity, from the Holy Spirit in the full measure of his Divine nature. The law is spiritual, for it has a spiritual origin and a spiritual power. In contrast, Paul is carnal, sold under sin.

Paul is saying that in his present redeemed state he is still a creature of the flesh to some degree. He elaborates upon this and here's the part that seems to be so confusing: **I do not understand what I do. For what I want to do I do not do, but what I hate I do** (verse 15). Paul is articulating here something that is very commonplace. We are creatures with mixed desires. We are never left with only one desire working in our hearts or in our minds. The whole business of making choices is a very complex thing, and that complexity is intensified by the fact that we have several choices or desires coexisting within our hearts at any given moment.

This is why the secret of sanctification is to develop within our hearts a growing intensity of desire to please God, to be obedient to Christ. That's why we are called to fill our minds with the Word of God that we may know more of the loveliness of God, the majesty of God, the sweetness and excellence of Christ. The more we know him, the more we understand how excellent he is. The more we begin to have the mind of Christ, the more we begin to approve the things that God approves and disapprove the things of which he disapproves. Then our hearts will begin to come into line with our heads.

But no Christian in this world achieves a 100% consistent desire to obey God only. There is a powerful desire left over from the fallen nature. When we have been born again and the Spirit has been shed abroad in our hearts, we have new natures, new desires, new inclinations, new attitudes, new love for the things of God. But that love is not perfect, it is not pure, it is not yet completely realised in our lives. There is a constant daily struggle and warfare with the old self whose desires are battling the desires of the new self. It is precisely this battle, with which every Christian has struggled, that Paul is setting forth here.

And if I do what I do not want to do, I agree that the law is good (verse 16). What he is saying is very complex: we have already explained what he means by doing what he doesn't want to do. The very fact that he has this desire not to do it, indicates that part of him agrees that the law is good. The very antipathy and hatred that he has in his heart towards sin, is testimony to the goodness of the law.

Verse 17 almost sounds like a disclaimer: **As it is, it is no longer I myself who do it, but it is sin living in me.** Paul is not denying personal responsibility for his sin. What he is saying is that the real I, the new I, the person that I am in Jesus Christ, is not doing that. It is the old self who has been put to death with Christ that is gaining the upper hand here. Now, that does not mean that there are two distinct personalities, nor does it mean that the Christian is schizophrenic. A person who lived twenty years ago in Cincinnati and now lives in Boston is still the same person. He does not behave exactly in the same manner as he did twenty years ago, but he is still affected by influences from his past life.

Paul continues: **I know that nothing good lives in me, that is, in my sinful nature.** Paul knows something good dwells within him: God the Holy Spirit dwells within him and he has a new nature that dwells within him. But there is nothing good dwelling in his sinnature. **For I have the desire to do what is good, but I cannot carry it out. For what I do is not the good I want to do; no, the evil I do not want to do - this I keep on doing** (verses 18,19). This is the same problem, just stated in opposite directions.

Again, he repeats the struggle: **Now if I do what I do not want to do, it is no longer I who do it, but it is sin living in me that does it** (verse 20). Paul is not denying personal responsibility for, or personal activity in, sinning. But he is having this conflict between the real Paul who is being sanctified by Jesus Christ and the Paul who was the Pharisee and an enemy of God.

So I find this law at work: When I want to do good, evil is right there with me (verse 21). By law here he means a proverbial axiom. It seems that whenever we desire to do good, we experience the closest proximity to evil. Sometimes it is in our most dedicated moments, in our most precious hours of devotion to Christ, that the most wicked thoughts will creep into our minds. Such things take away our peace with God and our assurance of our redemption, because we ask ourselves how this can happen, how we can find ourselves so enticed to wickedness, right in the middle of the battle for righteousness.

It is verse 22 that convinces me, and the vast majority of theologians historically, that Paul was speaking of his present state as a Christian, and not recalling a struggle prior to his conversion: **For in my inner being I delight in God's law.** No unregenerate person delights in the law of God in the innermost self. This statement can only be made by a regenerate person, so I am convinced that Paul is speaking of his present condition. Notice that he qualifies 'self' here by distinguishing between the innermost self and the other self, his old fallen nature: **but I see another law at work in the members of my body, waging war against the law of my mind and making me a prisoner of the law of sin at work within my members** (verse 23). Paul is not saying that the soul is righteousness whereas the body is wicked. When he makes this distinction between 'members' and 'innermost' he is talking about the core of his being versus the periphery of his being. The peripheral power of sin is still raging and is very potent, but in the core of the regenerate man dwells a self that has been made over in the image of God.

So he bursts out in exclamation: **What a wretched man I am!** (verse 24). It would be easy for us to read these words, comment on them theologically, and miss the passion that is pouring out of the pen of the apostle. Here is a man who is grief-stricken at his own sinfulness. Again, this is not the posture or the attitude of an unregenerate man. Only the Christian knows the anguish of godly remorse for sin. Only the Christian can say and mean it, 'I am not a man but a worm' (Psalm 22:6). Only the Christian can cry out like Isaiah, 'Woe is me for I am undone!' (Isaiah 6:5). How characteristic this is of redeemed souls!

Other people moan and lament and complain, one doesn't have to be born again to consider oneself wretched. But when Paul makes this judgment about himself, he is making it out of a sense of moral anguish and profound remorse for his sin. This is the deepest kind of broken and contrite heart expressing itself here, such as an unredeemed person can never have. An unredeemed person may have a broken and contrite heart for the loss of something or for a fear of something, but not a genuine remorse for having offended God. Only the convicted sinner can cry out like that.

Who will rescue me from this body of death? (verse 24). What is this 'body of death'? We have already noted one commentator's explanation (comments on 6:6). He tells us that in antiquity there were rare occasions when somebody was convicted of a particularly heinous form of murder, in which one of the punishments was that the corpse of the victim should be chained to the killer. Part of the killer's sentence was to walk around in this gruesome condition of having to carry on his back the decaying, putrefying corpse of the person that he had killed. You can imagine how that would drive a man insane, not only to be faced with his victim, but chained to his victim while the body was rotting.

Whether or not that is what Paul had in mind, certainly the analogy is an apt description of what it is to be a Christian. From the day that we are born again, we have to carry around this putrefying, dead, old nature with us, that gets in our way and makes us sick and brings us to all kinds of wicked circumstances. The question is, Is there anybody out there who can deliver us from this state of wretchedness? Notice that the chapter doesn't end there, but immediately after this exclamation of remorse the apostle breaks forth in doxology, in a hymn of praise and thanksgiving. He answers his own question, 'Who will rescue me from this body of death?' **Thanks be to God - through Jesus Christ our Lord!**

His conclusion to this section is: **So then, I myself in my mind am a slave to God's law, but in the sinful nature a slave to the law of sin** (verse 25). Now that is scary. In spite of the fact that a real change has taken place in our lives, that we have been born again to a lively hope, that the Holy Spirit is within us, changing us, we still sin. What are the consequences of that? According to the law of God, if we sin, we die. We must face the wrath of God. So Paul brings us back to the basis of our justification and what it effects.

Romans 8 begins with one of the most triumphant and glorious verses in all of sacred Scripture: **Therefore, there is now no condemnation for those who are in Christ Jesus.** That is the gospel in a nutshell. The declaration that in Christ Jesus there is for us no condemnation.

Now Paul, in chapter 7, has made it very clear that there is still sin in our lives. How does the word 'therefore' fit in with this passage? Is the conclusion coming from the seventh chapter, or from the whole previous discussion on justification? I prefer the latter, namely, that the whole previous discussion is in view. Paul is not saying that there is nothing in the Christian worthy of condemnation. There are plenty of things in my life, even since I have been born again, that deserve condemnation. I continue to sin, and insofar as I continue to sin, what I merit for my sin is the condemnation of God. If God were to judge me right now according to my behaviour, I would be condemned. But I have a Saviour, and because I am in Christ Jesus, there is no condemnation.

It is because I have been justified by faith, because the righteousness and merit of Jesus Christ have been imputed to me that there is no condemnation. When God looks at me he sees me covered with the righteousness of Christ. That is why there is no condemnation.

What does Paul mean by the phrase 'in Christ Jesus' that we see so often in the New Testament? There is a little quirk in the Greek language that we often miss when we read the English translation. Whenever the Bible says, Believe in the Lord Jesus Christ, the word for 'in' is *eis*, and literally it means, 'into'. Think of it this way: you are standing outside the gates of Jerusalem. In order to go in to Jerusalem you have to pass through the gate. You have to move from outside to inside. Whenever the Greek uses the word *eis*, it means moving from one place to another, moving into. But once you go into something, then you are clearly in it, and there the Greek word is *en*, which is also translated by the English word 'in'. Once a person has faith that moves 'into' Christ, then he is securely 'in' Christ Jesus, having what we would call a mystical union with Christ. Faith moves me from outside of Christ to inside of Christ, from outside the kingdom to inside the kingdom. So anyone who is in (*en*) Christ has no condemnation.

Because of this, people say: If it is all done by Jesus, what do I need to worry about? There is no judgment, there is no condemnation. Now, condemnation is a negative form of judgment. All the term 'judgment' means is to evaluate, to render a verdict, to examine. But we will all be brought before the judgment seat of Christ who will evaluate our lives to the degree to which we have been obedient or disobedient. When I am brought before the Judge, I will know that

I have passed from the negative judgment. I don't have to worry about going to hell, I don't have to worry about being condemned. But I still have to be evaluated.

That doesn't bother me at all. I look forward to the fact that I am going to be evaluated, because I know that God will reward me in a way that I will never be upset about. If I see you in heaven with ten times more reward than me, there will be no way that I can be jealous. By that time I will be so sanctified that I will be able to delight in your exceedingly great reward, knowing that Christ is giving you what pleases him and what will please you. So my evaluation on that day is not something I fear, although certainly I would not like to be totally embarrassed by my lack of obedience. On the other hand, I don't fret over the possibility that Christ is going to say to me, 'Depart from me into everlasting torment', because there is no condemnation left for those who are in Christ Jesus.

THE CHRISTIAN AND THE HOLY SPIRIT (8:1-27)

Therefore, there is now no condemnation for those who are in Christ Jesus becomes the jumping off point for an explanation of the significance of the removal of all condemnation from those who are in Christ Jesus. He links his explanation to the work of the Holy Spirit in specific ways in the lives of believers.

(1) Delivered from the power of sin

Paul continues by saying: **because through Christ Jesus the law of the Spirit of life set me free from the law of sin and death** (verse 2). Paul contrasts two principles, what he calls two laws. On the one hand, there is the law of the Spirit of life in Christ Jesus, and on the other hand, there is the law of sin and death. While we were in the flesh, we were exposed to the full penalties of the law of God, which included eternal death. We were in bondage to sin. Now another law has been made manifest, namely the law of the Spirit of life in Christ Jesus, which is the principle of the gospel. Paul is showing the power of the gospel to set us free from the bondage that we experience in our flesh.

For what the law was powerless to do in that it was weakened by the sinful nature, God did by sending his own Son in the likeness of sinful man to be a sin offering (verse 3). Here Paul speaks of the impotence of the law to save us. The law cannot save fallen man. Why? Where do we find the weakness of the law? Wherein lies its impotency? 'It was weakened by the sinful nature'. The lack of ability of the law to save us resides in the lack of our ability to be obedient. The weakness is found in us, in the *sarx*, in our fallen nature.

But since our fallen nature could not obey the law, and thus the law could not become an instrument of salvation for us but only an instrument of damnation, God sent his own Son 'in the likeness of sinful man to be a sin offering'. Paul doesn't make an absolute identity between the flesh of Christ and the flesh of man, because the word 'flesh' in the context does not refer to our physical bodies, but to our sin-nature, our corrupted state of humanity.

God sent his Son, who took to himself a human nature - a body and all the other components of human nature, with one noticeable exception: he did not take to himself sinful human nature. The incarnate Christ was without original sin. Christ came like us, in the likeness of sinful flesh, but not as sinful flesh. If he had come as sinful flesh, he himself would have been a sinner and could not have saved himself, let alone us.

And so he condemned sin in sinful man (verse 3). The cross of Christ was where God poured out his judgment upon human sins. Believers' sins were imputed to Jesus and God condemned them. That is why there is now no condemnation left for anyone who is in Christ, because the condemnation has already taken place on the cross.

Why? **in order that the righteous requirements of the law might be fully met in us, who do not live according to the sinful nature but according to the Spirit** (verse 4). Christ did not only come to set us free from the penalty of sin, he also came to set us free from the power of sin. With the Holy Spirit residing in us, we may fulfil righteousness by the way we live. The law is not simply set aside as Antinomians would have us believe, but in the cross we have been set free for righteousness.

Paul continues on this contrast between the Spirit and the sinful nature: **Those who live according to the sinful nature have their minds set on what that nature desires; but those who live in accordance with the Spirit have their minds set on what the Spirit desires** (verse 5). Those who are in the Spirit are delighted by the things of God and follow after the things of the Spirit. The Holy Spirit lives within such, and when he comes into their lives, he does something to each human spirit. Their human spirit is changed and they have a new delight, a new appetite, a new sense of longing and yearning for spiritual things.

The mind of sinful man is death, but the mind controlled by the Spirit is life and peace (verse 6). Paul is calling attention to one of the best-kept secrets of the human race. Everybody in this world wants life and peace and they go through a million different avenues trying to find them. But Paul is telling us that the key is to be spiritually minded. To have our minds focused on lofty things, on the things of excellence, goodness, truth and beauty is the secret to life and to peace. Now that may sound like a call to be sophisticated or cultured, to understand fine arts so that we can quote the great poets and the great novelists. That is not what I mean, and I don't think it is what the apostle meant. He is saying that there is a peace that flows from the contemplative life, the life that focuses on the good, the true and the beautiful.

Romans 8:7 falls like a hammer on Arminianism, Pelagianism, or semi-Pelagianism. The conflict between Arminianism and Calvinism has its roots long before Calvin and Arminius. We find it originally in the dispute between Augustine and the monk, Pelagius who was convinced that, although sin is a serious matter in which all people participate, man is basically good and has the ability, even after the Fall of Adam, to live a perfectly righteous and moral life. In other words, Pelagius believed that man does not need grace in order to be redeemed. Grace does help man live up to the demands of the law, and is there as a remedy for those who are weak and require it, but the possibility exists of fallen man achieving perfect obedience to the law. Although the church condemned Pelagius and sided with

Augustine, the issue has returned in various and sometimes more subtle forms.

There was never a person called 'Semi-Pelagius' but semi-Pelagianism refers to an attempt to produce a middle ground position. On this view, the fall has affected man significantly and so without grace he cannot be saved. But the grace that is offered, is offered to people who, despite being seriously weakened by sin, are capable of responding to the offer of the gospel. Verse 7 begins: **the sinful mind is hostile to God.** Remember Paul is speaking of our mind by nature. He goes on to explain how the sinful mind is hostile to God: **It does not submit to God's law, nor can it do so.** Total depravity does not mean that man is as sinful as he could be, it is not utter depravity. The point of the debate is this: Does man in his fallen nature have the moral ability to obey God? The answer that the Calvinist gives is that man, in his fallen mind, suffers under a moral inability to do the things of God. Man in his natural state cannot be subject to the law of God, and he is therefore at enmity with God.

This is why the Bible stresses reconciliation, for reconciliation presupposes estrangement, some breach or schism between two or more parties. The estranged parties of which the Bible speaks are man and God. We are at enmity with God, estranged from God, because in our fallen nature we cannot obey his law.

Those controlled by the sinful nature cannot please God (verse 8). It is impossible for someone who is only sinful ever to please God. Arminians believe it possible for fallen men who are still in the flesh to choose Jesus Christ, to choose to be born again. We say no to that. Unless God first does a work of grace in our souls, and quickens us and gives us this new life principle, we would never choose Christ.

But Paul doesn't stop there. In verse 9 he turns his attention away from those who are of the sinful nature to the Christian, and says: **You, however, are controlled not by the sinful nature but by the Spirit, if the Spirit of God lives in you.** We noted earlier (see comment on 7:14) a serious distortion of theology that is rampant in the evangelical world today, namely, that there are two types of regenerate Christians - the spiritual Christians and the carnal Christians. Notice that Paul knows nothing of this: you are either controlled by the sinful nature or by the Spirit. The ultimate test of whether you are saved or not is this: is the Spirit of God dwelling in you? Paul couldn't be any more clear in this passage and he reinforces it in the second part of verse 9: **And if anyone does not have the Spirit of Christ, he does not belong to Christ.**

But if Christ is in you, your body is dead because of sin. Here we have to be really careful that we don't get confused. All through this passage Paul has been contrasting the Holy Spirit and the fallenness of corrupt human nature, and he has used the Greek word *sarx*, which can refer to body but usually refers to the fallen nature of man, particularly when it is set in contradistinction to the word 'Spirit'. But now Paul is talking about the physical body when he writes 'your body is dead'. Even if Christ is in you, your body will still go through death. Why? Because of sin. We have to pay the temporal punishment for our sin. We must die. That is the last enemy to be destroyed.

What does he mean by **yet your spirit is alive because of righteousness** (verse 10)? Let's go on: **And if the Spirit of him who raised Jesus from the dead is living in you.** Who raised up Jesus? God raised up Jesus by the Holy Spirit. The Holy Spirit quickened the corpse of Jesus in the tomb and effected his resurrection from the grave. Now listen to what Paul is saying: **And if the Spirit of him who raised Jesus from the dead is living in you, he who raised Christ from the dead will also give life to your mortal bodies through his Spirit, who lives in you** (verse 11). The same power that God used to raise the corpse of Jesus from the dead is living inside believers right now. That is the astonishing message the apostle is presenting here. The Holy Spirit who dwells in Christians is exactly the same person who raised Christ from the dead. Just as the Holy Spirit raised Jesus from the dead, so the Holy Spirit will raise the bodies of believers from the grave. If you are a believer, your body will die because of sin, but your body will be raised because the Holy Spirit dwells in you. Because that same power is indwelling you right now **your spirit is alive because of righteousness.**

This is Paul's conclusion: **Therefore, brothers, we have an obligation - but it is not to the sinful nature, to live according to it. For if you live according to the sinful nature, you will die; but if by the Spirit you put to death the misdeeds of the body, you will live** (verses 12, 13). The Spirit brings life and peace and so our indebtedness is not to the sinful nature, but to the Spirit. Notice the shift that has occurred here. Paul moves from focusing upon the character of God and His blessings bestowed upon believers, to the responsibilities and obligations that we have in living out the faith. This distinction, however, leads to another distinction. Our obligation does not require us to act on our own, independent of the work of the Spirit within us. It is our faith that must be exercised; we must work out our faith in fear and trembling, but all this is in, by, and through the indwelling power of the Holy Spirit.

(2) The Spirit of adoption

Verse 14 begins a glorious section of this chapter: **Those who are led by the Spirit of God are sons of God.** Today, there is a widespread notion permeating our culture, the essence of which is that true religion teaches the universal fatherhood of God and the universal brotherhood of man. But the Bible does not teach either the universal fatherhood of God or the universal brotherhood of man. There is one verse in the New Testament (Acts 17:29) in which Paul, quoting the secular poets of his day, says to the Athenian philosophers at Mars Hill, that we are all God's offspring, as indeed we are in the sense that God is the Creator of the human race. In that respect it is possible to say that all are the children of God.

But when the Bible talks about the fatherhood of God, it never does so in the sense of God's creation. To address God as Father involves a relationship of intimacy. To be a member in good standing in the family of God is a privilege never to be passively assumed or taken for granted. In fact it is the greatest privilege of all, to be able to come to God and address him as Father. And we are not able to do that by nature, because by nature we are children of wrath.

What about the universal brotherhood of man? Doesn't Christianity teach the universal brotherhood? No, it doesn't. I don't know any text in the Bible which teaches that all men are my brothers. The brotherhood in Biblical categories has to do with those who share the intimacy of fellowship with God, and with Christ who is the Son of God.

Where the confusion comes in is this: the great commandment tells us to love the Lord our God with all our heart, all our mind, all our strength and so on, and to love our neighbours as much as we love ourselves. What Jesus says, in answer to the question of the Pharisees about who is my neighbour, is that all men are my neighbours, and so the obligation to love all men, to honour all men, to be just toward all men, is imposed upon us clearly by Scripture. But the Bible doesn't describe that in terms of brotherhood. Paul, in verse 12 for example, uses the term 'brothers' to refer to a special group, those who are in the brotherhood and sisterhood of faith because they have a unique relationship to Christ and are those in whom the Spirit of Christ dwells. Who are the children of God? They are those who are led by the Spirit of God.

Paul elaborates further in verse 15: **For you did not receive a spirit that makes you a slave again to fear, but you received the Spirit of sonship. And by him we cry, "Abba, Father".** This is what is accomplished at justification by the indwelling of the Holy Spirit. When the Holy Spirit comes into my life and enters into me, I receive the Spirit of adoption. It is not something I possessed already; it is something that is added to my life, a gift that God gives when the Holy Spirit comes and dwells within me. God adopts me. By nature I am not a son of God. The only way I can enter the family of God is to be adopted. The only Son of God, by nature, is Christ. All the other children of God are not natural children, but adopted children. I can draw near to the Father through the Spirit, and can cry out, 'Abba, Father.'

The Spirit himself testifies with our spirit that we are God's children (verse 16). Paul touches here on something that is very important to our understanding of the Christian life. The Holy Spirit

testifies with our spirit that we are the children of God. The work of
the Spirit is not only to make us children of God, and then to take up
a dwelling place within our hearts, but also to give us an inner
assurance of our standing with God. It is vitally important for the
Christian to have assurance of salvation for **we are heirs - heirs of
God and co-heirs with Christ, if indeed we share in his sufferings
in order that we may also share in his glory.**

To be an heir is to be rightfully in line to inherit what is in store
for you. Because of our adoption into the family of God we are no
longer strangers, nor are we of our original father, the devil. Instead,
we possess an inalienable right to receive all that God has promised
to give to each of his children, beginning with our elder Brother,
Christ. What we know of this inheritance is largely symbolic, and
much in Revelation speaks to the riches that will be bestowed upon
us. Chief among them will not be things, but greater intimacy with
Christ than we presently enjoy.

(3) Suffering and glorification

Suffering is a very common theme in the New Testament, particularly
in the writings of the apostle Paul. As Christians we are baptised into
the death of Christ, and we are called, in a certain sense, to participate
in the sufferings of Christ, in the tribulations of the kingdom of God.
The purpose of these sufferings is not to accrue any merit but rather
to solidify our identification with Jesus and to work out the redemptive purposes of God. Tribulation is to be expected in the Christian
life. Paul, however, says that if we share in Jesus' sufferings we will
also be glorified with him. Just as Jesus has been exalted and been
given the promise of the fullness of the kingdom of God, so we will
participate in the glory that the Father gives to the Son.

**I consider that our present sufferings are not worth compar-
ing with the glory that will be revealed in us** (verse 18). Paul is not
saying that there is a level of pain and suffering that is equalled or
balanced out by a future promise of reward or blessedness. He is not
saying that for every ounce of suffering we patiently endure in this
world, we will reap the benefit of an ounce of glory in heaven. Paul

says that the ratio is not one of equality; in fact, the ratio is such that they are not even worthy of comparison. The principle that he states here is the principle of the *how much more* - that is to say, the blessing that God has stored up for us is many times greater than the suffering we are called to endure in this world. Our suffering is minute, virtually insignificant, compared to the deposit of glory that is established on our account in heaven.

In verse 19, Paul further elaborates this concept by expanding the application of this future glory to which we look and for which we wait. In a rather unusual, and I think fascinating, way he says: **The creation waits in eager expectation for the sons of God to be revealed.** What Paul has in mind here, as we can deduce by careful analysis of the verses that follow, is the created realm, apart from men and angels. It is that part of creation, both animate and inanimate, personal and impersonal, which is under the dominion of man - the rocks, the trees, the hills, the valleys, the seas, the plants, the animal kingdom. These aspects of the created order participate in the anticipation of the future manifestation of glory. And it is not a mild expectation, but an earnest expectation. The phrase here is one that is intensive. The whole creation, the birds, the animals, the snakes, the grass, the hills and the valleys are waiting for our full measure of redemption.

For the creation was subjected to frustration. The creation is, at present, experiencing futility, the weakness or frailty that afflicts it as a result of the corruption of man. For example, death stalks the world and there is much decay and trouble, even within the order of nature. For the most part God richly cares for the birds of the air and the fish of the sea, but they also participate in calamities. Just think of what happens when men pollute the streams of the earth, or the air of the earth, and how this creates suffering for the beasts of the field and the birds of the air and the fish that live in the streams.

Notice that the creation was made subject to these weaknesses, frailties and corruptions, **not by its own choice, but by the will of the one who subjected it** (verse 20). There is some debate as to whether or not the one who subjects the creatures to this vanity is man, because it is man's sin. Or is it, ultimately, God? I believe that Paul is not speaking of man's will. We did sin wilfully and willingly, and we as human beings have been made subject to vanity willingly. But that is not the case with the birds and the fish; they are not moral creatures, making the moral decisions of which men and women are capable. They did not fall into this adverse condition as a result of their sin, but they fell as a result of our sin. They were not willing participants in the transgression against the law of God.

So our sin spills over and adversely affects our subordinates. Man was given dominion over the earth, to dress the earth, to keep the earth, to till the earth and to name the animals. Man was established as the king of this environment, and when the king, or the ruler, falls, the effects of his sinfulness spill over and harm the subordinates of the king.

In fact, the illustration is used repeatedly throughout Scripture, that man who is supposed to be superior to animals, in many instances is judged to be inferior, inasmuch as the ox knows his master and his cradle, but men don't even seem to know who their Creator is. The stars obey the laws of God, they follow the orbits and elliptical movements that God has designed for them. The birds fly south in the winter when they are supposed to fly south in the winter, and they don't exercise rebellion against their Creator.

In verse 21, Paul makes an incredible statement: **the creation itself will be liberated from its bondage to decay and brought into the glorious freedom of the children of God.** Part and parcel of what Christ has effected for us, is not only the redemption of our souls and of our bodies, but redemption of our terrestrial environment including the plants, the fields, the hills and the creatures who populate the world. The Scriptures tell us that there is a future time when God will pour out his wrath upon the world, and so we can expect some kind of significant conflagration to afflict this planet.

However, that is not the end of the story. The Bible does not teach the annihilation of this planet, but rather its renovation and redemption. The Scriptures promise a new heaven and a new earth: a cosmic transformation whereby the work of redemption effected by Christ will not only bring renewal, sanctification and glorification to man, but also renewal, sanctification and glorification to our natural world, to our natural environment.

Little children, for example, who lose pets often ask me the question, Will their dog or their cat be in heaven? Most theologians answer that question by saying, 'No, of course not, because they don't have souls.' I don't know whether they have souls or don't have souls - I know they are not created in the image of God in the sense that we are - but I have every reason to expect a new earth that is populated by glorified dogs and cats and canaries and redeemed snakes, if you will! But we often fail to notice this magnificent promise that the Bible gives us concerning the future, not only of the redeemed sons and daughters of Christ, but of our planet.

Paul continues in verse 22: **We know that the whole creation has been groaning as in the pains of childbirth right up to the present time.** This is a graphic description of the suffering that is inflicted upon the earth. The earth is a place where there is much sorrow, and the sorrow that afflicts our lives is described here as a sorrow that impacts the whole creation, and elicits groans from the world. If I can press this to its simple application, it means that the deer in the woods, and the lion in the jungle, groan, as they wait for redemption and deliverance from the bondage of corruption.

But notice that the groaning and the pain of which Paul speaks is like 'the pains of childbirth', a specific kind of intense pain. When the apostle speaks of the groaning of the creation, it is like the groan of the expectant delivering mother. Even though the created world is going through agony, it is an agony that does not end in termination or annihilation; it is an agony that ends in the unspeakable joy of birth, of new life, of renovation and redemption.

And Paul goes on, **Not only so, but we ourselves, who have the firstfruits of the Spirit, groan inwardly as we wait eagerly for our adoption as sons, the redemption of our bodies** (verse 23). There is a sense in which we are still waiting for our adoption, and that waiting provokes within us certain groans. What Paul teaches here is that redemption in Biblical terms is not something that takes place all at once, but rather in stages. We have been reborn, we have experienced faith, we have been justified, and in our justification we are united with Jesus Christ. So there is a sense in which we are saved, but we have not yet experienced the full measure of our salvation. We still struggle with sins, as Paul indicates in chapter 7. We still suffer from disease, illness and death. Yet we are promised a future glorification when there will be no more sin, or sickness, or sorrow, or death. Death, it says, will be no more.

However, that element of our salvation, the future consummation of the fullness of glory, is something we have not yet experienced. Yet we have what Paul calls 'the firstfruits of the Spirit'. We do not simply have a promise of the future with no present participation in that future. Rather, we have a foretaste of the glory to come, by the newness of life that we have already experienced in Christ through the Holy Spirit. But it is a taste which is mixed with an ongoing struggle against sin, mixed with a coat of suffering that still causes us, in spite of the joy of our salvation, to weep, to suffer, to hurt.

The firstfruits of the Spirit is like a down payment, with a Divine promise that the full measure of the blessing will most certainly come. Christians still suffer from the effects and consequences of the Fall upon their mortal bodies. They know what it means to grow old; they know what it means to experience degeneration and decay; they know what it means to suffer the ravages of disease. But they do not look, like the Greeks, for redemption from the body to a bodiless existence in some kind of amorphous soul; they expect a salvation that redeems both soul and body. The glory given to Christ was manifest in a glorified, resurrected human body, and his glory is the firstfruits of what we are to experience. We too will inherit bodies that are incorruptible and immortal, that will not be subjected to pain, disease, suffering and death. We know these things will come to pass because God has promised them. But in the meantime, having experienced the taste of the firstfruits of the Spirit, like the rest of the created order we groan in the expectancy of childbirth, waiting for the full measure of the manifestation of the sons of God.

For in this hope we were saved. What does that mean? Some people reading this might say, 'I thought the Bible taught salvation by faith, not by hope?' I want to underscore that the word 'save' in the New Testament, is used somewhat differently than in the popular vocabulary of evangelical Christians. We know that the verb 'to save' is used in virtually every available tense in the Greek language. There is a sense in which we were saved, are saved, are being saved, and shall be saved. Also, salvation in its broadest meaning can refer to any deliverance from any kind of calamity - you can be saved from illness, saved from defeat in battle. Above all, to be saved is to be reconciled to God, saved from his wrath, and given the privilege of entering into his family.

Paul is saying that in our present circumstances, despite having the firstfruits of the Spirit, we still suffer. Now what saves us from despair? What is it that protects us from surrendering to the sorrows that beset us in this world? The saving factor for the Christian, which preserves him in the midst of his present circumstances, is his hope.

We need to mark carefully the difference between the meaning of the word 'hope' in the New Testament, and the way the word normally functions in our language. There are lots of things that we wish were true, but some of the things that we wish were true cannot possibly be true. There are things that we wish for, in terms of the future, that might come to pass, but might not. There are no guarantees.

Now this is where the Biblical concept of hope differs from the cultural concept. When the Bible speaks of the hope that saves the Christian, it is talking about our confidence in the promises of God for the future. This hope is solid because it rests upon the promises of God which nothing can ever frustrate. When God says that something is going to happen in the future, it is going to happen. The hope of the Christian is strong enough to carry him through the present suffering and sorrow.

But hope that is seen is no hope at all. Who hopes for what he already has? But if we hope for what we do not yet have, we wait for it patiently (verses 24,25). Here is the real difficulty of the Christian life. We know that when we die we are going to heaven; we know that God is going to renovate his creation; we know that he is not going to fail in the promises he has made. But in the meantime, we hurt, we suffer, we get discouraged and it is so easy for us to become impatient.

Impatience is a sin that afflicts us in both obvious and not so obvious ways. Some of the most serious distortions of Christian truth are a direct result of people's impatience.

What provokes people, for example, to go around teaching that God always wills healing and that Christians, if they are truly believers, will never be sick? The logic of that is that if they were never sick, they would never die, and we should expect that they would be translated into heaven in the same way as Enoch and Elijah. That wrong teaching is a result of human impatience with present suffering. It is as if we were claiming for the present what God has promised for the future.

The same thing happens with perfectionism: people claiming that they can have total victory over sin in this world. We certainly will be glorified as God has promised, but in the meantime we struggle with sin as well as with sickness and death. It is impatience with the struggle that produces these wrong theologies.

But it is not merely hope and patience that make it possible for the Christian to endure the present tribulations and sufferings of this world. Paul speaks of another crucially important dimension in verse 26: **In the same way, the Spirit helps us in our weakness.** One very important part of the ministry of the Holy Spirit is to sustain us in the midst of tribulation. He is the one who stands with us in our moments of darkness and of trial. He helps us to persevere. One of the important ways that he does it is indicated by the next clause: **We do not know what we ought to pray for, but the Spirit himself intercedes for us.**

Now what Christian doesn't enjoy seeing answers to prayer? Yet what Christian has never been frustrated by getting an answer different from what he desired? Is there a secret to answered prayer? If so, it is praying through the Spirit. Now what I mean by praying through the Spirit is not glossalalia (speaking in tongues), but that when we pray, we are in close touch with the Spirit of God working in us to assist us. The Spirit teaches us to pray as we ought to pray. The more we grow in grace, the more we cultivate the life of the Spirit, the more accurate and effective our prayer life becomes because we pray according to the Word of God and according to the mind of God which is given to us, inwardly, through the Holy Spirit.

Paul says that **the Spirit himself intercedes for us with groans that words cannot express** (verse 26). Who is doing the groaning? Is it our groaning or is it the Spirit's groaning? Christ, our great High Priest, now our primary Advocate who stands for us in the presence of God, promised before he left his disciples, another Advocate, the Holy Spirit. As Jesus intercedes for us before the Father, the Holy Spirit intercedes for us. It works like this: I pray to Jesus, Jesus speaks to the Father on my behalf. But how do I know what I should pray as I approach Jesus? The Spirit helps me form my prayers and direct them to Jesus. So both the Spirit and the Son are helping me to get my prayers to the Father on the throne of grace.

And he who searches our hearts knows the mind of the Spirit. Who is it that searches the hearts? This is a reference to Christ. He knows the mind of the Spirit. There is a communion, if we can use these figures of language, in the mind of God, the mind of Christ and the mind of the Spirit. There is a harmony of thought in the Trinity.

because the Spirit intercedes for the saints in accordance with God's will (verse 27). It is one thing for me to pray, 'Thy will O God' - but I don't know what the will of God is except as it is set down for me in Scripture. However, the Spirit knows both the mind of God and my mind in a way that I don't know the mind of God nor even my own mind. So the Holy Spirit works to facilitate the communication that takes place between God the Father and his children.

What a tremendous assistance that is to us in this time of pain and patient waiting for the future hope to be realised! While we are waiting, the Holy Spirit is living in us and is helping us to speak with our God as we go through the valley of the shadow of death. The Spirit keeps our hearts buoyant, our souls comforted and our minds at peace, because he teaches us to pray according to the will of God.

GOD'S SOVEREIGNTY AND THE CHRISTIAN RESPONSE (8:28-39)

And we know that in all things God works for the good of those who love him, who have been called according to his purpose (verse 28). This verse is so rich in comfort and substantive in meaning that it is frequently memorised by itself. But if we take this particular verse out of the context in which it is written, we could distort the meaning. There are three elements that require specific attention.

The first element is the meaning of the phrase, 'in all things'. One natural conclusion from such a statement is that every single thing which happens to us, by us, with us or for us, in this world, is added together by the sovereign God and brought to a great and wonderful conclusion. Well, I am not denying that God does that. But in the context of this verse, the use of the phrase 'all things' does not refer to each and every thing that happens.

Rather Paul is using this phrase 'all things' in the same way he uses it throughout his writings, as a summary statement to capture the essence of what he has just said. So if we are going to understand what he is saying here, we have to apply the 'all things', not to a universal sense of all things, but to the 'all things' that he has just described.

Obviously what the apostle has in view is the infirmities and the sufferings of the people of God. These sufferings that we endure in this world are not worthy to be compared with the glory that God has laid up for us in the future. These present sufferings are the 'things' that Paul has in mind. They are actually in a sense blessings in disguise, because the sufferings in this world are used by God for our ultimate good and for our ultimate benefit.

This does not mean that everything which happens to us is good in and of itself. Suffering is a tragic, physical evil. I am not supposed to say to another believer who is suffering, 'Rejoice, this is a wonderful benefit that you are experiencing here, because it is working together for your good.' We are not to praise God for the presence of suffering, particularly in the case of others, because that would lead us to the same smug attitude that is so destructively manifest in Job's friends. Rather if I see another suffering, I must do everything in my power to alleviate that suffering.

Now that would seem to be working against this wonderful benefit God has given him. But Paul is saying that God uses these things, triumphs over them, brings victory out of them and adds them together for our greater glory. In other words, God redeems the evil that befalls us.

So we should be comforted and consoled by the fact that our suffering is neither futile nor ultimately tragic. It may be very painful and difficult to endure for the moment. But God stands sovereign over our suffering.

The second thing we need to note is that there is a restriction here. God is not promising to bring goodness out of all suffering for everybody. Rather he says, **that in all things God works for the good of those who love him** (verse 28b). It is not in the final analysis a matter of mental assent but of affection for God. Obedience, discipleship and living the Christian life are a consequence of loving God. If you love me, Jesus said, keep my commandments (John 14:15). Our obedience is based upon a prior love. The love of God is the motivating force for living a Christian life. It is not the desire to merit one's own salvation, nor even an altruistic beneficent attitude towards our fellow men. The ultimate motivator for Christian service, Christian ministry and Christian obedience, is a personal affection for God.

The whole point of studying Scripture is that we might love God more. The better we know him, the easier it is for our hearts to be inflamed with affection for him. It is difficult, nay impossible, to love an unknown quantity. Love involves a personal relationship. Love is something that takes place between subjects, not objects, and is the personal quality on which Christianity is based. So those who love God have the promise that all of their suffering and all of their difficulties are being worked together for their good by the very God that they love. The bottom line of what we are trying to develop in our Christian growth is a deeper affection for God. That's what worship is all about.

The third aspect of this verse to be noted is a second distinction that makes it a passage of particular rather than universal application:

who have been called according to his purpose (verse 28c). When the Bible speaks of God's call, it never means simply the external call whereby the invitation to fellowship with God is given. Those who are called by God experience, what we call in theology, effectual calling (see comments on 1:1).

The last clause does not refer to a different group from the clause preceding. All those whom God calls according to his purpose love him, and all those who love God have been called according to his purpose.

The foundation for the comfort and certainty of future joy is God's plan of redemption, which Paul summarises in verses 29 and 30: **For those God foreknew he also predestined to be conformed to the likeness of his Son, that he might be the firstborn among many brothers. And those he predestined, he also called; those he called, he also justified; those he justified, he also glorified.**

A woman once raised this question with me, Does the Bible teach the doctrine of predestination? My answer to her was not a simple, Yes, followed by a lengthy explanation; my answer was more emphatic: 'Of course the Bible teaches the doctrine of predestination. I say that as dogmatically as I possibly can because the assertion is indisputable. I don't know anyone who has ever read the Scriptures, or particularly the book of Romans, who has tried to argue that the Bible has no doctrine of predestination.' Now the reason why no-one does so is because such an argument would be futile. John Calvin, Martin Luther and Augustine didn't invent predestination, it is a Biblical term.

So the answer to the question, Does the Bible teach predestination? is simple. But not everybody agrees about what kind of predestination is in view. Biblical scholars and Christian theologians throughout history have been sharply divided on this issue.

Verse 29 has been a very important proof text for those who would deny the Reformation concept of predestination. Most people equate predestination with Calvinism, because Calvin is seen as the author and propounder of the doctrine of predestination. But there are different beliefs concerning predestination. For example, the view which is common to the Roman Catholic Church, to Methodists, Arminians and Lutherans is what is known as the *prescient view* of predestination. As the word implies, it is a doctrine of predestination based upon a concept of foreknowledge, and the classical proof-text for the prescient view of predestination, is verse 29.

The view goes something like this. From all eternity God has prior knowledge of the actions and responses of human beings. This is part of God's omniscience, since he knows everything from an eternal perspective. Since God knows in advance with respect to time what we will do as human creatures, he knows in advance who will and who will not respond to the gospel. So the idea is this: God looks down the corridors of time from his vantage point in eternity and he sees the different responses people make to the gospel of Christ. On the basis of his prior knowledge of how we will respond freely to the invitation of the gospel, God then predestines those whom he knows will say yes to salvation. Predestination, according to this view, is not an actual foreordaining that people will believe, but only a foreordaining that those who believe will be saved. God does not work the faith into their hearts. That is something they do by their response, by their will, by their choice.

The Reformed community would answer by saying that foreknowledge, or prescience, is not an explanation of predestination, but is in fact a denial of predestination. The word has been explained away because on this view the destiny of people is, in effect, determined by the choices that they make and not by any choice that God makes in advance.

But we are still left with the problem of how to answer the fact that the advocates of the Arminian view appeal to this text, where *foreknowledge* is at the beginning of what we would call the order of salvation: **For those God foreknew he also predestined ...**

First of all, Paul is saying here that each one of these categories is all-inclusive, that is, all those whom God foreknows, he predestinates, and all he predestinates, he calls, and all he calls, he justifies, and all he justifies, he glorifies. It is very important to understand that, in the structure of the language here, everyone in each category belongs totally to every other category. The prescient advocates say that God foreknows who will choose, and on the basis of who will choose, he predestinates.

Now the Scripture doesn't supply that information, it is supplied by the prescient advocate. He puts something in the text which is not there and I am saying that such an addition or qualification to the text is utterly gratuitous. All the apostle says is that everybody God foreknows in some sense, he predestines in some sense, and everyone that he predestines in some sense, he calls in some sense, and everyone that he calls in some sense, he justifies in some sense, and everyone he justifies he glorifies.

What can we learn from this? Let's work backwards. First of all, if a person is justified, can he lose his justification? This passage tells us very clearly that everyone whom God justifies, God will glorify, so that once a person is justified there is an absolute certainty of receiving the fullness of salvation.

Who are justified? All those who are called. When Paul refers to being called by God in this context, he is not referring to the outward call of the gospel which falls upon the ears of the believer and the unbeliever. He is speaking about that inner calling which results in regeneration.

Who are those who receive this inward work of the Spirit? What comes prior to this kind of calling? Predestination. Notice in the order of salvation, prescient advocates would say that all whom God has foreknown he has called. But they are thinking of the outward call, arguing that all who respond to it God predestines to be justified. In so arguing, they have reversed the order here so that it simply doesn't flow from the text. Paul says that everyone who is called is justified. Now he can't mean the external call because not everyone who hears the gospel is in fact justified. So he must be speaking of the internal call.

Who receives that inward calling? Everyone who is predestined to receive that inward calling. There is a clear link between predestination and calling, and between calling and justification. So we can say that only the predestined are justified; only the predestined are glorified.

But why is foreknowledge stated first? To answer that, we have to ask the question, What does foreknowledge mean?

The verb *to know* has more than one meaning in Scripture. There is first of all the cognitive meaning of knowledge, simply to be aware of something, to have cognition. In the sense of 'being aware of', we would have to say that God is aware of all men's actions. God certainly knows in advance what everybody does. But 'foreknew' describes some, not all humans. It, therefore, cannot refer to pure cognition, it is more than that.

There is also the intimate sense of knowing, where the Bible says Adam knew his wife and she conceived. Some would interpret foreknowledge as saying that those whom God has loved in advance, he did predestinate to be called. (Some believe that God loves all men but it is clear from Paul's statement that not all are predestinated.)

Then there is to be known as to be selected. This is a really simple explanation of predestination. God looks at the mass of fallen humanity and selects some to receive the grace of calling, justification and glorification. But before he can select anyone, God must have an idea in his mind of the identity of those whom he is choosing. God does not predestine unknown quantities; God predestines persons that are known to him. Therefore, it is a logical necessity that foreknowledge of the people comes before predestination. To add that it is a foreknowledge of what people were going to do before he predestines them, runs absolutely contrary to the rest of the list.

It is safe to say that the classical doctrine of predestination, in the Reformed sense, is not minimised or eliminated by the fact that the word 'foreknowledge' precedes the word 'predestination'. It would have to precede the word 'predestination', because God must know me before he can predestine me to anything.

For what are such predestinated? **to be conformed to the likeness of his Son, that he might be the firstborn among many brothers** (verse 29). This very important verse is often neglected, not only by Arminians, but by Calvinists as well. Here the goal of election is set forth, and we have a Biblical answer to one of the greatest mysteries that puzzles us. If our salvation has nothing to do with our own merit, or our own foreseen good works, but is purely of grace, then why does God save me? What is his purpose, if it is not based on my work or my activity?

The only reason why God has saved me is for the sake of Jesus Christ. The ultimate reason for predestination is the honour and glory of Jesus. Jesus is the reason for the universe. The goal of creation is that Christ might have the pre-eminence.

God the Father gives his people as a love-gift to his Son. Jesus says, All that the Father gives to me, come to me (John 6:37). Christ was aware of the fact that certain people were given to him by the Father. And that's where our election is based, in the love of the Father for the Son.

Now that has glorious implications for us which should cause us not to despair but to rejoice, and Paul elaborates on those in the verses that follow.

What, then, shall we say in response to this? (verse 31). That is, what should our response be to this announcement of Divine sovereignty working itself out in history for our redemption? There are several responses to any presentation of the doctrine of predestination. Usually, there is a howl of protest and people react negatively to the whole concept. Even those who do acquiesce in the doctrine of predestination, do it with a spirit of being more or less forced to surrender to the clarity of the teaching of Scripture. The normal human reaction to predestination, then, is one of reluctance at least, or even belligerence.

But that is not the apostle's response. It is certainly not his purpose to grind his teeth against Divine sovereignty, rather he looks on the bright side. He says: **If God is for us, who can be against us?** (verse 31). Divine sovereignty is the ultimate source of comfort for the Christian believer, because it means that God is in control of his destiny. What could be more comforting to the Christian than to know that the outcome of his life is not in the hands of fortuitous circumstances, but is in the hands of a benevolent God?

One of the most frequent objections to Divine election is that it is a kind of fatalism. Fatalism is a very pessimistic view of reality, and originally meant that the affairs of men are determined and dictated by the arbitrary, capricious and whimsical activities of the Fates, a sort of junior-grade deities, who took delight in causing untold grief to their human targets and objects. Then there is the more abstract and sophisticated sense of fatalism which says that the affairs of man are dictated by the blind, impersonal forces of nature. In modern language, fatalism means that there are times when we are victims of circumstances, victims of the accidental movement of atoms and the random activities of impersonal forces.

So whether we think of fatalism as the result of impish sub-deities or blind impersonal natural forces, either one would put a cloud over the pursuit of happiness. To think that all of my labour, all of my effort in this world, can be set aside in one moment of collision with these blind impersonal forces. That's pessimistic!

Paul is saying that our ultimate destiny is in the hands of a holy, omnipotent, sovereign, righteous, loving, personal God and that this is a cause for rejoicing. If for one second there was one molecule running around this universe out of the control of the sovereignty of God, I would have to surrender to despair. If there is one molecule outside the control of God's sovereignty then there is no guarantee whatsoever that the promises of God will in fact ever come to pass. That single molecule may be like the grain of sand in the kidney of Oliver Cromwell, that brought down an empire.

The good news is found in the words, **If God is for us**. Paul is describing the ultimate sense of experiencing someone who is for us, and in this case it is God. This is the message of predestination: God does not leave me to impersonal, fortuitous circumstances. God determines, in a very real way, my destiny which is glorification. Whatever else happens to me in this world, I know that God is for me. That knowledge is humbling, as well as comforting.

Some people object to this on the grounds that it represents a foundation for people to boast. The charge often made to advocates of predestination is that predestination is a doctrine of arrogance. In reality it is the denial of predestination that involves arrogance. The person who receives these benefits solely on the basis of God's sovereign election, has to understand that the only thing ensuring and guaranteeing future bliss and felicity is the grace of God. It is the Arminian who has God choosing people who are worthy of the choice; it is the Arminian who has something of which to boast before God. But the Calvinist does not. His only response is to say, **If God is for us, who can be against us?**

The answer is of course, Nobody.

A perfectly reasonable answer to the question, however, would be that everybody in the world can be against you. God was for Jesus, but look at all the people who were against Jesus and are still against Jesus. God is for his people, and yet his people have been thrown to the lions, they have been used as human torches to illumine the gardens of Nero; the Christian church has been the object of all kinds of animosity and persecution. The whole world can be against us, as Jesus himself said to his disciples, If they hate me, they are going to hate you (John 15:18, 19). Paul is not saying that if God is for a person, nobody in the world will ever rise up against that person.

The meaning of this idiom is, who can *prevail* against us? All kinds of people will be against us, but who can overcome the sovereignty and the power of God? We have the old cliche that one person with God is a majority.

He who did not spare his own Son, but gave him up for us all - how will he not also, along with him, graciously give us all things? (verse 32). Notice Paul uses a word in verse 32 that would be easy to miss if we read over it too quickly. It is the word *idion* - he that spared not his *own* Son. Why does Paul put in that qualifier? Why does he not just say, He that spared not his Son?

Well, in this chapter he has expounded the whole concept of adoption. But there is a distinction that the apostle makes here. God has an only-begotten Son who is uniquely the Son of God and that's what the Greek means here when the apostle speaks of his *own* Son. His *own* Son is distinguished from all those who are sons of God by *adoption*.

Paul is saying this: Look at the extent to which God has gone to ensure our ultimate victory. He has spared nothing to bring it about, not even his own Son. Here Paul refers to the inheritance the Father has laid up for the Son being shared with us, and our participation in the benefits of what rightfully belongs to Christ alone. God delivers up his own Son for us, and in doing so he is willing to give us everything that he has promised and set apart for his Son.

Who will bring any charge against those whom God has chosen? (verse 33). Paul is saying that there is no-one who can lay any charge to God's elect that will stick. It is not that no-one will ever lay a charge against God's elect. One of the most frequent sins a Christian must endure in this life, at the hands of other people, is that of slander. In fact, one of the names for Satan means the Slanderer (devil), and as Christians we are constantly exposed to the criticism, the insults, the slanders and the calumnies of those who are hostile toward us. Remember the words of Jesus in the Beatitudes, his benediction on those who bear the pain of false accusations: 'Blessed are you when people insult you, persecute you, and falsely say all kinds of evil against you because of me' (Matt. 5:11). Jesus anticipated that those who follow him will be the victims of the same kind of false accusations that he himself received.

Occasionally, in response to my radio ministry, we receive unbelievable letters that are filled with hostility. When I first started I wasn't really sure how to handle them. I remember talking to George Wilson who runs the Billy Graham organisation and he told me that Billy Graham gets letters like that all the time. George said, 'Make sure that you don't let your critics determine your agenda. Listen to legitimate criticism, but if you begin to minister on the basis of seeking to ingratiate yourself with people, you will soon prostitute any commitment you have to Christ.' That was sound advice.

But what about when we really do sin and are guilty? Here is where Satan is most concerned to bring his accusations. What is the difference between the conviction of the Holy Spirit for sin and the accusation of Satan for sin?

The Holy Spirit's work is to convict us of sin and righteousness, in order to lead us to repentance. The result is that we go to God to confess our sin and ask for his forgiveness. The conviction of the

Holy Spirit is positive, it is redeeming. The aim of Satan, on the other hand, as he points out exactly the same sins of which the Spirit has convicted us, is to oppress us, to paralyse us, to destroy us with guilt.

Suppose the Spirit has convicted me of my sin, and I have confessed it. God has promised to forgive my sin, but Satan starts telling me, 'How can you be a Christian? Look at what you did!' As he starts taking away my peace, it is at that point I am to say, 'Satan, who shall lay any charge to God's elect? Get out of here! You have nothing to say because I am a justified man.' **It is God who justifies.** That is the point the apostle is making here. God, the supreme Governor, the supreme Judge, has declared that I am justified.

Who is he that condemns? The ultimate Condemner of sinful people is God; only God can condemn in the final sense. But Paul reminds us in verse 34 that **Christ Jesus, who died - more than that, who was raised to life - is at the right hand of God and is also interceding for us.** Christ was condemned for me; my sin was condemned by God on the cross. So what possible condemnation is left to be heaped upon me? There may be all kinds of people in this world who condemn me with their mouths, and who pray that I would be condemned by God, but that prayer is in vain, because the only one who can condemn me has already condemned me in Christ.

What is the right hand of God? What is the role of one who stands at the right hand of God? It is as though God were the king and his prime minister stands at his right hand. In the Biblical imagery here that is exactly the idea we have: Christ has been appointed by the Father to be the Judge of the world. So the Judge of the world stands at the right hand of God. Paul is speaking in legal terms, and says that the person who has been given the supreme authority to charge and to condemn, to stand in judgment over the world, is Christ.

But Christ is our Advocate, as well as our Judge. Even now he is making intercession for us. So my sin has been covered from every conceivable angle.

This leads logically to the next rhetorical question: **Who shall separate us from the love of Christ?** (verse 35). Here we stand before God, justified, having no condemnation to fear, with Christ as our Advocate. What is there in this world that can demolish or destroy the love Christ has for his people? In the rest of the chapter, Paul lists various things that could possibly separate us from the love of Christ.

He does not mention living in sin by those who profess faith as being a cause of separation from Christ. It is common today for many to make a profession of faith, and then to repudiate it by their lives. What are we to make of them? They could belong to those who have made a spurious profession of faith and their true colours are being shown. Or they could be authentic Christians who are in the midst of a serious and radical fall, but who later will be restored. The one thing I am sure of, however, when I see a person make a profession of faith and then later repudiate it, is that I am not witnessing an example of a person who is truly converted and then losing his conversion. The Scriptures make it abundantly clear that that cannot happen. The perseverance of believers is not due to the intrinsic power of faith, but due to the grace of God, who has promised that he will finish what he starts.

Paul does not give a totally exhaustive list but he begins, **Shall trouble or hardship or persecution or famine or nakedness or danger or sword?**

There seem to be a number of Christians whose commitment to Christ is only as strong as the intensity of their latest feeling of being blessed. It is great to sense being moved by the presence of the Holy Spirit. But none of us lives on a plane of constant intensity of the feelings flowing out of religious experience. Sometimes our ardour waxes cold, and we don't feel the presence of Christ.

I will use myself as an example. I have to speak over 300 times a year. Do you think it is remotely possible that my feeling of spiritual intensity, my feeling of closeness to Christ is equally strong every time I speak? Of course not. There are times when I feel so overwhelmed by a sense of awe and adoration for Christ, that I can't wait to speak. There are other times I feel so far away from Christ; perhaps I am tired, sometimes I am just not in the mood, often I feel spiritually vacant and poverty stricken. But it says on my calendar that I have to give a lecture or a sermon or a lesson. At such times,

I am thinking, 'What am I doing standing up here trying to encourage other people when I am going through the dark night of the soul myself?' But I have found that the worse I feel, and the less I feel like it, the more I really feel dependent upon the power of God.

We can't be fair-weather Christians. So when trouble or hardship or persecution or famine or nakedness or danger or sword come, they cannot separate us from Christ's love. Nor should they separate our love from Christ. The true Christian continues to love Christ throughout all these things. It is a two-way affair here. Trouble tends to increase my ardour for Christ, because my sense of need for Christ is intensified. When I face hardship, I do not flee from Christ, but rather run to Christ. When I am persecuted, I may be tempted to deny Christ with my mouth to get relief from the persecution, but in the midst of persecution is where I most need the presence of Christ.

Paul says in verse 36: **As it is written: "For your sake we face death all day long; we are considered as sheep to be slaughtered."** That is a capsule summation of the life of the apostle Paul. He was like a sheep accounted for slaughter. This is what it means to be a Christian. We are going to have to face trials, tribulation, distress, nakedness, sword, all these things. But why do we do it? For Jesus' sake, because we love him. But Jesus is not like the general who tells his troops to charge into enemy machine gun nests while he is seated comfortably in a bomb shelter. No, Jesus has gone before us, he was the sheep who was slaughtered. He was killed in a way that we can never be killed, he suffered in a way that we can never taste, he drank a cup that can never touch our lips. Our response of gratitude and love for our Lord is that we are glad to be counted as those who are facing death all the day long and are considered as sheep to be slaughtered.

No, in all these things we are more than conquerors (verse 37). The phrase 'more than conquerors' is a translation of a single compound word in the Greek, *hupernikon*. It has a prefix, *huper*, that is emphatic and intensive (which comes across into the English language in the word, 'hyper'); and it has a root, *nikon*, meaning 'conqueror'. So literally, Paul is saying that in all of these things we are 'hyperconquerors'.

The word used in the Latin version of the New Testament is *supervincimus*. We are not just more than conquerors but superconquerors. We are supermen. The New Testament says it is the Christian who is the superman; it is the Christian who rises to the supreme level of conquest; it is the Christian who has at his disposal the power to conquer which no one else can find. In fact Christianity, instead of diminishing our manhood, our strength and our authentic existence, enhances them. In Christ we don't conquer people in bloodbaths of fights but we conquer trouble, hardship, persecution, famine, nakedness, danger and the sword. How much more strength does it take to conquer distress or persecution or peril than it does to beat up somebody on the street corner?

But what is the key to being supermen, being *supervincimus*: through him who loved us. The means by which we conquer is not our own strength, but rather Christ gives the capacity to overcome.

Paul brings this section to a grand conclusion: **For I am convinced that neither death nor life, neither angels nor demons, neither the present nor the future, nor any powers, neither height nor depth, nor anything else in all creation, will be able to separate us from the love of God that is in Christ Jesus our Lord** (verses 38, 39).

Do you know what happens to people when they are persuaded? They become convinced, and people who are convinced have convictions; and people who have convictions live according to principles. How else can you explain the life and ministry of Paul, apart from the fact that he was a man who had been persuaded. That's what we need in the church - people who are convinced that nothing can separate them from the love of God that is in Christ Jesus our Lord.

Again, Paul gives a list of things that could possibly disrupt and rupture our relationship with Christ: death, life, angels, demons, the present, the future, powers, height, depth, anything else in all creation. He could have said it in one sentence: 'Brethren, nothing can separate us from the love of Christ.' That's the point he is making. There is nothing in this universe that can separate us from the love of God that is in Christ Jesus our Lord. When we read this, we know that we are ultimately safe and secure in Christ.

4
ISRAEL IN THE PLAN OF GOD
(9:1-11:36)

THE BLESSINGS OF ISRAEL (9:1-5)

Chapter 9 is most acutely clear with respect to the doctrine of predestination and divine sovereignty. I was an Arminian for five years after I was converted to Christianity and fought against the doctrines of grace in general and against the concept of predestination in particular. Finally, in the context of debate and discussion, I was confronted with the content of chapter 9 of Romans, and there was no avenue of escape from it.

It begins in a very unusual way, where Paul writes: **I speak the truth in Christ - I am not lying, my conscience confirms it in the Holy Spirit**. The apostle is taking an oath. Now you will recall from the teaching of Jesus that no oath is ever to be taken lightly, and that men are held accountable for the veracity and the consistency with which they handle vows and oaths (Matt. 5:33-37). The Old Testament says that it is better not to vow, than to vow and not pay (Eccles. 5:5). So Paul here, as a matter of emphasis, underscores the seriousness and soberness of what he is about to say, by swearing an oath.

When he says, 'I speak the truth in Christ - I am not lying', he is not alluding to divine revelation. He is simply saying that as a Christian, he promises he is telling the truth. He uses the Jewish literary form of a positive affirmation followed by the negative, a parallel that is designed to indicate emphasis. Paul adds to this the fact that his conscience is bound and subordinate to God the Holy Spirit. He wants it to be clearly understood that he is fervent in what he is about to say.

Now why does the apostle take such a solemn and formal oath? You would think it totally unnecessary for the apostle Paul to do this. The point that he is underscoring with such emphasis and with the oath is this: **I have great sorrow and unceasing anguish in my heart** (verse 2). Paul is saying, ' I swear to you that I am a burdened man, that I walk around with great sorrow and with a constant sense of grief in my heart.' This is the apostle who is always placing such stress on the importance of rejoicing in the Christian life. Yet he is a man with constant pain and continual grief.

What is the cause of this continuous grief that afflicts him? **For I could wish that I myself were cursed and cut off from Christ for the sake of my brothers, those of my own race, the people of Israel** (verses 3,4). If the apostle has already come on strong, he goes over the edge in verse 3. He is willing to experience the ultimate anathema, the final act of excommunication from God himself, for his brethren. He is saying, 'If I could suffer damnation instead of my kinsmen according to the flesh, I would do it.' But of course, Paul could not make atonement for anybody.

This verse destroys any possibility of the dreadful calumny that some have committed against Christ and against the Spirit of God by trying to ground a spirit of anti-Semitism in Scripture. There is no anti-Semitism with Jesus - he himself was a Jew. Paul also was a Jew and he harboured no ill will or resentment against his own nation. If there was ever a man who would have been justified in being angry with his kinsmen it was Paul. When you consider their bitterness against him, you would think that in normal circumstances a human being might retaliate with an equal sense of bitterness. But that's not Paul's attitude; Paul's attitude is one of compassion.

Theirs is the adoption as sons; theirs the divine glory, the covenants, the receiving of the law, the temple worship and the promises. Theirs are the patriarchs, and from them is traced the human ancestry of Christ, who is God over all, forever praised! Amen (verses 4,5).

How can anyone have an anti-Semitic attitude when we stop and consider the contribution that has come to the world through the nation of Israel. Israel, as a nation, was God's *adopted son*. When he called Israel out of Egypt, he adopted the nation in a certain sense, because it was through Israel that his work of redemption was to be carried out.

What *divine glory* do you suppose Paul had in mind? We have to speculate a little here but in all probability the glory of which Paul speaks is the Shekinah glory, that brilliant, effulgent, radiant cloud that indicated an appearance of the presence of God. The Shekinah glory was in the pillar of cloud and in the pillar of fire. The Shekinah glory hovered over Mount Sinai and came over the Mercy Seat in the Holy of Holies. This glory belonged to the people of Israel. You didn't find the Shekinah glory among the Babylonians or among the Phoenicians, or among the Philistines or among the Egyptians. It pertained to the Israelites because with them God placed his radiant glory.

The *covenants* refer to the covenants that God made with Moses (Ex. 19-24) and David (2 Sam. 7:12-16). These intimate agreements were made between God and Israel. God didn't make a covenant with the Philistines or the Babylonians, but he made covenants with Israel.

The Jews possessed *the law*, a rule of ethics that was not the invention of insightful men. It came from on high and was mediated through angels (Gal. 3:19). God himself uttered the commandments and wrote them with his own finger on tablets of stone, and gave them to Israel (Ex. 34:1). Israel has given the ten commandments to the world. We still consider the ten commandments to be the foundational legal structure for western civilisation, and they were given first to Israel.

Israel was also consecrated as a priestly nation, and a priestly tribe was set apart to minister in the *temple*. The service of God was given to the Jews.

The *promises* about the redemption of the world came to and were mediated through Israel. This is all part of the heritage of the Jewish people. Israel was the fountainhead of world salvation. Salvation is of God, but it comes through Israel.

A Christian cannot think of himself as being cut off from the Old Testament. It records the history of redemption culminating in the appearance of Jesus Christ. Abraham is the father of the faithful; Isaac is a patriarch of the covenant; Jacob is the father of the twelve tribes; Moses is the mediator of the law; David gives us the psalms; Jeremiah speaks of the new covenant; Isaiah prophesies of the coming

Messiah. All of these great heroes and heroines of faith (Heb. 11) that
are such a rich part of Christian heritage, are Jewish.

The ultimate point Paul is making is that our Lord was a Jew.
Touching his *human ancestry* he came to us from Israel. Paul refers
to the glorious dual nature of Jesus. He specifies the fact that Christ
came from Israel according to his *human ancestry*. But he is the same
Christ, *who is God over all, forever praised! Amen*. When Paul says
'over all' he doesn't mean over all Jews, he means over everything.
The word is in the neuter form and indicates the sum total of the
universe. Jesus Christ is over the entire universe.

THE JUST CHARACTER OF GOD (9:6-16)

The problem Paul has in view is that the Jews were very certain of
their future because of the covenant promises God had made. They
had come to the conclusion that by the very fact of their birth into the
nation of Israel, they were guaranteed all of the promises of salvation.
But Paul shows that it **is not as though God's word had failed.** God
had promised to bless Israel but the point Paul makes is that **not all
who are descended from Israel are Israel. Nor because they are
his descendants are they all Abraham's children** (verses 6,7).
Those who are the children of the flesh are not the children of God,
but the children of the promise are counted as the seed: **On the
contrary, "It is through Isaac that your offspring will be
reckoned." In other words, it is not the natural children who are
God's children, but it is the children of the promise who are
regarded as Abraham's offspring** (verses 7,8). Abraham had more
than one child: he had Ishmael as well as Isaac, but Ishmael did not
receive the promise as Isaac did (Gen. 21:12-13). God's promise is
given sovereignly, not biologically.

The argument is this: not everyone who is of the seed of Abraham
receives the promise of Abraham. Abraham had two sons by different
mothers: Ishmael and Isaac. Ishmael did not receive the promise of
redemption; Isaac did: **For this was how the promise was stated:
"At the appointed time I will return, and Sarah will have a son"**
(verse 9).

On this basis we would think that all the children of Isaac will receive the promise. But we are reminded that Isaac had two children by the same mother. **Not only that, but Rebekah's children had one and the same father, our father Isaac** (verse 10). Paul wants to dispel any confusion arising from the fact that Abraham's children, Ishmael and Isaac, were half-brothers. Some might have said, 'The reason why it was given to one and not the other was because there were two different mothers.' But that was not the case with Jacob and Esau, because they had the same father and mother. Not only did they have the same parents, but they were twins, born virtually at the same time. **Yet, before the twins were born or had done anything good or bad - in order that God's purpose in election might stand: not by works but by him who calls - she was told, "The older will serve the younger." Just as it is written: "Jacob I loved, but Esau I hated"** (verses 11-13). Dramatically, the firstborn is passed over and the second-born receives the promise of God.

The choice has nothing to do with the actual good or potential good, the actual evil or potential evil, of Jacob and Esau. It has to do with the purpose of God. It is of his sovereign good pleasure.

Some have tried to get around this position by saying that Jacob and Esau were representatives of nations. On this interpretation Paul is not talking about the election of individuals but of nations. Even if that were the case, all the questions that surround the problem of predestination of individuals would still apply to the predestination of nations, only on a higher scale. But the apostle is clearly writing of the selection of individuals. There may be national repercussions as a result of it, but the election of which he speaks whereby one man is elect, while another is passed over, has nothing whatsoever to do with the virtue, foreseen or otherwise, of these two individuals.

When the Scripture speaks of God's *hating*, it means that he did not bestow favour upon Esau. God did not give to him grace and the benefits of salvific love. It doesn't mean that God hates in the sense that human beings hate.

Of course, this raises the question: Is there arbitrariness in God? Is he capricious? Do his choices border on the irrational with no legitimate reason whatsoever? Absolutely not! God never does anything without a reason. It is beyond the character of God to act in a whimsical, capricious manner. God's decisions are always taken in accordance with his character. But the spectre of arbitrariness is here because the Scripture makes it very clear that there is no reason in the elect why God has chosen them. But the fact that there is no reason in them, does not mean that there is no reason at all. God has a reason for doing what he does. But the point is that the reason does not lie within us.

This raises a second question: 'Is God unjust?' People think that this is a necessary inference from the doctrine of sovereign predestination. God, willy-nilly, saves some and damns others and in violating the canons of justice, is in fact, unrighteous. So people think that by rejecting the doctrine of predestination, somehow they are holding to a higher view of God.

The Arminian believes that the ultimate basis for our salvation is whether or not we choose to receive Jesus Christ. Whoever chooses Christ will be saved, and whoever refuses Christ will be damned. Those who choose Christ will be elect, and those who do not choose Christ will lose any possibility of election. In the Arminian view of theology, election is based upon human decision. This is a serious distortion of what the apostle Paul is teaching here.

Jesus made it clear that no one can come to him unless it is given to him by the Father (John 6:65). Our natural state of sinfulness is one of utter moral dereliction. We do not have the moral power to come to Jesus if left to ourselves. The gift of grace, with which predestination is concerned, means that God gives the ability to come to Jesus Christ to some people. He does not give that ability to everyone. He gave it to Jacob; he withheld it from Esau. It is not that God brings some people into the kingdom who don't want to be there, kicking and screaming against their will. The point of regeneration is that God changes the heart. God quickens to spiritual life and plants a desire within for Christ.

But if God gives this desire to some but not to all, it doesn't seem right. There is something basically unfair about it. This is what Paul has in mind when he raises the rhetorical question: **Is God unjust?** (verse 14). Has God any obligation to give this opportunity of being born again to all men?

The reply must be another question: Why would God ever be under any obligation to give us anything after we have fallen, having committed cosmic treason, resulting in the desires of our hearts being only wicked continuously? It is absolutely essential that we understand this: God Almighty owes us nothing. We have no claim upon grace. If we had, then we would not be talking about grace but about justice. Grace, by definition, is something that God is never obliged to give, but something that he gives freely and voluntarily.

Only a perfect man can ever claim that God in justice should give him a reward. But all men are sinners. If God deals with them strictly according to righteousness, they are finished, and are doomed to everlasting punishment in hell. If God is going to save anybody, the only way he can do so is by grace.

No one deserves to be saved, for all are under the condemnation of God. If God delivers justice to everybody, all will perish. But suppose that God, in his desire to be merciful, decides to be merciful to some, but not to others. For example, if there are ten people who are guilty, and God sovereignly decides to pardon one of them and sentence the other nine, who has received an injustice? The nine who are sentenced receive what they deserved - the just punishment for their sins. The nine received justice, the one received mercy. But none received injustice.

It is unthinkable that God could ever be unrighteous or unjust: Paul says strongly, **Not at all!** He bases his argument on an earlier Scripture: **For he says to Moses, "I will have mercy on whom I have mercy, and I will have compassion on whom I have compassion"** (verse 15). This is the basic essence of the doctrine of predestination, showing it to be a doctrine of grace. Some people think that predestination inclines Christians to pride, but how could this be? Any understanding at all of divine election recognises that it is purely by the grace of God. The doctrine of predestination reminds us of the merciful character of God.

It does not, therefore, depend on man's desire or effort, but on God's mercy (verse 16). This verse should put an end to the debate for ever. God could not make it any clearer. Salvation is by grace and by grace alone. Bless that holy God, who gives his sovereign mercy, bestowing it upon those whom he will. Those who are devoid of that mercy will perish and justly perish. They will act according to their sinful nature: they will refuse to capitulate to Christ, they will flee from the kingdom of God, they will harden their hearts until the day of wrath. Our only hope is to be found in the God who shows mercy.

THE SOVEREIGN POWER OF GOD (9:17-21)

What follows is one of the most difficult portions of the entire epistle, because we enter into that perilous corridor in which the apostle speaks about hardening the heart of Pharaoh. It is what some would call the shadow side of election and predestination. It is important, therefore, that we come to a clear understanding of what is being revealed to us by the apostle. **For the Scripture says to Pharaoh: "I raised you up for this very purpose, that I might display my power in you and that my name might be proclaimed in all the earth"** (verse 17).

In Exodus, God commanded Moses to go to the court of Pharaoh to instruct him, in the name of God, to let the people of Israel go. Because Pharaoh refused, God sent a series of plagues on Egypt. Each time Pharaoh would relent and agree to allow the Israelites to depart, but then we read the refrain that God hardened Pharaoh's heart, resulting in Pharaoh changing his mind and stopping the Israelites from departing.

Paul is saying that the purpose of God in elevating Pharaoh to his position of power was not to reward Pharaoh's righteousness, or because he merited his prestigious position. Rather, God put him in that position for God's purposes. Here we have an insight into God's providential rule as the Lord of all history. He raises kingdoms up, he brings kingdoms down. Pharaoh could not become the most powerful man in the world, apart from the providential rule of God.

And the purpose of God in establishing Pharaoh was to show God's power. Pharaoh was the most powerful man in the world at that time, but when his power was brought to bear against the power of God, Pharaoh appeared impotent, and God's manifestation of his own authority reigned supreme.

God was using an evil man to bring about his good purposes and redemptive activity. This is a common theme of the Bible. It is not that God creates evil, nor ever does evil, nor even inclines the heart to evil, but rather that God brings good out of evil, overruling the evil machinations of men to bring about his own purposes.

A classic example of this is the story of Joseph. His brothers, filled with jealousy and envy, sold him into slavery. Joseph was taken down to Egypt and remarkable events transpired by which Joseph was elevated to the level of prime minister and was set in a strategic position to bring relief and redemption to his own family at a time of crisis and famine in the promised land.

Finally, Joseph had a meeting with his brothers when they recognised him and repented of their evil deed. Joseph responded to their confession by saying, 'You meant it for evil, but God meant it for good' (Gen. 50:20). God's holy, powerful providence can make use of the wicked intentions of men to bring about the good purposes of his own plan. This does not mean that men are mere automatons or pawns in the hands of God, or that Divine providence excuses men from the guilt of their own wickedness. The intentions of Joseph's brothers were clearly wicked. But God made use of the evil of which they were guilty to bring about his divine plan of redemption.

Of course, the supreme example of God's control of evil is in the betrayal of Jesus by the hands of Judas. Judas was not forced, he did exactly what he wanted to do. He manifested his own treachery, his own lust for power and his own selfish motives in taking thirty pieces of silver for handing Jesus over to his enemies. But in so doing, there is a sense in which Judas did the world the greatest favour it has ever known. By means of this betrayal, Jesus was crucified, an act which, considered in terms of the intentions of Judas and the intentions of those who crucified Jesus, was an act of diabolical wickedness, yet from God's perspective was the supreme salvific event in world history. Without the cross we have no salvation. Does that mean, then, that we should go up to Judas and say, 'Congratulations, Judas, thank you so much for your benevolent act on behalf of mankind; if it weren't for you we wouldn't be redeemed.' No, we should still regard Judas' actions for what they were: self-centred and wicked. Rather than showing any evil in God, this shows the overwhelming power of God to bring about his good purposes by means of wicked men.

In verse 18, we have the repetition of what Paul has said earlier: **Therefore God has mercy on whom he wants to have mercy.** God has the divine right to exert executive clemency, the right to show mercy to whomever he will. This is of the very essence of mercy which, by definition, is voluntary and not required. But we have something added on that makes the text so much more difficult: **and he hardens whom he wants to harden.** The flip-side of grace is this concept of hardening. Some allege that God is unjust in hardening somebody's heart and then punishing him for doing what he couldn't possibly stop from doing once his heart was hardened.

Such an idea is utterly repugnant to everything that the Bible teaches about the character of God. The question is, Shall the judge of all the earth ever do wrong? God is incapable of committing an unjust act. There is no dark side to his personality, by which he would commit an outrageous act of injustice, such as would be the case if he hardened somebody and then punished him for being hardened. We have to make a distinction between active hardening and passive hardening, and understand that what we are reading here in the text is an example of God's punitive judgment against a wicked man.

Pharaoh was already wicked, he was already ill-disposed towards the things of God. Out of Pharaoh's heart came only wickedness continually. To do something evil was Pharaoh's sheer delight. The only thing that could stop him would be the restraints and constraints that God placed upon him. This brings in the concept of 'common grace'. We distinguish between special grace and common grace. Special grace is for the redeemed: the grace of salvation. Common grace is the favour or the benefits that all men, indiscriminately, receive at the hands of God. One of the most important principles of common grace is the restraint of evil.

All God had to do to accelerate the wickedness of Pharaoh was to remove the restraints from him. God had been keeping Pharaoh's wickedness in check, providentially. Even though Pharaoh was powerful, he was not all-powerful, he was still under the control of the providence of God. Pharaoh would have liked to perform more wickedness than he actually did. God wanted Pharaoh to resist the Exodus, in order that Israel would understand that deliverance came not through the beneficence of Pharaoh, but through the redemptive grace of God. All God had to do was remove the restraints. He did not have to create fresh evil in the heart of Pharaoh. The evil disposition was already there, and so through a providential act that was both an act of punishment on Pharaoh, and an act of redemption to Israel, God removed the restraints and therefore passively hardened Pharaoh's heart.

You may say, 'That's not fair! If God knew that Pharaoh was going to commit a sin, shouldn't God have stopped him?' So I ask you the question, 'Why should he?' If God stops Pharaoh from committing sin, and therefore reduces the number of his sins and the consequent amount of punishment, he would be doing Pharaoh a favour, and a favour is what we call grace. So had God not hardened Pharaoh's heart, he would have been gracious to Pharaoh. But Paul is emphasising the point that grace is voluntary. God doesn't owe Pharaoh any grace. So God lets him go on, knowing full well that he is going to sin, and knowing full well that when he sins he is going to be brought into judgment. Hence God's activity towards Pharaoh is an act of punitive judgment. Pharaoh gets justice. The people of Israel get mercy. So there is no injustice involved in this act of hardening.

The problem with predestination is that it is all settled before we are born in terms of who will be saved and who will not. We are dealing with an eternal plan of salvation. Some are predestined to salvation; others are not included in that predestination to salvation but are reprobates, that is, they are non-elect.

We are dealing here with what is called 'double' predestination. Double predestination is distinguished from single predestination. There are those who say that the only predestinating with which the Bible is concerned, is single predestination, predestination to eternal life, and that there is no concept of predestination to damnation. Others believe in double predestination but think that it means this: God from all eternity determines to create faith in the heart of the elect and bring them to salvation; and by the same symmetrical, equal form of ultimacy, creates evil in the hearts of the reprobate and ensures that they don't come to salvation. In other words, God causes faith in one and causes unbelief in the other. Now that is not the Biblical doctrine of predestination.

The Calvinistic (and Biblical) doctrine of double predestination simply says that there are two sides to predestination. There are those who are predestined to salvation, called the elect, and there are those who are not predestined to salvation whom we call the reprobate. But the way in which God acts towards both groups is not the same. He intervenes in the lives of the elect to bring them to faith, as an act of mercy, an act of grace. The others he passes over, allowing them to work out their own sinful dispositions and he withholds his mercy and grace from them.

A great deal of confusion surrounds this issue of predestination because of a very important element. We have a tendency to think of God's eternal decrees as if he were contemplating an innocent human race. This view is called, technically, supra-lapsarianism: that from all eternity God looked at this morally neutral, innocent human race, and decreed to make some of them sin, and perish, but to make some of them believers, and bring them into eternal salvation.

What we call the Calvinistic or Reformed view of predestination is called infra-lapsarianism. Infra-lapsarianism emphasises this point that when God makes his decrees about salvation and reprobation, he does so considering the mass of humanity as fallen. Obviously God made the decision before the Fall, but he makes the decision in light of the Fall. God considered a fallen race when he made the decree of salvation. And out of this mass of fallen humanity, he chose to exercise grace toward some and bring them to salvation, but to withhold that mercy from others and punish them for their wilful disobedience and sinfulness.

Paul responds: **One of you will say to me: "Then why does God still blame us? For who resists his will?" But who are you, O man, to talk back to God? "Shall what is formed say to him who formed it, 'Why did you make me like this?' " Does not the potter have the right to make out of the same lump of clay some pottery for noble purposes and some for common use?** (verses 19-21). Paul rebukes his opponents by pointing out the wickedness of the calumnies that are raised against God in the first place. If you understand the doctrine of predestination as Paul teaches it, and you hate it, then you are merely demonstrating your own fallenness by attacking God and assailing his character. The assumption made by those who reply against God is firstly, that God is unjust, and secondly, that God owes us mercy. Those two errors need to be seen for what they are and we need the antidote to understand that firstly, God is never unjust, and secondly, God is never obliged to be merciful. If we understand those two points we should have clear sailing through these difficult passages.

Now notice that Paul says, 'Does not the potter *have the right* to make out of the clay ... ?' Paul is not asking whether or not the potter has power over clay, or whether or not God has power over his creatures. That's obvious. He is talking about authority. 'Does not the potter have authority over the clay?' He can make what he wants to make out of that lump of clay. Does not God have authority over men? Supralapsarians jump on this passage and say that God does indeed make evil men and then punishes them for their wickedness. God certainly has the power to do that but he does not have the authority to do so, if we understand that his authority is tied to his character. If God had the authority to create innocent beings, force them to do wickedness and then punish them for their wickedness, he would violate his own holiness and justice.

But he does have the authority to appoint sinful man to dishonour, just as the potter has the authority to take a piece of clay and mould it and shape it to its ultimate end. Once I sin against God, God can dispose of me anyway he wants. He may use my punishment to the glory of himself. He can harden my heart, he can bring disaster into my life. He has every right to do so, just as the potter has that kind of right over the clay. The reason why he had the authority to do so, is that it is within the scope of his character and of his justice. It was perfectly just for God to make Pharaoh an object of wrath.

THE SOVEREIGN GRACE OF GOD (9:22-33)

What if God, choosing to show his wrath and make his power known, bore with great patience the objects of his wrath - prepared for destruction? (verse 22). Is there anything wrong with God enduring sin? In other words, perhaps we should be raising this objection: why does God tolerate Pharaoh for five minutes? Why does God allow a wicked person to continue to exist? That's the real theological question.

What if he did this to make the riches of his glory known to the objects of his mercy, whom he prepared in advance for glory (verse 23). Paul says God did this to make known the riches of his glory to the objects of his mercy. God forbears with wickedness for a gracious end. God was forbearing with Pharaoh so that he would show mercy on those upon whom he would show mercy. There is a sense in which even the wickedness of the wicked is redeemed by God to be a blessing to the righteous. That is why all things work together for good to those who love the Lord. God is able to bring good out of the wickedness of his enemies to the everlasting benefit of his people, **even us, whom he also called, not only from the Jews but also from the Gentiles?** (verse 24). There is a wideness to God's mercy. Not only does God pour out his mercy upon the children of promise in Israel, but he pours out mercy on Gentiles, people who are strangers to the covenant.

As he says in Hosea: "I will call them 'my people' who are not my people; and I will call her 'my loved one' who is not my loved one," and, "It will happen that in the very place where it was said to them, 'You are not my people,' they will be called 'sons of the

living God' " (verses 25,26). Paul is quoting Hosea to describe Gentiles, who were strangers to the covenant of God, outside the camp of Israel. They were not the people of God, and yet now God says to them: 'You are my people, you are my beloved.' They will be called sons of the Living God. That, of course, is the legacy Christ has given to his people, to be called the children of God.

Paul then quotes from Isaiah: **Isaiah cries out concerning Israel: "Though the number of the Israelites be like the sand by the sea, only the remnant will be saved. For the Lord will carry out his sentence on earth with speed and finality"** (verses 27,28). The apostle is reminding his readers of the remnant concept. The prophets had called Israel to repentance and warned them that the judgment of God was going to fall upon the nation. Yet the hope was held out that, even in the midst of the judgment, God would preserve for himself a remnant. So even though the Gentiles are now being called, there is also still a remnant being called out of Israel.

The apostle further cites Isaiah, in verse 29: **It is just as Isaiah said previously: "Unless the Lord Almighty had left us descendants, we would have become like Sodom, we would have been like Gomorrah."** What happened to Sodom and Gomorrah? The lawlessness and the pagan practices of Sodom and Gomorrah so provoked the anger of God that he brought judgment from heaven and annihilated these cities. Paul is saying that were it not for God's gracious preserving of a remnant in Israel, the whole nation would have become like Sodom and Gomorrah.

Verses 30 and 31 bring us to a significant conclusion. Paul again asks, rhetorically, **What then shall we say? That the Gentiles, who did not pursue righteousness, have obtained it, a righteousness that is by faith; but Israel, who pursued a law of righteousness, has not attained it.** Now that sounds shocking; it doesn't make sense. It seems as if God is totally capricious here. On the one hand, Paul acknowledges that Israel pursued righteousness, but didn't get it. The Gentiles, on the other hand, didn't pursue righteousness, but they did get it. But this is still part of Paul's whole treatment of whether salvation is by works or by the grace of God. But how is it possible that God would give salvation to those who did not pursue righteousness, and withhold it from those who did pursue righteousness?

Actually, Paul asks the same question in verse 32: **Why not?** Why didn't Israel receive salvation if in fact they pursued righteousness? The reason they did not receive it, Paul says, is **Because they pursued it not by faith but as if it were by works.** That was the tragic error of Israel. And it is also the tragic error made by multitudes of people in the Christian church today. The Jews pursued righteousness, but they pursued it in exactly the opposite way from that in which it is to be found. They pursued it in their own strength, by their own works, by their own merit, and consequently fell into a spirit of self-righteousness.

They stumbled over the "stumbling-stone". As it is written: "See, I lay in Zion a stone that causes men to stumble and a rock that makes them fall ... ". Christ came to his own people as a rock and a Saviour. Instead of standing on the rock and seeking shelter in the rock, they tripped over the rock, and it became a stumbling-stone to them. With the appearance of Jesus it was clear that there was only one way to get to heaven, namely, by exercising faith in Christ alone. That's what his contemporaries could not handle, because he was saying to them, 'Your works are not pure enough to merit entry into the kingdom of God.' This infuriated them because the doctrine of justification by faith alone is a violent assault upon human pride. Instead of allowing Jesus to lift them up, they tripped over him.

Chapter 9 ends with this statement: **and the one who trusts in him will never be put to shame.** Some people are embarrassed to admit that they are Christians. They feel ashamed of the fact that they have put their confidence in Christ, and need to depend upon grace in order to be reconciled to God. But the Bible promises that if we put our trust and confidence in Christ, we will never be embarrassed in God's sight.

THE UNBELIEF OF ISRAEL (10:1-21)

Chapter 9 started with Paul stating his concern for his brethren according to the flesh, his fellow Jews, and chapter 10 begins in a similar vein. He says, **Brothers, my heart's desire and prayer to God for the Israelites is that they may be saved.** He is still pouring out his personal anguish over the situation of his fellow kinsmen.

For I can testify about them that they are zealous for God, but their zeal is not based on knowledge (verse 2). There is a certain sense in which this verse is terrifying. Paul is describing people who are under the judgment of God, and yet have a zeal for God. The problem with their zeal for God was that it was based on bad theology. Israel neglected the truth of God and were slothful and indolent with respect to their study of the things of God.

Since they did not know the righteousness that comes from God and sought to establish their own, they did not submit to God's righteousness (verse 3). God did not accept the Israelites because they put their faith in their own law-keeping, and not in the Saviour. But **Christ is the end of the law so that there may be righteousness for everyone who believes** (verse 4). The law which itself reveals the pattern of good works should drive us to Christ. Christ is the point of the law; Christ is the goal of the law; Christ is the meaning of the law. So if you try to follow and obey the law, but avoid Christ, you have missed the whole point of the law.

Paul further elaborates in verses 5-7: **Moses describes in this way the righteousness that is by the law: "The man who does these things will live by them." But the righteousness that is by faith says: "Do not say in your heart, 'Who will ascend into heaven?'" (that is, to bring Christ down), "or 'Who will descend into the deep?'" (that is, to bring Christ up from the dead).** This is difficult to understand. I am not sure exactly what Paul means here, but there was a tradition among the Pharisees that if any single Pharisee kept all the Jewish laws perfectly for one day, that man's righteousness would be so pure that it would induce God to send the Messiah. The idea was that if a person was good enough he could have the merit to climb right up to heaven and bring the Messiah down, or if the

Messiah had gone into hell, he could bring him back up. But who has that kind of righteousness, that kind of merit? We can't climb up into heaven and bring the Saviour down from heaven. The whole point is that only God can send a Saviour from heaven, and only God can bring one back from the dead. Only God can save you and that is where your faith must be.

But what does it say? "The word is near you; it is in your mouth and in your heart," that is, the word of faith we are proclaiming (verse 8). His point is this: the word of God is not obscure, not all that difficult to grasp. Where do we find the word of faith in the Christian? In two places. We find it in the heart and in the mouth. It is possible to have faith in the mouth and have no faith in the heart. But you cannot find faith in the heart that is not also in the mouth. It is impossible to be a Christian and to have the word of God hidden in your heart, yet for it never to come out of your mouth.

And how important it is to believe in your heart, and to speak with your mouth, as Paul goes on to explain. The question, What must we do to be saved?, is nowhere in Scripture stated more succinctly than in these verses: **That if you confess with your mouth, "Jesus is Lord," and believe in your heart that God raised him from the dead, you will be saved. For it is with your heart that you believe and are justified, and it is with your mouth that you confess and are saved** (verses 9,10).

There are times when we are called upon to open our mouths and make simple declarations. When I got married I had to say before God and certain witnesses 'I do' or 'I will'. A Christian is to publicly reveal that he has been saved. One way to do this is to say, 'Yes, Jesus is Lord'.

The second necessary condition that must be fulfilled if salvation is to take place is to believe in the heart. The word for 'believe' is *pistauo*, which means 'to put your personal trust and confidence in'. This is why justification is by faith. Now where is that faith? In the heart. Paul is not using the heart as a term to describe merely the seat of emotions. When he speaks about the heart, he is speaking about the core of one's being. It includes the mind but it involves more than the mind. From the depths of my being, I trust that God raised Jesus from the dead.

This is why orthodox Christianity declares belief in the resurrection of Christ to be essential. If a person denies the resurrection of Jesus Christ from the dead, then he cannot possibly be a Christian. Christians can make mistakes in theology and not everybody is perfectly orthodox. Indeed, if we had to wait until we were perfectly orthodox before we were saved, none of us would be saved. But the denial of the resurrection of Christ is an intolerable error. You cannot be saved if you do not believe in the resurrection of Christ.

As the Scripture says, **"Anyone who trusts in him will never be put to shame". For there is no difference between Jew and Gentile - the same Lord is Lord of all and richly blesses all who call on him, for, "Everyone who calls on the name of the Lord will be saved"** (verses 11-13). Again, Paul has in view the problem of Jews and Gentiles. The way of salvation is the same for Jew and for Gentile.

But Paul isn't finished. He raises some more questions. **How, then, can they call on the one they have not believed in?** Do you see the logical thinking here? Nobody is going to call upon somebody for salvation without the belief that that person can save. If I don't believe that Jesus is a Saviour, I am never going to call upon him. So before anyone will ever call upon Christ he has to believe that Jesus is capable of saving.

And how can they believe in the one of whom they have not heard? Before you can believe in somebody you have to at least have heard of him. Paul is being as elementary as he can possibly be. The message is one of the simplest that the apostle Paul ever wrote, but it goes right over the heads of most people in the church who don't see any reason why the church should be involved in evangelism.

And how can they hear without someone preaching to them? (verse 14). The top priority enterprise for the Christian church is the preaching of the gospel of Jesus Christ, because people cannot believe or even hear about Jesus unless Jesus is preached. So the church must be committed to the preaching of the gospel to all men. Jesus gave the Great Commission to go into all the world to preach the gospel to every living creature. There are still thousands of tribes and people in this world who have never heard a single word about Jesus Christ. In fact, every day in human history a record is broken: more people died today without hearing the name of Jesus Christ, than on any day since God created Adam and Eve, and tomorrow will break today's record.

But there is one more part of this chain of causes and effects and necessary conditions that the apostle spells out here: **And how can they preach unless they are sent?** Not every Christian is responsible to go to the mission field, and not every Christian is called to be a preacher. But the body of Christ has the responsibility to send preachers and teachers and missionaries into the world.

Paul ends this verse with an abbreviated quotation from Isaiah: **As it is written, "How beautiful are the feet of those who bring good news!"** (verse 15). The imagery is of a runner coming from a battle with news either of victory or defeat. The lookout on the city wall waited anxiously for any sign of the outcome of the battle, and the first thing that he saw was the dustcloud being stirred up by the churning feet of the runner. The lookouts were able to tell from a great distance whether the news was good news or bad news. Somehow they recognised, by looking at the action of the feet of the runner, whether the news was good or bad. If it was news of a calamitous defeat, there was a kind of plodding stride, the heavy, weighty, cumbersome step of the runner as he approached. If the news was good news the feet were flying, the dust was being kicked up and there was an enthusiasm in the stride of the runner as he approached. The most beautiful sight for the lookout was to see feet that were flying in joy and excitement because that meant good news.

God appoints human messengers as vessels of the greatest treasure that we could possibly find: the truth of our redemption. There is no greater privilege in all the world than to bear that treasure to someone else, to tell them the story of Christ.

But not everyone thinks the feet are so beautiful: **But not all the Israelites accepted the good news. For Isaiah says, "Lord, who has believed our message?"** (verse 16). Not everyone who hears the gospel believes the gospel. This is one of the most frustrating features about preaching, about teaching, about evangelism. It also raises a couple of questions, one theoretical and one very practical.

The theoretical question is one theologians have debated for centuries: are there few that are saved, or are there many? I am not sure of the answer to that question. Jesus said the gate that leads to life is narrow, and few there be that find it (Matt. 7:13-14). But there are other passages that speak of great multitudes that will be saved (e.g. Rev. 7:9). In the final analysis, I really don't know, although the Scriptures seem to me to indicate that a minority are saved rather than a majority. But I do know that those whom God has ordained to salvation will certainly be saved. The number of the elect is God's business, not mine. My business, practically speaking, is to obey the mandate and to preach the gospel in season and out of season.

Practically, it is tough when it seems as though no one is listening. It is easy to speak when everybody responds enthusiastically. But when we witness over a long period of time, and people are not very serious about responding, it can be so discouraging that we want to give up and we begin to lose the commitment. But we are to remember verse 17: **Consequently, faith comes from hearing the message, and the message is heard through the word of Christ.**

Then Paul asks in verse 18: **But I ask: Did they not hear?** There is a play on words here in the original language between the Greek word for hearing and the Greek word for obedience. The verb 'to hear' is *akouein* which simply means 'to hear'. The verb 'to obey' is *hupokouein*. It is simply the root for hearing - *akouein* - with a preface *hupo* (that word comes across to English in the word, 'hyper'). Literally, then, the Greek word for obedience means 'hyper-hearing'. Those who really hear are the ones where the message gets through and penetrates their hearts. In fact, the word *hupokouein* is found in verse 16, where it reads that they have not all *accepted* the gospel - literally they have not all 'obeyed' the gospel. Although we see a frequent contrast in the Scriptures between law and gospel, here we have an indication that the gospel is to be obeyed. There is an implicit command in the gospel, a call to obedience to Jesus Christ.

Did Israel hear? **Of course they did: "Their voice has gone out into all the earth, their words to the ends of the world"** (verse 18). In Romans 1, Paul refers to two kinds of revelation: general revelation, which God gives of himself in nature (verses 19, 20); and special revelation, which is found specifically in sacred Scripture (verse 2). Not only did the Jews have the benefit of general revelation, but they also had the benefit of special revelation.

Again I ask: Did Israel not understand? Here was the threat of Moses in response to the fact that so many people in Israel had heard the announcement of God, but did not obey it. Moses warned them saying, **"I will make you envious by those who are not a nation; I will make you angry by a nation that has no understanding."**

And Isaiah boldly says, **"I was found by those who did not seek me; I revealed myself to those who did not ask for me"** (verses 19, 20). This is the mystery of the expansion of the gospel to the Gentiles, those who were strangers and foreigners to Israel.

But concerning Israel he says, "All day long I have held out my hands to a disobedient and obstinate people" (verse 21). If there is a difficulty here with the text it is the problem of the relationship between the doctrine of election and the question of human responsibility. The word 'responsibility' is a word that is composed of two words: ability and response. Responsibility involves an ability to respond. However, the Biblical doctrine of election teaches that we are morally unable to respond to the offer of the gospel because of our sinful corruption. Yet the Scripture also talks about God inviting everyone to come to Jesus Christ in the universal offer of the gospel. Here we have it in verse 21: 'But concerning Israel he says, "All day long I have held out my hands to a disobedient and obstinate people".' Paul uses the imagery of God with his palms open, beseeching people, exhorting them, inviting them, telling them, to come to him. And he stands there not just for a second, not just for a moment, not for a five-minute altar call, but all day long.

The reason why people don't come to God is not because God fails to invite them, nor is it a logical conclusion from the doctrine of predestination, but it is rooted in disobedience and obstinacy. It is precisely because man is in a state of rebellion that he will never respond to the offer of the gospel, unless God sovereignly conquers that rebelliousness in his heart. To state it another way: anyone can be saved if he wants to be saved, but therein lies the problem. No one wants to be saved, unless God sovereignly and unilaterally plants a desire in the rebellious heart to come to him. If we were left to ourselves, if there were no election, if there were no predestinating grace, none of us would ever come to Christ, simply because we would never want to come, because we are by nature disobedient and rebellious.

GOD'S GRACE TO A REMNANT OF ISRAEL (11:1-10)

Paul then asks another question: **I ask then: Did God reject his people?** As a nation they are involved in wanton disobedience and rebelliousness. Paul answers his own question: **By no means!** Paul says he can prove that God has not rejected his people Israel: **I am an Israelite myself, a descendant of Abraham, from the tribe of Benjamin.** There is, within the nation of Israel, some whom God determines in advance to save, to overcome their rebelliousness; and exhibit A for that is Paul. Who was more rebellious than Paul? Who set out to destroy the Messiah and his people more rigorously than did Paul? And yet, when God intervened in his life on the Damascus Road, giving him the vision of the risen Christ, his life was changed.

God did not reject his people, whom he foreknew. Don't you know what the Scripture says in the passage about Elijah - how he appealed to God against Israel: "Lord, they have killed your prophets and torn down your altars; I am the only one left, and they are trying to kill me"? And what was God's answer to him? "I have reserved for myself seven thousand who have not bowed the knee to Baal" (verses 2-4). Elijah had been so discouraged in his ministry because the people as a whole were rejecting his message. He was complaining to God because God's chosen people had killed God's chosen messengers, torn down the altars to God and replaced them with altars to Baal. He believed he was the only one left serving God.

But God had reserved for himself seven thousand who had never bowed the knee to Baal. God is saying, 'I have preserved a vast multitude of people who are authentic disciples, true believers, who are faithful to me. Don't get yourself so puffed up, Elijah, that you think that you are right and everybody else is wrong.'

The Elijah syndrome is a syndrome of arrogance; it is a syndrome that lacks charity and works on the basis of hasty judgment. Of course, we have to be astute enough to recognise heresy when we hear it, but even at that point we are to realise that authentic Christians are capable of serious error, and we are not to write people off as being enemies of God too quickly. This is the warning that Paul is giving here. **So too, at the present time there is a remnant chosen by grace** (verse 5). There is a small number of Israelites whom God has chosen, because of his mercy and not because of what they have done: **And if by grace, then it is no longer by works; if it were, grace would no longer be grace** (verse 6).

What then? What Israel sought so earnestly it did not obtain, but the elect did. The others were hardened (verse 7). The people of Israel did not find what they were looking for. It was the small group chosen by God who found it and the rest grew deaf to God's call. What happened was that in their disobedience they did not just remain the same but grew more and more immune to God's word. This was anticipated in the Old Testament (Deut. 29:4, Isa. 29:10): **As it is written: "God gave them a spirit of stupor, eyes so that they could not see and ears so that they could not hear, to this very day"** (verse 8). This blindness and deafness is visited upon people as a judgment for their earlier and prior refusal to see and hear. It is what we would call 'poetic justice'. Paul quotes from one of the imprecatory psalms (Psalm 69:22-23) to confirm the rightness of God's actions in judgment: **And David says: "May their table become a snare and a trap, a stumbling-block and a retribution for them. May their eyes be darkened so they cannot see, and their backs be bent forever"** (verses 9,10).

THE SPIRITUAL RESTORATION OF ISRAEL (11:11-36)

One of the great controversies among Christians is how we are to understand Biblical prophecies of the future, with specific reference to the Jewish people. Does God have in his plan another chapter to be written for Israel as a nation, as a people? Is what is going on today in Palestine significant to Biblical prophecy? Or is it just part of the normal passage of secular history?

Some take the position that there is no more to be done of any special character with the Jewish people, other than the conversions of individuals from Judaism to Christianity. Others are convinced that the Christian church has become the new Israel, the spiritual Israel, and all Biblical prophecies in the Old Testament and the New that refer to the future of Israel, find their fulfilment totally and exclusively in the Christian church. Still others are of the opinion that God indeed does plan a new redemptive work, specifically targeted at the Jews, and with a view to their restoration in the kingdom of God. Personally, I have been persuaded that God does intend to write another chapter for the Jewish people. I do think that what is happening in Palestine today is significant, and I have been persuaded that there will be a restoration of the Jewish people to faith in Christ before the end of the age.

In verse 11 Paul asks a crucial question: **Again, I ask: Did they stumble so as to fall beyond recovery?** The Jews obviously stumbled, but did they fall to their ruin? Charles Hodge put it like this: 'As the rejection of the Jews was not total, so neither is it final.' What Hodge means when he says the rejection was not total is that even though Israel as a nation fell away, God preserved for himself within that nation a remnant. But the key affirmation of Hodge is that just as it was not total, so neither is it final. They have not so fallen away as to be hopelessly destroyed. God did not design to cast away his people entirely when he redeemed the Gentiles.

What is Paul's answer to his own question? **Not at all!** It is unthinkable that the Jews may have stumbled to their ultimate ruin. That statement is a keynote to what follows; Paul is preparing his readers for a startling conclusion.

Rather, because of their transgression, salvation has come to the Gentiles to make Israel envious (verse 11). Jewish people have not followed after the things of the Messiah, but God so loves Israel that he is now provoking them to jealousy, so that they would desire what the Gentiles have received in their place. Notice that Paul distinguishes between ethnic Gentiles and Jews and these words cannot be spiritualised. Paul is clearly speaking of two different groups of people in terms of their ethnic background.

But if their transgression means riches for the world, and their loss means riches for the Gentiles, how much greater riches will their fullness bring! (verse 12). Again we see the extraordinary and marvellous way in which the hand of Providence works in history. This text should scream at us that God is sovereign over history. God is able to bring good out of evil, and he uses his power and sovereignty to bring about redemption. Paul is making a kind of comparison that is very familiar in the New Testament: 'How much greater the blessings will be then, when the complete number of Jews is included.' In other words, Paul is saying that if the apostasy of Israel brought great blessings to the world, how much greater blessings will come through their restoration. This is the theme of this section of Romans 11, the restoration of the Jewish people.

I am talking to you Gentiles. Inasmuch as I am the apostle to the Gentiles, I make much of my ministry in the hope that I may somehow arouse my own people to envy and save some of them (verses 13,14). Paul realised that it was not a small thing to be called the apostle to the Gentiles. He is assuring his Gentile readers that they are not second-class citizens. No, he took pride in his work. But he is saying, 'Perhaps I can make the people of my own race jealous, and so be able to save some of them.' Now there are some interpreters of Scripture who believe that all Paul means by a restoration of Israel is that throughout the ages there will always be converts from Judaism. However, Paul goes on in verse 15: **For if their rejection is the reconciliation of the world, what will their acceptance be but life from the dead?**

To illustrate his teaching he uses extended analogies: **If the part** of the dough offered as firstfruits is holy, then the whole batch is holy; if the root is holy, so are the branches (verse 16). The Jews were the firstfruits; they were dedicated to God. Gentile converts are the rest of the loaf, and they belong to God too. Israel is the roots of the tree; it was offered to God. Believers (Jews and Gentiles) are the branches, and the branches belong to God too. So the Jews do not have any special privilege over those who are brought in later.

But notice what he says next: **If some of the branches have been broken off, and you, though a wild olive shoot, have been grafted in among the others and now share in the nourishing sap from the olive root, do not boast over those branches** (verses 17, 18). Do you see the picture? The tree is an olive tree. Olive trees are magnificent, particularly their root systems, and the trunk of the olive tree is massive, strong, and very beautiful. With these root systems and trunks, olive trees have gorgeous branches bearing lovely fruit. Paul's picture is of a cultivated tree. The non-productive branches, that were not bearing fruit, were cut off. But the tree was not left in that condition, or it would be disfigured and become stunted in its growth. God's work is not merely to cultivate by cutting off the dead branches, but by grafting new branches on to the tree. Paul says, A wild olive shoot has been joined to it.

Who are the wild olive branches? The Gentiles! They were strangers and foreigners to the covenant of God, they were not privy to the great teachings of the Old Testament Scriptures and the effects of God's sanctifying influences in the history of Israel. They came out of paganism, wild olive trees, and they have been grafted on. Notice, it is not that God cuts down the tree and plants a new tree. God doesn't do that; he keeps the substance of the tree and grafts on wild olive branches.

If you do, consider this: You do not support the root, but the root supports you (verse 18). What are the roots? The roots are in Abraham, in Isaac and in Jacob, down through David, Jeremiah, Isaiah and Amos. They are our forefathers. Even though their blood is not in our veins, their truth and their heritage are in our hearts.

You will say then, "Branches were broken off so that I could

be grafted in" (verse 19). Any Christian who has tried to justify anti-Semitism because the Jews rejected Jesus, has never read seriously this piece of Scripture. It is unthinkable for a Christian to hate Jews. Why? Because they have given us salvation. Salvation comes from Israel, from God's activity in the Old Testament.

Granted. But they were broken off because of unbelief, and you stand by faith. Do not be arrogant, but be afraid. For if God did not spare the natural branches, he will not spare you either (verses 20,21). The appropriate response to the rejection of the Jews is not pride but fear. If God did not spare the Jews who are like the natural branches, do you think he will spare the Christian church, if it becomes an instrument of unbelief?

Paul continues: **Consider therefore the kindness and sternness of God: sternness to those who fell, but kindness to you, provided that you continue in his kindness. Otherwise, you also will be cut off** (verse 22). What a strange conjunction of words! How kind and how severe God is. He is severe towards those who have fallen, that is, he is severe in his judgments on apostasy. Paul is warning Gentile believers that they ought not to take the occasion of God's kindness in including them in his kingdom as a reason for arrogance.

And if they do not persist in unbelief, they will be grafted in, for God is able to graft them in again. After all, if you were cut out of an olive tree that is wild by nature, and contrary to nature were grafted into a cultivated olive tree, how much more readily will these, the natural branches, be grafted into their own olive tree! (verses 23,24). Which is easier: to graft a wild olive tree on to a cultivated tree, or to graft the branches from a cultivated olive tree back on to the tree? Paul is saying, 'Look what God has done: he has grafted you in, you who were wild. You think that he can't regraft the Jewish people back? Of course he can.'

Verses 25-31 are the most important passage in this epistle, and probably in the whole Bible, concerning whether or not there will be a restoration of the Jews to Christ.

I do not want you to be ignorant of this mystery, brothers, so that you may not be conceited: Paul uses 'mystery' in the New

Testament sense of the word. It means something that once was hidden and required special revelation to make it known. What is that revelation? He says, **Israel has experienced a hardening in part until the full number of the Gentiles has come in** (verse 25). Many take the view that in this verse the apostle is not predicting any future conversion of the Jewish nation, but is simply declaring that the Jews will continue to enter the Christian church as long as the Gentiles continue to come in. But it doesn't require any revelation to deduce that there will always be converts from Israel as long as the church exists. Paul was preparing his readers for something far more emphatic, far more significant. When Paul says that Israel has experienced a partial hardening he is not referring to spiritual Israel but ethnic Israel. It will last 'until the full number of the Gentiles has come in'. This very strongly suggests that there is a terminal point to that partial hardening.

How are we to interpret the phrase, 'the full number of the Gentiles'? Look at Luke 21:24: 'Jerusalem will be trampled on by the Gentiles until the times of the Gentiles are fulfilled.' What does it mean, the fullness (or times) of the Gentiles? To my mind it is this: God begins with the Jewish nation as his chosen people. The Jewish nation, in large measure, falls into apostasy; the olive tree that God cultivated becomes rotten and many branches are cut off. God doesn't cut down the tree, but he grafts in the wild olive branches. He brings Gentiles into the community of faith and he has a definite number of such. When the last wild olive branch is grafted on to the tree, then God is going to do something again with the original tree.

And so all Israel will be saved. The context indicates that Paul must be speaking of the Jewish people. He does not mean every Jew that ever lived, but the nation of Israel. Now why do I say that 'Israel' in this phrase refers to the Jews? All through his discussion Paul is talking about Israel in part: part of Israel has been blinded, part of Israel has been cut away, part of Israel has been stubborn, part of Israel has been excluded from the kingdom of God and its blessings. The Jews as a people are presently under judgment. But as there was a national judgment, so there will be a national restoration. Their rejection, even though it was a national rejection, did not include the rejection of every individual. So the restoration doesn't necessarily mean that every individual Jew will be saved, but the nation as a nation will be restored to God.[1]

Paul quotes from the Old Testament (Isa. 59:20,21; 27:9; Jer. 31:33,34): **as it is written: "The deliverer will come from Zion; he will turn godlessness away from Jacob** (verse 26). The descendants of Jacob are Jews. Jacob is the father of ethnic Israel. God has in covenant determined to remove wickedness from the descendants of Jacob: **And this is my covenant with them when I take away their sins."**

Today, Israel and the church are not on friendly terms: **As far as**

---

1. I don't know whether this restoration is going to be sudden or gradual, or even if it is going to follow the return of the Jews to their own land. There is still quite a bit of debate about that. I remember sitting on my porch in Boston in 1967, and watching on television the Jewish soldiers coming into Jerusalem, dropping their weapons and rushing to the Wailing Wall, and weeping and weeping. Immediately I telephoned one of my dear friends, a professor of Old Testament theology, who does not believe that modern day Israel has any significance whatsoever. I asked him, 'What do you think now? From 70 AD until 1967, almost 1900 years, Jerusalem has been under the domination and control of Gentiles, and now the Jews have recaptured the city of Jerusalem. Jesus said that Jerusalem will be trodden under foot by the Gentiles, until the fullness of the Gentiles be fulfilled. What's the significance of that?' He replied, 'I am going to have to rethink this situation.' It was indeed startling.

Well, 1967 was many years ago, and we have not seen the restoration of the Jewish nation, although we have seen the greatest concentration on eschatology that the church has ever known. There have been periods before in church history when people, for one reason or another, were excited about the nearness of the return of Jesus, and were disappointed to find out that it was not as close at hand as they had thought. Perhaps it will be another thousand years before the Jews have complete control of Jerusalem. Maybe present arrange-

the gospel is concerned, they are enemies on your account; but as far as election is concerned, they are loved on account of the patriarchs, for God's gifts and his call are irrevocable (verses 28,29). God made a covenant with his people and he made promises to save them as a nation. In his electing grace, he will keep that covenant and will bring about the restoration of the Jewish people. God chose the Jews as his people, and the purpose which he had in view can never be altered. It was his purpose that they should be his people for ever, and for that to take place there must be a future restoration and their inclusion in his kingdom. This covenant of God will be fully and finally accomplished.

See how God's plan works out? The Jews are given the blessing; they reject the blessing and the blessing is given to the Gentiles; the Gentiles are brought in, but then after that the Jews are brought back: **Just as you who were at one time disobedient to God have now received mercy as a result of their disobedience, so they too have now become disobedient in order that they too may now receive mercy as a result of God's mercy to you. For God has bound all men over to disobedience so that he may have mercy on them all** (verses 30-32).

Paul concludes chapter 11 in an appropriate way. It is his style of writing, in the middle of very weighty and heavy exposition of doctrine, to break out into doxology. **Oh, the depth of the riches of**

---

ments are just a temporary interlude. It is possible that the Arabs will drive the Jews out of Jerusalem and the Jewish people will be put in exile again, and this present attempt to recover the Promised Land will be abortive - who knows? I don't know what the significance of it all is. But I will tell you this: we should be watching very carefully. It is a remarkable event in history that the city of Jerusalem is now back in Jewish hands, under Jewish control. As Jesus said, Jerusalem will be trodden under foot until the fullness of the Gentiles be fulfilled (Luke 20:24). And Paul says that after the fullness of the Gentiles have come in, there will be a restoration of the Jewish nation. All of these things are put in context by Jesus when he tells his followers to watch and pray, for their salvation is drawing near.

the wisdom and knowledge of God! How unsearchable his judgments, and his paths beyond tracing out! "Who has known the mind of the Lord? Or who has been his counsellor?" "Who has ever given to God, that God should repay him?" For from him and through him and to him are all things. To him be the glory for ever! Amen (verses 33-36). Paul is rhapsodic here about the depth of wisdom and riches that God is revealing. It is not some commonplace conclusion that anybody could figure out just by looking at the fact that certain Jews and Gentiles are being converted. No, God has a plan, a plan that is startling and fantastic. God's greatness is the subject of this doxology of praise. All things were created by him; all things exist through him; all things exist for him. Behind all of the machinations of human history stands the sovereign electing God. He is the Creator of everyone and of all things, and all things exist by his power and through his power.

5
LIVING THE CHRISTIAN LIFE
(12:1-15:33)

Frequently, people will ask me who I think is the greatest theologian in the history of the church. I know that they are thinking of such giants as Augustine, Luther, Calvin, Edwards and so on. But there is really no difficulty in answering the question: the greatest theologian that the church has ever had is the apostle Paul. But if you change the question a little and ask, Who is the greatest teacher of practical application of Christian truth? Wesley? Wilberforce? Again, the answer is simple. The greatest practical teacher of Christian truth in the history of the church is the apostle Paul. This is what makes Paul so extraordinary. Whenever he gives us deep and profound doctrinal teaching he always follows it with very specific, concrete, practical application.

In chapter 12, we see that remarkable transition in style which is so typical of the apostle. For eleven chapters he has taken us through the weightiest type of doctrinal study, and he ended that doctrinal section at the end of chapter 11, fitly and appropriately, with a doxology. But what does it mean for our lives? What should be our response in terms of our hearts, in terms of our behaviour, in terms of lifestyle? How are we supposed to react to the revelation of truth that Paul has just spelled out?

LIVING SACRIFICES (12:1-2)
Usually, when the apostle gives a conclusion flowing from a **Therefore**, we look to the immediately preceding verses for a clue to the conclusion. But is Paul basing his conclusion on the last few verses of chapter 11? I don't think so. Rather Paul is looking to what he has told us about the plan of redemption in all the previous chapters. He realises that there needs to be an appropriate response. And it goes like this: '**Therefore, I urge you, brothers, in view of God's mercy** - I am begging you by the grace of God - **to offer your**

bodies as living sacrifices, holy and pleasing to God.

The sacrificial system of the Old Testament is over. The detailed descriptions that were given to the people of God on how to fulfil their obligations, in the temple and in the places of worship, pointed ahead to what was going to take place in the future. They were shadows of the full-orbed light that was yet to break through. They anticipated and typified the perfect sacrifice that was offered by our Lord on the cross once and for all. So when the perfect sacrifice was made, that was the end of the Old Testament sacrificial system. No longer do worshippers come with sheep, goats, bullocks and cereal offerings, and burn them before the Lord as sacrifice for their sins.

But there is still a New Testament sacrificial system. It is not a sacrifice that we give in order to make an atonement, but a sacrifice that we give because an atonement has been made for us. God does not ask us to bring in our livestock and burn it on the altar; he asks us to give ourselves, to put ourselves *alive* on the altar. To be a Christian means to live a life of sacrifice, a life of presentation, making a gift of ourselves to God. Some people think that all it takes to be a Christian is to scribble a cheque or to give a few hours of service here and there on special projects for the church. But that's not what believers are called to. My life is to be set apart and consecrated to God. That is what is acceptable to him; that is what delights him; that is what pleases him; that is the appropriate response to him and for him.

To do so is described by Paul as **your spiritual act of worship.** The New American Standard Bible renders the last clause as: 'your spiritual service of worship'. Other translations say, 'your reasonable service'. In fact, both ideas are included in this activity for it is logical worship. It is logical in this sense: it is what God deserves. It is reasonable for us to give ourselves away to God. God is not saying that spiritual sacrifice and spiritual worship are above and beyond the call of duty. It is the duty of every Christian to present himself as a living sacrifice to God.

Paul, in verse 2, shows what real worship and devotion does not entail before he proceeds to tell what it does look like. **Do not**

conform any longer to the pattern of this world. Believers are not to align themselves to the structures and forms of this world. There is a certain sense in which we are not supposed to be 'with it'. Of course, some people interpret this passage to mean that the real test of spirituality is to show the whole world that we are out of it, in the sense of being irrelevant, insignificant, odd and peculiar. But that is not what Paul is talking about here.

We have to be very careful with this business of conformity and nonconformity. We are by nature conformists. We tend to pinpoint the drive to conformity among those passing through adolescence. But we are conformists from the time we are born until the time we die. We always feel peer pressure, the tug and struggle to be in line with contemporary tastes and standards. That's why watching contemporary culture and its customs is a very dangerous way for a Christian to educate his or her own conscience, because something that may be part of the acceptable standard of life in a given community may be radically alien to the kingdom of God.

The other danger to recognise is that nonconformity can be as vicious a trap as conformity. There is such a thing as nonconformity for nonconformity's sake. We all want to be different, so that in the group we will stand out. There are Christian distortions at this point. Often Christian ethics is determined simply on the basis of antithesis - if the world wears lipstick, the Christian doesn't wear lipstick, to show that she is spiritual rather than worldly. If the world goes to movies, Christians don't go to movies, to show that they are more spiritual, more pious. That's nonsense, that's the kind of attitude the Pharisees had, which distorted the truth. Christ calls us to a special kind of nonconformity: a refusal to conform to the sinful patterns of the world, to patterns of disobedience.

But notice that the call is not simply a negative prohibition but also a positive affirmation. Look at the text again: **but be transformed by the renewing of your mind.** To be transformed means to go above and beyond the forms and structures of this world. Christians are called to be light to the world, to be the salt of the earth, to show a more excellent way. This is not so much a call to drop out of society and culture, as a call to excellence, dedicating our lives to the glory of God. The means by which we are to be transformed is through the renewing of our minds. We have to relearn things from a new perspective. We need new values. We need to train our minds so that we begin to think God's thoughts after him.

Why is it so important to have a new mind? **Then you will be able to test and approve what God's will is - his good, pleasing and perfect will** (verse 2). The question burning in the heart of every Christian is, What is the will of God? If you want to get a theological discussion going in a real hurry with people, all you have to do is ask - what is the will of God for my life?

Do you want to know what the will of God is? You have to study the word of God. You have to think like God. You have to have a new mind. And if you want a new mind you have to study the word of God more rigorously than you have ever studied anything in your life. There is no magical way to know the will of God, apart from knowing the word of God.

Why do you need a new mind? So that you can know the will of God. This is why truth is so vital, why theology is so important. Theology is not speculating about the philosophical aspects of the character of God. It is studying who he is, what his character is, what he loves, what he hates. If God reveals that something is good, then we know it is good. When God reveals that something is bad, then the debate is over. We are not to wrestle within ourselves whether it is right or wrong. If God says it, then we know what the standard is of righteousness. If you want to live a godly life, then it is indispensable to your spiritual growth that you dig into the Scriptures deeply, to understand what God is revealing. This is part of the sacrifice of the Christian life. There is a sacrifice of your body and there is a sacrifice of your mind. It is not a sacrifice of the mind in the sense that you vacate your intellect, but in the sense of giving your mind as a present to God, to be instructed by him, so that your thinking will honour him.

LIVING TOGETHER AS CHRISTIANS (12:3-11)

Paul now explains what becoming a living sacrifice means for interpersonal relationships between believers. **For by the grace given me I say to every one of you.** What a marvellous statement! Paul could have claimed the full authority of his apostleship. He was speaking with nothing less than the authority of Jesus Christ who is the Lord of the Church. But he would not have any authority except through the gift God has given him. Whatever leadership or capacity he had was because God had been gracious to him.

Do not think of yourself more highly than you ought, but rather think of yourself with sober judgment, in accordance with the measure of faith God has given you (verse 3). If we want to keep things in perspective there are two things that we always have to remember. We have to remember first of all who God is, and second, we have to remember who we are. If we really know who God is, it should not be too difficult to figure out who we are. When we know who God is, then we know that we cannot make a move in this world of any significance, without the grace of God. Knowing that we are utterly dependant on grace for any achievement or success that we enjoy in this world, how can we be anything but humble. This verse prohibits pride and arrogance, a boastful exalted opinion of ourselves.

But the implication of the text goes deeper than that. What is also prohibited is too low an opinion of ourselves. If we only read the first part of the verse, we might think that we are worthless and insignificant. But our significance comes from God and whatever God assigns to us is valuable. You may not be as significant as you would like to be, but you are significant. A sober judgment means to make a sober evaluation of our gifts, our strengths, our weaknesses. To think of ourselves in terms of sober judgment is very difficult to do because we have a tendency to see ourselves through rose-coloured glasses for five minutes, then put down the rose-coloured glasses and put on jaundiced eyes!

I have found, in working in the church now for several years, that it is a mistake to try to get people to perform against the pattern of their motivated skills. Sometimes we do terrible disservices to people by trying to force them to perform in areas where they are simply not gifted to perform.

Part of this lies with our own tendency to think more highly of ourselves than we should. If I have achieved a certain degree of competence in a particular activity, then I want that to be the standard. We have a tendency to exalt our own strengths, believing them to be the important ones, the ones that really count. That is absolutely deadly to the body of Christ. We must understand that God has allotted to each person a measure of faith, and that people have different personalities, different strengths, different weaknesses and different gifts. There is a diversity within the body of Christ, and maturity as Christians demand recognition of this. In fact we are told elsewhere that we should prefer one another over ourselves, that we should stand in awe and admiration at other gifts which people have that we don't have. Instead of being jealous of them or deprecating them, we should honour and respect them.

Paul uses what must have been his favourite analogy of the church – the body of Christ. **Just as each of us has one body with many members, and these members do not all have the same function, so in Christ we who are many form one body, and each member belongs to all the others** (verses 4,5). The human body is made up of different parts and each part has a very important function to perform. My body would be hurt in its entirety if I lost my eyesight. The quality of my life would be diminished significantly if I lost my hearing. I would struggle much more than I do now through life, if one of my legs were amputated. Every part works together for the good of the entire body. It is the same in the church. All members together form one body and each member's contribution is essential for a healthy church.

We have different gifts, according to the grace given us. God is the one who makes us different, because we differ according to the grace given to us, and it is God who gives us the grace. So he gives one person the grace and the gift to be effective in evangelism, which he doesn't give to another person. The other person is given another gift. What makes me different from other people is not my greatness, but God's graciousness. Therefore, we should enjoy and honour all those differences of abilities, talents and gifts in the body of Christ.

If a man's gift is prophesying, let him use it in proportion to his faith. If it is serving, let him serve; if it is teaching, let him teach; if it is encouraging, let him encourage; if it is contributing to the needs of others, let him give generously; if it is leadership, let him govern diligently; if it is showing mercy, let him do it cheerfully (verses 6-8). The prophecy of which Paul speaks is not to be confused with the predicting of future events, but rather that which a person had received from God for instruction, exhortation, or comfort. Those who considered themselves recipients of this gift were always to conform their message to the objective standard of the faith once delivered, and were to be judged by their conformity to that standard of faith. In no instance should their prophesying contradict the objective revelation of the Scriptures.

The teaching that Paul refers to here of course is founded upon the Scriptures, and in his case, especially the Old Testament. Since the formation of the whole canon the well defined limits of what constitutes the scriptures must be carefully observed. Teachers may only teach that which is found in and is in harmony with the Old and New Testaments. As James would say, 'Let not many of you become teachers, my brethren, knowing that as such we shall incur a stricter judgment.' Too many are exercising this function today, all the while transgressing biblical orthodoxy and bringing dishonour to Christ. These false teachers were never really gifted for teaching, and actually usurp this role from those who ought to teach.

The gift of encouraging or exhorting refers primarily to teaching that addresses the conscience and the feelings; it is intended to move the listener to practical, comforting ends. Doctrine applied to life provides an incentive to live righteously, and becomes a positive exhortation or encouragement to the people of God.

If you have a gift, then the command from God to you is this: if you have a gift, then you are to exercise that gift. God does not give you that gift to hide it under a bushel. If you have a gift you are to use it. But the command is not simply given to you, it is given to me about you. I am to make sure that you are given the room and the freedom to use your gift. I should be doing everything in my power to help and assist you fulfil your gift; you should be helping me to fulfil my gift.

What if you don't know what your gift is? I say to you, try different aspects of the life of the church. If you don't know what your gift is, try being involved in evangelism, try being involved in Sunday School teaching. You may have to try a few things before you discover where your niche is. And listen to the body of Christ. The body of Christ will begin to communicate to you where your gift is, and where you can be used of God.

Lots of folk want to have the gift of teaching or the gift of evangelism or the gift of preaching. I haven't had too many tell me that what they would really like to have is the gift of *giving*! But it is a gift. There are some people who are so extraordinarily generous. They are generous with their time, they are generous with their service. They are so thoughtful in consideration of other people, and they are very gracious in their financial giving. When they give money, or time, or whatever, they don't begrudge it, they enjoy it. They enjoy it! What a delight it is to meet a person like that.

It is one thing to be a leader, it is another thing to be a *diligent* leader.

I don't like to receive reluctant mercy: *if it is showing mercy, let him do it cheerfully*. Real mercy is expressed in a spirit of joy and cheerfulness, the way God gives mercy to us.

LOVING RELATIONSHIPS (12:9-21)

Love must be sincere. Demonstrations of love must be genuine, authentic and believable. Hypocrisy is fraudulent and a sham. The idea behind the Biblical word here is playacting. Don't let your love be a kind of playacting. Some Christians have a reputation that is all too deserved for coming across as being plastic. They use such phrases as, *Oh bless you brother, God loves you*, without thinking about them. But it is playacting. Others don't sense from them authentic love. Love is the top priority in the Bible. It is by a life of loving fellow believers that all men will know that we are Christ's disciples (John 13:35). And that is why we need to be certain that we communicate to other people that we are loving.

Hate what is evil; cling to what is good. Here our passions are to be involved. If we love evil, we will do evil; if we hate evil, we will refrain from evil. At the same time, we are to hold fast to what is good, not merely approve it in passing, but grab it, hang on to it, cling to it with all of our might.

Be devoted to one another in brotherly love. How many people do you know that you would describe as being 'devoted' to you? I know that I am devoted to my family and that I am ready to do all I can for them. But Paul is saying that there is a real sense in which our families now are larger. We are to have this brotherly and sisterly love and devotion to all those in the body of Christ. We need to devote ourselves not merely to our own family, but to our brothers and sisters in the faith.

Honour one another above yourselves (verse 10). To have this attitude is a blow against personal pride. There is nothing wrong in wanting to be honoured, but we can't be jealous or covetous about honours. We should rejoice in any honour that our brother or sister gets.

Never be lacking in zeal, but keep your spiritual fervour, serving the Lord (verse 11). Lots of people are zealous, but there is no diligence or responsibility in their zeal, they are just running all over the place, like chickens with their heads cut off. It is not enough to be zealous, nor is it just enough to be diligent. There are some people who are methodical in routine, but there's no zeal, no warmth, no ardour, no spirit. God wants to see discipline, but he also wants to see passion, to see hearts that are on fire, that are excited about what he has done.

Be joyful in hope, patient in affliction, faithful in prayer (verse 12). These verbs emphasize the believer's responsibility in Paul's list of virtues enjoined upon believers. Virtue is practised, it is done over and over again. So Paul's exhortation binds us to repeated praise for our blessed hope of salvation, even when present circumstances include trials and tribulation. This present strength in time of trouble results from wholehearted and unceasing prayer. It is not the result of human stamina that we stand fast. Rather, it is our standing in need of grace and mercy that causes persistent prayer.

Share with God's people who are in need. Practise hospitality (verse 13). What the apostle is speaking of here is *koinonia*, fellowship. We are to be sensitive to what is going on around us in our community of faith. We are called to bear one another's burdens, and to be alert to needs that are afflicting the people of God with whom we are in contact. We are to be generous persons, not selfish or miserly. We are to help make a contribution to the lives of those around us. Of course there is nothing new in this admonition from the apostle's hand. It is consistent with what God has been teaching his people from the beginning of the Old Testament.

Included in this is the specific injunction to be given to *hospitality*. In the Old Testament, hospitality was an extremely important virtue. In fact, it still is in the Middle East. One of the great reasons for this was that, in the ancient world, travel was exceedingly difficult and dangerous. We are to make sure that the needs of the visitor in our gates are taken care of. With all of the modern conveniences, and all of the modern comforts, travel is still a burdensome experience for people, and Christians need to be alert to precepts of hospitality.

Bless those who persecute you; bless and do not curse (verse 14). The word for 'blessing' is the same word from which we get the English word, *eulogy*. If there is any dimension in which Christians are to transcend the normal behavioural patterns of fallen man, it is with respect to how they deal with their enemies, with those who have injured them. To say something good about one who has persecuted us, takes as much grace as any virtue ever did, because our natural human tendency is to get even.

To curse others does not mean simply to insult them, it is to wish that God consigns them to unmitigated wrath and punishment for ever in hell. For any to wish for the damnation of another soul is an unthinkable grievance against the grace of God. Who am I to desire that someone else be damned when I escape damnation only through the grace of God and through the work that Christ has performed for me? It is one thing for God in his holiness and justice to exercise damnation. When he does it, we can be sure that the damnation is perfectly just and according to all righteousness.

We must be very careful in our attitude towards our enemies and, particularly, with what we say. As we know from the teaching of Scripture, the tongue is one of the most difficult things to control. How many times have you said nasty things about people you wished you could have recalled the minute they were spoken? The answer is to develop the good habit of trying to find something worthy of eulogy, worthy of blessing, even in the most diabolical of people.

Rejoice with those who rejoice; mourn with those who mourn (verse 15). This is another of those injunctions, however, that is much easier said than done. It takes real sensitivity, real grace and discipline to listen and watch for the moods of other people, and to express empathy. Empathy means to feel with another person. Paul is not referring to sympathy, but empathy, where we enter into the feelings of others.

Live in harmony with one another (verse 16). Here is a Biblical call to seek unity of belief, of concern, of feelings. Now that is very difficult. We know how easy it is to disagree and to enter into debate and arguments that can tear relationships apart. There is no way we are always going to agree with everybody that we meet, but there is a way to handle disagreement. We can seek unity and try to find that place where our minds can come together. And even if we do disagree, we should have a certain attitude in the context of that disagreement, an attitude of charity. For the sin of disagreement can become the occasion for more sin, where it degenerates into a free-for-all of hostility and divisiveness. So unity is something which we should seek.

Some people, however, feel that disagreement doesn't matter; all that matters is unity. But Paul was zealous to deal with issues, and to get at the truth of the matter. Disagreements can be over important issues. There is nothing wrong with a godly argument. An argument is an attempt to get at the truth through the exchange of ideas, through criticism of false ideas and so on. It is one thing to have a good, healthy, positive argument; however, it is another thing to have an argumentative spirit that seems to thrive on disunity, discord and conflict.

Going back to the previous wrong attitude of a contentious spirit, we are to remember that it is arrogance that produces an argumentative spirit. Pride is seen where we just are not interested in anybody else's opinion, and where we just assume that anybody that disagrees with us must be wrong. What Paul is saying here is that we need to be teachable. We are called to have convictions, but those convictions have to be established on a sound basis and received with a humble heart and a humble attitude. I admit that it is difficult to be firm in our convictions and yet, at the same time, to hold those convictions with humility.

That's what Paul meant when he said, **Do not be proud, but be willing to associate with people of low position. Do not be conceited** (verse 16). That other person may have an insight that I have never ever really considered. Maybe that person has eyes to see through my blind spot. That's what I think humility is: to be able to listen to people and give an honest hearing and consideration to what they are saying.

Do not repay anyone evil for evil (verse 17). There is never any justification for fighting evil with evil. Just because somebody treats me in an evil manner does not justify my responding in kind. I am not to return evil for evil, but I am to return good for evil. I never have the right to do wrong; I never have the right to do evil. I always have the obligation to do what is right.

Be careful to do what is right in the eyes of everybody (verse 17). The old translation was 'Provide things honest in the sight of all men'. Here I think we have an improvement in translation, because the old rendering suggests to the English reader that our means of labour and providing for the needs of our family, is to be done in an honest way. But Paul is not specifically referring to earning one's livelihood. His teaching has broader applications than a mere work ethic; it means that in everything we do we should be careful to do what is right. Translated loosely, Paul is saying, 'Act with integrity in the sight of all men. Let your honesty be a model to the world.' There is a sense in which even the pagan applauds certain civic virtues of righteousness. Even the pagan will appreciate a man who keeps his word. The pagan will appreciate a man who does his business dealings with integrity. Pagans can appreciate righteousness, at least where they are the beneficiaries of that righteousness.

If it is possible, as far as it depends on you, live at peace with everyone (verse 18). None of us can possibly be at peace with all men. The Prince of Peace was murdered by hostile people who hardly were at peace with him. Paul was beaten with rods, was stoned and received 39 lashes several times. It is impossible for us to live a Christian life without offending people, and creating conflict. But there is a distinction that John Murray makes here which I think is important, and it is this: 'It is one thing if I give offence to somebody; it is another thing if a person takes offence at what I do.' It is a subtle distinction but a very important one for this reason: it is easy for us to become guilty and paralysed because we find that people are taking offence at what we do. People took offence at Jesus; people took offence at Paul.

The subtlety runs both ways. On the one hand we could be paralysed by guilt because people were offended by what we are saying or doing. They have no legitimate basis for taking offence, but because they are offended we think that we have done something wrong and so we are afraid to open our mouths. But the other side of that is equally devastating. If we are guilty of unnecessarily offending people and we refuse to face up to it and hide behind the fact that some people will take offence illegitimately, we will deceive ourselves and say, 'Oh well, the reason people are mad is because they are mad at the truth of the gospel.' Here's where we must be scrupulously honest and very careful. When peace is broken we have to ask the hard question - Is peace broken because that person has taken illegitimate offence, or is peace broken because I offended illegitimately? And if there is any doubt in our minds it is better to err on the safe side and to think that we have caused offence.

Do not take revenge, my friends, but leave room for God's wrath, for it is written: "It is mine to avenge; I will repay," says the Lord (verse 19). Concerning this passage there is a great deal of confusion. The spirit of vengeance is deeply rooted in our human hearts. It is seen in the expression: 'Don't get mad, get even'. To retaliate is so natural to our make-up that it is one of the most difficult attitudes to overcome in the Christian life.

There is a fine line of distinction among three words that we use in our vocabulary frequently. We need to know the difference between 'justice', 'vengeance' and 'vindication'. In particular, there is a lot of confusion when the term 'vindictive' is used as an adjective, and is regarded as virtually synonymous with the word 'vengeful'. A vindictive person is characterised by a desire for blood; to see his enemies suffer, to see his enemies crushed under foot. But vindication is not the same thing as revenge.

Justice means giving a person their due. If it is a reward that is appropriate, they are to be rewarded. If it is recognition, they are to be recognised. If it is punishment, they are to be punished. God promises to execute perfect justice in the day of judgment. Now justice is the broad category; vindication is a specific sub-division of justice. Vindication means to be exonerated from a false accusation. To be vindicated means to be shown to be in the right. God promises to vindicate his people when they are victims of false and unfair accusations.

Of course the person who can most look forward to total vindication at the final judgment day will be our Lord himself, because he was the only man who was totally innocent of any sin, and yet he was attacked, criticised, and even convicted by the law courts of this world, and executed. The resurrection was the first great step of vindication for our Lord. God declared him worthy of life and vindicated him by bringing him back from the grave. But God also promises to vindicate his people.

But let's say that somebody accuses me of something that I didn't do. I plead innocent and go on trial and the judge and the jury declare me to be innocent. I have been vindicated. At that point, I have had no revenge against that person. He has not been punished for falsely accusing me. If the courts, in addition to declaring me innocent, would punish the false accuser, then that would be revenge. Revenge is when the person who has injured me, is himself injured. I am vindicated when I am declared to be innocent; I am avenged when the person who hurt me is punished.

It is important to understand this difference because I am never allowed to be my own avenger. Because the Bible repeatedly says that we ought not to be vengeful, many have concluded that vengeance, considered in and of itself, is evil. But vengeance is not evil, it is a form of justice. Just punishment is when the severity of the punishment equals the severity of the crime, and when that just punishment has been exacted, vengeance has been accomplished.

Paul is saying that vengeance is legitimate. But if we want vengeance, we have to let that vengeance be in God's hands, and not in our own. Now to be sure, he uses human instruments as instruments of vengeance - the state and the courts are human institutions that God himself has established, not only for vindication of the innocent, but for vengeance and punishment for the wicked, which we will see in chapter 13. But the thing that we have to keep in mind here is that an individual cannot take it upon himself to be his own avenger.

The comfort here is that God's promise to avenge his people should be enough for us to know that we will be avenged perfectly. We will be vindicated without our adding to sin ourselves. That outlook has to be our consolation in the midst of conflict and of persecution.

Paul amplifies this further: **On the contrary: "If your enemy is hungry, feed him; if he is thirsty, give him something to drink. In doing this, you will heap burning coals on his head"** (verse 20). This is a tough verse and it is capable of various interpretations. One of the most common is that if you really want to have revenge on your enemy, then you must respond with good, and the more good you do, the more God is going to punish him. But there is something devious about that interpretation. It isn't right that the motivation for doing good to our enemy is so that we can really do him harm. I don't think that is what Paul is saying. Rather Paul is teaching that what we are doing is putting an avalanche of restraint upon him. It is true that the more we return good for evil, the more God will be moved to come to our aid. But at the same time we are exercising restraints upon our own wickedness which in turn will, in normal circumstances, restrain our enemies' wickedness.

Do not be overcome by evil, but overcome evil with good (verse 21). God, in response to our evil, has poured out goodness upon us. We are to be imitators of God and of Christ. We are to show in our relationships with our fellow human beings, the same attitude and behavioural pattern that God has shown to us.

THE CHRISTIAN AND HUMAN GOVERNMENT (13:1-7)

In Romans 13 we find the clearest statement in all of Scripture concerning the function, the role and the origin of civil government. We are commanded, every one of us, to be subject to the higher powers. **Everyone must submit himself to the governing authorities, for there is no authority except that which God has established. The authorities that exist have been established by God. Consequently, he who rebels against the authority is rebelling against what God has instituted, and those who do so will bring judgment on themselves. For rulers hold no terror for those who do right, but for those who do wrong. Do you want to be free from fear of the one in authority? Then do what is right and he will commend you. For he is God's servant to do you good** (verses 1-4).

The word translated as 'authorities' is the word, *exousia*. The same word is used to describe the manner of Jesus' preaching: he spoke as one having authority. If we break the word down in terms of its origins we discover that it is a compound word, made up of a prefix and a root. *Ex* is the Greek prefix meaning 'from' or 'out of'. The root is *ousia* which is the present participle of the verb 'to be'. It refers to the concept of being.

In Greek philosophy there was much concern for discovering *ousia*, which is 'being', the ultimate stuff out of which the universe is made. English words such as 'substance' or 'essence' are translated into the word *ousia*. Those of you who are students of church history will remember the tremendous debate in the fourth century that culminated at the council of Nicaea with the important confessional statement with respect to Jesus. That creed declared that the second Person of the Trinity is *homoousios* with the Father, that is, he is of the same being, of the same substance. English translations of the Nicene creed read, he is 'co-substantial' with the Father, or 'co-essential' with the Father.

The word for 'authority' or 'power' is derived from that root by adding the prefix *ex*, so that it becomes ex-ousia, which means literally, from the substance, or out of the essence. When it was said of Jesus that he spoke as one having *exousia*, it meant that there was substance to his statements, that he was not simply speaking from thin air, or from a vacuum. He spoke with substantial power, with substantial authority.

The two words by which the term *exousia* is translated, power and authority, are very important terms for our understanding the nature of government. What does authority mean? In the English word, authority, we find the smaller word, author. So authority has something to do with authorship and ownership. God is the ultimate author of all things, for he is the Creator who owns what he creates and who has the right to rule and to govern his creation. That's the root meaning of authority.

In its actual functional meaning, authority means that one has the right to impose obligations, to issue commands which others are responsible and morally accountable to obey. Parents have authority over their children; so they have the right to command obedience from their children. Teachers in schools have authority over their students; they have the right to give assignments, to state requirements, and the students are responsible and culpable if they fail to accomplish them. Therefore, the whole concept of authority is important to Christians, for the Christian life is profoundly concerned with obedience. And obedience means conforming to authoritative obligations that are set before us from a source of authority.

I want to call attention to the other possible interpretation of this word, which the King James Version uses - 'Let every soul be subject unto the higher powers'. Instead of translating the word *exousia* as authority, the King James' translators used the word 'power'. Now, in our understanding of the very nature of government, classically, the bottom line could be stated like this: government is force. Christians have an obligation to understand that government is force, particularly when we are functioning in what could be called a free and democratic society where people have a right or privilege to participate in their own government.

To govern means to impose obligations that are backed up with sanctions if a person refuses to obey. Coercion is forcing people to obey laws. We not only have laws, but law enforcement agencies. The purpose of law enforcement agencies is to coerce obedience to the law, to force people to obey the mandates of the government. The government is force in that it alone has the right to use coercion to bring people into certain patterns of behaviour. It is obvious in a dictatorship that the will of the dictator must be obeyed or force will be applied. It is much more subtle when that force is disseminated among a group of people, or to what we would call a majority. But in our country, the majority can assemble the means of force and use it against a minority. That's why we are warned against the potential of what is called 'the tyranny of the majority'.

When does a government, or the individual ruler, have the right to impose legislation upon the rest of the people? When it legislates what God has ordained it to do.

There is an astonishing statement in verse 1 that is very difficult for us to apply consistently: **The authorities that exist have been established by God**. Does it mean that Hitler's and Stalin's governments were ordained of God? Does it mean that the ruthless dictators who have arisen in the Third World today are ordained of God?

Remember that Paul is writing to people who were living under a government that ultimately beheaded him. Paul was executed by a tyrannical Roman government. The Christians to whom Paul is writing paid with their lives in the Circus Maximus in Rome, when they were used as fodder for the gladiators and the lions. Though

Rome had a marvellous legal system, its rulers imposed ruthless policies upon their own people. Can we agree with the apostle Paul that the authorities that exist have been established by God?

Paul is saying something very profound. First of all, behind this statement is the absolute conviction of Scripture that God is the Lord of history. In the providence of God there is no government that can ever come to power except through God's ordination. Now we have to make a very crucial distinction here. When Paul says that the powers that be are ordained of God, he does not necessarily mean that the powers that be are approved of by God. God, I am sure, was furious at the injustices propagated by the Roman government, just as I am sure he was infuriated by the policies of Hitler and Stalin.

But there is a certain sense in which even Hitler's regime was ordained of God, in the sense that it could not happen without the Lord of history's permission. Now that permission may, from God's perspective, be an act of judgment against the world, or against the particular people. He told Israel, when they were particularly sinful as a people, that he would judge them by delivering them into the hands of tyrants.

But even if Christians find themselves in the unenviable position of being under the tyranny of an unrighteous and unjust government, they still have a fundamental responsibility to render civil obedience. That is what this chapter in Romans is about. This is not a matter that can be dealt with simplistically. There are principles that are not too difficult to discern, but the application of those principles can be extremely difficult at times.

What are the basic principles? Well, the fundamental principle is that Christians are, as a people, to be noted for their civil obedience. One of the strange ironies of early church history is that, while the Roman government was persecuting the Christian community, the church apologists were writing defences of Christian behaviour to the emperors. The Christians were not interested in disobeying the civil magistrates in civil matters; they paid their taxes, they did everything that a good citizen was supposed to do. They got into trouble when they refused to obey commands to worship the state or the emperor, rather than Christ. In that situation, they were to obey God rather than men. That is the second principle. Principle number one is that we should obey the civil magistrates, but principle number two, which balances it, is that we must always obey God. If there is a conflict between what the civil magistrate commands and what God demands, it is our moral duty to disobey the civil magistrate.

This difficult business of civil obedience is complicated further by Peter's statement that we are to obey the civil magistrates that Christ might be glorified (1 Peter 4:12-19). How is Christ glorified by my obedience to my employer, or to my parents, or to the government? Remember that there is an authority structure in the universe. The ultimate authority rests with God alone. All other authority in the universe is delegated authority, derived authority. If I refuse for no just reason to submit to the authority of my employer, or my parents, or my teachers, or my government, ultimately I am in defiance of God, and I become a participant in lawlessness which is the spirit of the antichrist. Christians are to be part of the complex of righteousness, not the complex of lawlessness. We become models of submission to authority which the world is not. We are called to obey God, and by obeying civil magistrates we show our spirit of submission and obedience to God himself.

Why is there government?

Why do we have a government? Remember that government is something that God has imposed upon the world. There are two major views which have historically competed for acceptance among Christians, one held by Augustine, and the other by Thomas Aquinas.

Augustine's viewpoint was that government is a necessary evil. Not that in and of itself government is evil, but government is made necessary by evil. Which is to say that in an unfallen world, there is no need of human government. There is much to commend this theory because the first use of force that we find in sacred Scripture is found after the Fall. We recall that God governed directly his creatures, Adam and Eve, by imposing law upon them from the very beginning of creation. So law existed from the very beginning and there was government in the sense that God was the law enforcement agency behind those laws. But there were no lesser authorities under God; we don't see any governors, or kings or emperors in the Garden of Eden.

But then they disobeyed God and as a punishment for their act of disobedience they are expelled from Eden. What happened then? God placed an angel with a flaming sword at the entrance to Eden to guard it from further trespassing by Adam and Eve and their progeny. So the first law enforcement officer who appears in Scripture is an angel, a minister of God, sent from heaven with an instrument of coercion, an instrument of force at his command, to enforce the barring of access into Eden. The first action of government is to use the methods of force to restrain evil.

When we work that out, we see that the first responsibility of government is to preserve, to maintain and to promote human life. So government exists to make the continuity of life possible, because in a fallen world people are left open to anarchy, which really means the unlimited and unrestrained power of the strong over the weak. And so the human institutions of government that are set up are necessary because of evil.

Against that, however, is the view that Aquinas offered. His theory is that even had there been no Fall, human government would still have been necessary. He argues that point on the basis of the fact that in Creation, there is a division of labour. There was a division of labour in the Garden, and even in the earliest records of society, when we see the sons of Adam and Eve, Cain and Abel, had different occupations. One had livestock and the other had produce, and the livestock was necessary for everybody and the produce was necessary for everybody. For society to function for everybody's wellbeing, it has to have certain organisational dimensions that enhance this division of labour, and will help balance and provide for the general welfare for the world.

If there is a division of labour built into creation, as Aquinas says, then that means, by implication, that man has been created for commerce. As soon as men are involved in any kind of trade or business, questions of contracts come up, questions of exchange of property. Men have to work that out in an equitable arrangement, so now they are involved in principles of justice. So they set up law courts, with law enforcement behind them to make sure trade and commerce is carried on in a just and equitable way. Therefore, another aspect of government is to set up legal systems to protect not only life, but property. Added to that division of labour there is a capacity for sin, which means that there is a capacity for injustice, and wherever there is a capacity for injustice then men seek something to promote justice. So government is also there to be an instrument of justice. And in that regard it is to be a positive instrument for righteousness and a negative influence against injustice.

Use of the sword
For he is God's servant to do you good. But if you do wrong, be afraid, for he does not bear the sword for nothing. He is God's servant, an agent of wrath to bring punishment on the wrongdoer (verse 4). The power of the sword is the exercise of force by government which is given to it by God. Paul, in the next breath, says the ruler is the servant of God. Of course, force is to be used only for righteousness, but that force is a legitimate dimension of ruling authority which this servant of God is given. The church has not been given the power of the sword, but the state has been given this authority.

Problem of war
Several theories concerning the Christian involvement in war have been postulated throughout church history and the debate continues even to our day.

There are those who take a pacifist position which says that under no circumstances is a Christian ever allowed to bear arms, and it is the duty of the Christian always to remain a conscientious objector, to refuse to participate in warfare.

The second position is one which we hear, sadly, from time to time: 'My country right or wrong, my country'. There are Christians who believe that any time a nation enters into war and conscripts its own citizens, it is the duty of the Christian to serve his civil government in whatever warfare it is engaged in. There were Christians in Germany who appealed to that principle of civil obedience to the magistrate, to justify their involvement in the Holocaust.

The third view, which I believe to be the Biblical view, is what is called the 'just war' theory. The basic principle of this theory is that all wars are evil, but not everyone's involvement in war is evil. It presupposes that in warfare, which is a dreadful thing, there are aggressors and there are innocent victims. There are those who take the offence, and those who are on the defence. The just war theory says that it is unjust for someone to wage war aggressively by attacking other nations' borders and subjecting them to murder on a grand scale. And so the theory sees a war of aggression as a violation of the prohibition against murder. If an individual wilfully and with malice afore-thought kills another individual, we call that murder and all of the negative sanctions of Scripture are called into play there. Well, if a nation, as a group, imposes murder on another group from another nation, that is equally murder and the sanctions of murder apply.

But the question arises, Does the civil magistrate, within the geographical boundaries of his own domain, have the right or the responsibility to use force to resist an aggressor and to protect his own people from being victims to hostile and aggressive acts? Again, if we look at an individual level we ask, Does the policeman have the right to use force to stop a murderer from committing his act of murder against a private citizen? And generally the answer to that question is yes. Again, by way of analogy, warfare in a defensive posture is then seen as self-defence or protection on a grand scale. The just war theory says that it is perfectly just for the government of a nation to wage defensive war.

But what is the Christian's responsibility herein? He is to remember the principles we have learned already from this section of Scripture: (1) that it is his duty to be as submissive to the government as he possibly can without violating the laws of God; (2) that the government does have a God-given right to bear the sword, and not only a right to bear the sword but a responsibility to bear the sword, because one of the primary tasks of government is to preserve, maintain, defend and promote life. If these principles are sound, then it would seem clear that the Christian's responsibility is to obey and to serve. Therefore the just war theory advocates that Christians who are called to serve in the armed forces in a righteous cause have a moral obligation to serve. They are not exempt from participation in a just action perpetrated by the state.

What happens if the state is itself the aggressor, and is involved in an unjust, unjustifiable act of warfare? If the state calls me to help it commit murder on a grand scale then, as a Christian, it is my duty to refuse to serve, no matter what the consequences may be.

Notice that in verse 4, the use of the sword is not only for restraint, but also as an instrument of vengeance. The civil magistrate, who holds an office that is enforced by instruments of violence, carries out a task of vengeance. This raises another difficult question with respect to Biblical teaching because the Bible says clearly, 'Vengeance is mine, saith the Lord, I will repay'. Christians are clearly prohibited from being private, personal agents of revenge.

But God, who has the right to vengeance, also has the right to delegate instruments of vengeance. This is precisely what we learn in this verse, that God delegates to the civil magistrate a certain measure of vengeance, making the civil magistrate a minister of vengeance on God's behalf. So it is within the province of the civil magistrate to seek retributive justice. It is within the province of the state to punish the evil doer.

Capital punishment

With respect to the issue of capital punishment, the debate usually centres on the question of the deterrent value of capital punishment. The advocates of capital punishment maintain that the threat of the death penalty is a deterrent to some from the commission of murder. Opponents of capital punishment point to various statistics that downplay the deterrent value of capital punishment and argue that it serves no useful purpose.

But the power of the sword, although given as a restraint, was not

only given as a restraint. There is a deeper moral question here, and
that is the question of justice. The basic Biblical support for capital
punishment does not rest upon the principle of deterrence; that would
be a secondary consideration. The primary consideration, biblically,
for capital punishment, is retributive justice. Capital punishment is
instituted very early in Genesis, in 9:6: 'Whoever sheds the blood of
man, by man shall his blood be shed; for in the image of God has God
made man'. God declared that if anyone murders another person, that
person is to be put to death. The reason is not for deterrence, but for
retribution, because man is made in the image of God. There is a
certain sense in which a murderer assaults the very being of God. And
there is nothing in the New Testament at any point that would indicate
a repeal of this principle of capital punishment, at least in terms of a
just treatment for murder. God has commanded the civil magistrate
to be his avenger in this case.

But there were certain safeguards and provisions in Israel for the
carrying out of the mandate. In fact the more I study the law code of
Israel, the more amazed I am by its wisdom, by its fairness and by
its justice. Even the law of the eye for an eye and tooth for a tooth has
nothing unjust within it. What could possibly be more just than that
- an eye for an eye and a tooth for a tooth? It's perfectly balanced,
perfectly symmetrical, perfectly harmonious and the scales of justice
were never in better balance than when that principle was being
applied to a culture and to a society.

But the safeguards against the unjust use of force are very severe
in the Old Testament. For example, for a person to be convicted of
a capital offence required two eyewitnesses (Deut. 17:6, 7). Circum-
stantial evidence was never grounds for capital punishment in the Old
Testament. It required two eyewitnesses whose testimonies had to
agree. The two eyewitnesses had their own lives on the line when they
bore testimony, because the rule in Israel was that if, in a capital case,
an eyewitness bore false witness, then he would himself be executed.

We don't have that kind of safeguard today in our Western
society. There are those who are justly concerned about inequities in
our systems in which the poor and minority groups tend to do very

poorly in legal trials that are of a capital nature, in comparison to those who have greater status in the community and greater wealth. It is still unusual in the United States for a prominent person, who has the ability to hire an excellent lawyer, to end up being executed. In our culture there are inequities in the exercise of capital punishment. And for this reason some Christians have taken the position that even though in principle they believe in capital punishment they argue for a moratorium on executions in the United States until such time as these inequities have been ameliorated, and we have a better law system.

But I think we are in shallow water here if we try to rule out capital punishment on a Biblical basis. I don't know of any document in history that is more clearly in favour of capital punishment than sacred Scripture. God gives to the civil magistrate the power of the sword to restrain and to avenge.

Therefore, it is necessary to submit to the authorities, not only because of possible punishment but also because of conscience (verse 5). There are two reasons why we must be careful to obey the civil magistrate. First of all, out of fear of coming under the wrath of the civil magistrate and being subject ourselves to punishment. But secondly, Christians are called to obey, not simply out of a fear of punishment, but as a matter of conscience. Their consciences must also include a respect for and submissiveness to the civil magistrate.

Taxation
This is also why you pay taxes, for the authorities are God's servants, who give their full time to governing (verse 6). God has appointed government for our wellbeing and government employees have to be paid, government budgets to be underwritten. The principal revenue for this is to come from the people, from taxation. Remember that governments do not as a rule produce anything; they don't sell goods and services in the marketplace. They exist for the welfare of the public and therefore government employees are, in a very real sense, called to be public servants.

It is interesting that in the Scriptures there are really only two groups of people whom God commands that the rest of the people support with their money. In the Old Testament, for example, it was mandatory in Israel that tithes be paid and distributed among the Levites, and so the public was to support the Levites in their vocation (Num. 18:24-26). They were the teachers of Israel, and those who were teaching were offering a public service, and God commanded that they be paid through the tithe. By the same token, taxes are to be paid to civil magistrates who also are carrying out public service responsibilities.

In passing, I want to comment about the financial support of full-time Christian workers. Throughout church history there have been movements such as the monastic movement which were ascetic and rigorous in worldly denial. Because of this, an idea emerged that pastors of local churches are to be paid a bare minimum wage. If you look carefully at the system God established in the Old Testament, you will see that the Levites who are the beneficiaries of the tithes, are to receive the firstfruits of the offering, and that their level of remuneration made them affluent people. It didn't make them the wealthiest people in the land, by any means, but neither were they called to a low income scale, relative to other professions in the ancient world.

Give everyone what you owe him: If you owe taxes, pay taxes; if revenue, then revenue; if respect, then respect; if honour, then honour (verse 7). Paul distinguishes here between taxes and custom duties that are to be paid. Now we know that today there is an enormous controversy about the principles of taxation and its extent. When Paul speaks of paying taxes here, the taxes he is referring to are, first of all, the head tax that was imposed by the Roman government upon their subjects, and secondly, property taxes that were imposed upon landowners in Rome. In addition, there were certain customs, duties and requirements placed upon merchandise. It wasn't quite a sales tax, but there was a tax on goods and merchandise. Paul is saying, Pay your property taxes, pay your poll tax, pay your merchandise taxes.

What about income tax? The idea of an income tax, as such, was not in vogue in Paul's day. But it has become a very controversial matter in our day for two reasons. First of all, the extent to which income taxation has risen in most Western countries and secondly, the structure of income taxes. Remember that the civil magistrate is to be an agent of justice and the government is to promote justice. Included among its considerations is economic justice.

The complaint of the wealthy class is that they are victims of injustice because they have to pay a graduated percentage of their income. So not everyone in the society pays the same amount, and not everyone pays the same percentage.

In contrast, the principle of the head tax in the ancient world was that every human being pays the same amount. The rationale behind this was that every individual has an equal responsibility to pay taxes to support the public service of government. Everybody benefits from the promotion of safety and the promotion of justice in a society.

Today there are political and economic rationale in using a head tax in certain nations. The idea is that if every human being is required to pay the same amount of taxes, then that is a tremendous restraint against governments growing to such an enormous size that they can become oppressive to the people. For example, if the government decides to raise taxes and they do it on the head tax basis, then such an increase in taxation is equal for everyone. So that when a government decides to raise taxes, it risks the wrath of the entire population.

On the other hand, if there is a tax increase that is differential, the rulers can set one group of the community over against another one, and diffuse any massive popular revolt against excessive taxation. You do this by giving one set of taxes to a minority and give a break to the majority. In most cases, the majority who vote on the basis of enlightened self-interest, will go along with it and won't revolt.

In the Old Testament concept of the tithe, wealthy people put more money into the work of the church, and so on, but not a greater percentage of their income. So there was an equality of taxation, percentage-wise, though not an equality in terms of volume.

There are Christian leaders who, for various reasons in the past decades or so, have advocated to the Christian public in the United States that they refuse to pay their taxes.

One crisis with respect to paying taxes came out of the Vietnam war and people's opposition to the amount of money that was being spent in that war effort. Many were concerned about their tax dollars being used to support what they judged to be an improper use of military force and might.

Another debate came out of the abortion crisis. When it became known that tax dollars were being used to fund abortions, people who had strong ethical objections to abortion saw economic boycott of taxation as a legitimate means to protest this crime against humanity.

A further question that Christians struggle with is in respect to paying their tithes. If I know that my tithe to the local church is being used to fund something that I believe is ungodly, should I continue to pay my tithe? If I know that my local church is giving a certain proportion of money to group causes such as the World Council of Churches, and seeing that revolutions are being funded by these dollars, and I am opposed to that, what do I do with my tithe dollar?

This is a complex matter to sort out. Let's see if we can discern some principles, however, that bear on the topic.

First, we go back to the book of the *Didache*, which was the first significant document circulating in the Christian church after the writing of the New Testament. The *Didache*, which is also called the Teaching of the Apostles, appeared towards the end of the first century, and is not Scripture. Although it does not have the authority of Scripture in the church, it has significance and influence for it is of great value to those seeking to understand the spirit and mentality of the first century church. It contains a precise expression of Christian ethics and Christian behavioural principles. For example, the *Didache* has a passage in it which clearly and unambiguously calls the abortion of the unborn an act of murder.

The *Didache* has much to say about the giving of alms, tithing and the giving of gifts. And one of the practical suggestions that it gives is: 'Let your donation sweat in your hand'. The practical principle there is that a person should be very careful where he gives his money.

He ought to be selective where he gives his money. And I think that that principle is an expression of practical wisdom.

There is a word in verse 7 that does have some ethical implications and may have bearing upon this question of paying taxes. It is the word *owe*. **Give everyone what you owe him; if you owe taxes, pay taxes; if revenue, then revenue; if respect, then respect; if honour, then honour.**

We use the word 'owe' in at least two distinct ways in our culture. For example, we speak of incurring a financial obligation to an organisation or group. When it is time to pay your subscription, you pay what you *owe*. When I engage in a commercial transaction, I buy something and they send me a bill, which informs me that I *owe* payment.

But there is a deeper concept in the principle of *owing*. What is justice? Justice means giving a person what is due them. If I promise to pay you fifty dollars for an object and you give me the object, you are then due my fifty dollars. Justice demands that I fulfil my obligation. Paul is describing the legitimate use of government and he is saying that we are supposed to pay our taxes in principle because governments are a good thing in principle. When the tax is just, it is my moral obligation to pay that tax. If the tax is not just, then I am not obligated to pay it.

Christians are to be courteous people, **if respect, then respect;** they are to be sensitive people, to be considerate people. I am not supposed to be arrogant, rude or impolite, but I am supposed to obey the laws and pay my taxes.

I am concerned about **if honour, then honour** because we live in a culture that has become a discourteous culture. We are to honour our parents; we are to honour those in authority over us; we are to honour the elderly; we are to give them respect. We are to maintain people's dignity by showing honour to whom honour is due. Christians cannot just assume that their obligations are fulfilled if they take care of material things like paying tithes and paying taxes. They must also show honour to other people.

LOVE IS A DEBT (13:8-14)

Verse 8 is a very strong statement: **Let no debt remain outstanding, except the continuing debt to love one another, for he who loves his fellow man has fulfilled the law.** In light of what the verse says, some Christians have tried to be very scrupulous at this point, and have adopted a policy in their life that they will undertake no debts. They will engage in no mortgage activities. They will not purchase a home until they can pay cash for it; they will not purchase an automobile unless they can pay cash for it; they carry no credit cards.

There are two ways of understanding Paul's instruction in this matter. The first view sees it as a prohibition against entering into debt; the other view interprets it as a mandate to pay all of your debts so that you have no debts outstanding. Which does the apostle mean? Does he mean that we are not allowed to borrow money? Or does he mean that once we borrow money we have an obligation to pay our debts?

I am not absolutely positive which of these interpretations is correct. Scripture, as a whole, however, certainly allows the concept of borrowing capital for purposes of investment. I don't think there is in the Bible a universal prohibition against borrowing money from another person. Therefore, I think that the point of this text is that we are to pay our debts.

There is an obligation that believers have: **the continuing debt to love one another, for he who loves his fellow man has fulfilled the law.** Paul is not saying the only law is the law of love, but he is being consistent with Jesus, with the Old Testament and with the other apostles by saying that the ultimate fulfilment of the law, the ultimate expression of the law is the love of people. This is why there are laws against murder and against stealing, for they indicate a concern of God that we do not violate each other, harm each other or damage each other, but that we manifest love to one another.

The commandments, "Do not commit adultery," "Do not murder," "Do not steal," "Do not covet," and whatever other commandment there may be, are summed up in this one rule: "Love your neighbour as yourself" (verse 9).

The heart of the law, that we love each other, is God's will for his people. Love cannot express itself through adultery. We know that in sexual ethics in our day, some people are convinced that love permits adultery. It is the great crisis in our culture today - What is the meaning of love? God says that love is expressed by avoiding adultery and other forbidden practices. Our love for God must express itself in how we deal with people, how we love people, how we treat them. God's laws are not just moral rules or abstract mandates, they are rules of love.

Paul gives a further expansion of the summary: **Love does no harm to its neighbour. Therefore love is the fulfilment of the law** (verse 10). Paul amplifies the statement by saying that love is not just a feeling, it has a behavioural aspect. When the Bible says I am to love my neighbour, it means I am to be considerate to my neighbour. It has to do with action: what I say, what I do with my money, what I do with my body, what I do that may bring harm and injury to another person. I am to care about other people. Christians should be the most caring, considerate and neighbourly people in the world. To be a lover of God requires that we show that love through being kind and considerate to people.

Now the reason Paul gives for the necessity of such a lifestyle is: **And do this, understanding the present time** (verse 11). The word for 'time' is the word *kairos* which does not refer to the normal passage of time but to a moment in time that is of special significance. It refers to a particularly important, decisive moment in history. The theme is the lateness of the hour. There is a temporal urgency about the gospel, and about our responsibilities to fulfil the law of love. Christians are called to be scrupulous in their obedience because of the lateness of the hour: **The hour has come for you to wake up from your slumber, because our salvation is nearer now than when we first believed. The night is nearly over; the day is almost here** (verses 11,12).

What is Paul speaking of when he talks about the lateness of the hour? There have been several suggestions as to the meaning of this phrase. Some think that Paul is saying, 'Look, we are growing old, we are older now than we were when we first believed, and we are approaching the ends of our lives. Therefore, the urgency to obedience becomes all the greater as we grow more mature and closer to our personal day of judgment.' I am not at all satisfied with that interpretation. I think it overly spiritualises the text.

Another interpretation is that he is referring to crisis events that are soon to take place in the first century. He is thinking perhaps of the destruction of Jerusalem that is at hand, and the time for the liberation of Gentile Christianity. But again, I am not persuaded of that.

Another element that has made this passage so controversial is the work of Albert Schweitzer in the nineteenth century, further developed by some of the New Testament scholars at the beginning of the twentieth century. Schweitzer developed a concept of what he called 'parousia delay'. The idea of parousia delay is this: the word *parousia* is used by the Biblical writers to refer to the appearing or the coming of Jesus at the end of the age.

We know that the early Christian community looked forward with great anticipation to the return of Jesus to this world. The theory is that the early church believed emphatically that the return of Jesus would take place very quickly, that is within the first generation of the Christian Church, in the first century. It is also argued that the apostle Paul was the chief expositor of the notion that Jesus would surely come by the end of the first century. Now this verse is one of those passages where it seems to suggest that Paul is teaching a very near time return of Jesus.

And when that appearance or coming of Christ did not take place, a crisis of faith developed in the early church. The people were disappointed because the prophecy of Jesus, and the prophecies of Paul regarding the return of Jesus simply did not take place. The coming of Jesus was delayed. And so in the later writings of Paul, for example, it was alleged that he had to alter his scope and change his thinking to allow for a greater time period to pass between the departure of Jesus in his ascension and his return at the end of the age.

Let me deal with the question of parousia delay in general. Albert

Schweitzer, in his study of the New Testament, came to the conclusion that Jesus had high expectations in fulfilling his vocation as Messiah, but that he died in broken disillusionment. His cry from the cross, 'My God, my God, why have you forsaken me?', was an expression of Jesus' final succumbing to despair, when he realised that God was not going to act to deliver him, and that he would die in ignominy. So, for Schweitzer, Jesus was a disillusioned man, who died and stayed dead in the first century.

The passages that drove Schweitzer to this negative conclusion about the ministry of Jesus, were Jesus' teachings concerning his own return and concerning the coming of the kingdom of God, in which Jesus said, for example, 'Some who are standing here will not taste death before they see the kingdom of God come with power' (Mark 9:1). Jesus taught in the Olivet Discourse about 'this generation (which) will certainly not pass away until all these things have happened' (Matthew 24:34). If we look at the prophecies of Jesus, however, we see that the destruction of the Temple and Jerusalem predicted in the Olivet Discourse did in fact take place within these time parameters. In the Olivet Discourse Jesus spent part of the time speaking about the destruction of Jerusalem, and another part of the time speaking about his own future return.

Some people put those two together and suggested that Jesus' return would be at the same time as the destruction of Jerusalem. But if we look carefully at Jesus' remarks in the Olivet Discourse, he doesn't say that. And if we examine carefully the writings of the apostle Paul, we find that, although Paul may have personally hoped for the return of Jesus in his own lifetime, he certainly didn't teach that concept. The Bible nowhere teaches, emphatically or explicitly, a timetable for the return of Jesus. It does not teach us that Jesus was going to come back in the first century.

Paul is saying that **our salvation is nearer now than when we first believed**. We are closer now to the final consummation of the kingdom of God than Paul was. There is a repeated theme in the New Testament, a call to vigilance and to diligence, realising that we are living in the last days. Since it has been almost two thousand years since the first advent of Jesus, we seem to think that the last days are taking a long time! But if we understand redemptive history from a Biblical perspective, it is necessary for us to make that very assertion, that we have been in the last days since the first century. The first century, with the advent of Jesus, ushered in the hour of the breakthrough of the kingdom of God. When Christ entered into the world, it was the pivotal moment in time. The period between the resurrection of Jesus and the time of his return is the end times.

What does Paul mean when he says 'our salvation is nearer'? We have to remember that the Bible speaks of salvation in the past tense, the present tense, and the future tense. Those of us who are already in Christ are already justified. We are in a state of salvation. But the fulness, the full measure of our salvation has not yet been experienced. When Jesus returns and consummates his kingdom, that will be a greater and fuller salvation than we have right now. Paul is not suggesting that people are not yet saved, and then later will be saved. He is talking about that final salvation which believers all look forward to.

Paul is echoing the teachings of Jesus with respect to the crisis of the breakthrough of the kingdom of God. The kingdom of God has begun. The hour is growing late. Paul frequently calls us to redeem the time because the days are evil. There is still evil in this world, there is still struggle in this world, and there is still some participation that each of us must endure in the night. But the night is growing into the dawn. We have already caught a glimpse of the Sun of righteousness who comes with healing in his wings. Christ has appeared; Christ has purchased our salvation; Christ has promised us a future inheritance in his kingdom. So the full dawn of day has not yet broken through, but we are, as it were, able to see the horizon and see the beginning edges of the sun come up for the dawn.

If we understand this teaching, it should make a difference in how we live. **So let us put aside the deeds of darkness and put on the armour of light. Let us behave decently, as in the daytime** (verses 12, 13). Do not live as if Christ hasn't come, as if the resurrection hasn't taken place. We have tasted of the kingdom of God, we have tasted the power of Christ in our lives, so let's stop doing the things that belong to the dark: **not in orgies and drunkenness, not in sexual immorality and debauchery, not in dissension and jealousy. Rather, clothe yourselves with the Lord Jesus Christ, and do not think about how to gratify the desires of the sinful nature** (verses 13,14). Paul frequently teaches by use of contrast. You used to live that way, but now you live this way; put off the old and put on the new; these are deeds of darkness not fit for the light of faith. So too our lives should manifest the same stark contrast from the manner in which the unregenerate live. Entirely too much licence is practised by the church today. 'Free from the law, O blessed condition. Sin as I please and still have remission' is the Antinomian theme song encouraged by growing numbers of evangelicals. Paul does not shrink from naming these vices as sin; nor should we. Flee such immorality in favour of being clothed in the righteousness of the Lord Jesus.

This passage at the end of chapter 13 was used by God to awaken the soul of one of his greatest saints. Augustine, in his youth, had rejected the Christian faith taught to him by his mother, Monica and, as a young man in his early twenties, gave himself to a wanton life of licentiousness. He fathered illegitimate children and turned himself over to sensuous pursuits and riotous living. On one occasion he picked up the Scriptures and the page opened to the end of the 13th chapter of Romans. His eyes fell upon this passage. He was convicted of his sin by the power of the Holy Spirit, and he became a Christian.

CHRISTIAN LIBERTY (14:1-15:7)

This section sets forth very clearly the concept of Christian liberty. Here Paul deals with matters that are very important for the peace and health of the church of Christ. He is dealing with how Christians are to behave with respect to issues that have no specific ethical import; they are morally neutral matters.

When people have scruples about things that are not matters of ethical significance we run into problems. But rather than considering examples from our contemporary culture, let's see what Paul was wrestling with in the first century. He begins with an apostolic command: **Accept him whose faith is weak, without passing judgment on disputable matters.** There is the first principle. He is saying that there should be a spirit of acceptance towards those who are immature, weak in the faith. In other words, mature believers are not to be contentious and argumentative with those who are still working through the difficulties of the early stages of their Christian development.

He goes on to explain the type of thing that he is referring to: **One man's faith allows him to eat everything, but another man, whose faith is weak, eats only vegetables** (verse 2). This is bad news for vegetarians! But the example here is that there are some people who, somewhere along the line, get the idea that they are not allowed to do certain things. Those ideas do not come from the word of God, but they come from their culture, or their parents, or from somebody telling them that they ought not to be engaged in certain activities. And they have not been informed of the full scope of what God commands and what God prohibits.

Let's state it another way: each one of us has a system in our heads of what is allowable and what is not allowable in the Christian life. We have a moral code by which we live. Now I doubt if any one of us has a moral system built into our heads that corresponds exactly and precisely in every detail to the moral code that God desires for us. We tend to overlook certain specific things that God commands or forbids, and we also bring baggage into our moral codes where God has left us free. We have this problem of Christians who are living side by side, but who are not operating with exactly the same moral code. One man thinks it is wrong to eat meat; another thinks that it is right to eat meat. One person thinks it is right to drink wine; another person thinks that it is a terrible sin to drink wine. How do we deal with this?

This verse is not saying that every person has the right to create their own ethical system. For example, if one person in the Christian community thinks adultery is a sin, and another person thinks that it is not, we should not have any disputes or arguments about it. The

New Testament makes very clear those things which God has clearly forbidden. What this text is dealing with are those moral issues where God has not prohibited or commanded. Let me use wine as an example.

The New Testament nowhere prohibits the use of wine yet there are multitudes of Christians who believe that one sip of wine is a sin, and they will go to lengthy gymnastics to try to show that the New Testament does not really condone the use of wine, that it wasn't real wine that Jesus made at the wedding feast at Cana, or that the disciples used in the upper room at the last supper, and so on. I am not going to get into that side issue except to say that it involves exegesis of despair in order to try and demonstrate that the word *oinos* in the New Testament, does not mean real wine.

The Bible clearly prohibits drunkenness; there is no question about that. But the use of wine is not absolutely forbidden. Today, there are those who take the position of voluntary total abstinence because we live in a culture that does not know how to handle intoxicating beverages. Some say that it is a matter of prudence to take a position over drinking wine, and I certainly respect that. But we cannot make that a rule to be imposed on all Christians, or as a sign of Christian godliness.

There were people in the first century church who were upset over whether they should eat meat that had been offered to idols in the pagan religious services. After the service was over the meat would be sold in the market, and some Christians thought that the meat had been desecrated by its use in a pagan environment. Paul is saying, 'If you want to eat the meat, you can eat it; if you don't want to eat that meat, you don't have to.'

Now here is the consequence that is difficult: if I believe that to eat meat is a sin, and then I go ahead and eat the meat, I have sinned. I have not sinned because eating meat is a sin, but it is a sin to do something that you believe is evil. If I think that something is evil and then I do it, then I have acted against my conscience, and to act against one's conscience is to commit a sin. At the same time, this gets complicated, because the conscience can be distorted and the conscience can be misinformed. But the only one who can bind my conscience ultimately is God; God is the Lord of my conscience.

In the text, the one who was overly scrupulous probably believed that he was strong in the faith because he did not eat anything apart from vegetables; he thought that he was being more righteous than his stronger brother. Paul sees this excessive scrupulosity not as a virtue, not as a mark of maturity, but as a mark of immaturity and of weakness of faith. It is a weakness in understanding the content of the faith.

But we read in verse 3: **The man who eats everything must not look down on him who does not, and the man who does not eat everything must not condemn the man who does, for God has accepted him.** In the exercise of my Christian freedom, God has left me free to eat meat. If I eat meat and my brother does not want to eat meat, I am not supposed to hold my brother in contempt because he doesn't behave the way I do. I am not to despise him. I am not to judge the person who refrains from eating meat, and the person who refrains from eating meat is not to judge me for eating the meat. God has accepted us both; we are both in Christ and we are to have that mutual acceptance.

Paul raises the rhetorical question in verse 4: **Who are you to judge someone else's servant? To his own master he stands or falls. And he will stand, for the Lord is able to make him stand.** In these questionable matters, these debatable matters, we are to leave the final judgment to the Lord. You refrain from your meat to the glory of Christ; I will eat my meat to the glory of Christ. We both belong to Christ and we will let Christ make the decision. We are not supposed to fight with each other over it.

One man considers one day more sacred than another; another man considers every day alike. Each one should be fully convinced in his own mind (verse 5). Most of the problems that Paul was dealing with were brought into the Christian community by Jewish converts who insisted on keeping the Jewish festivals. The Gentile Christians didn't want to keep the Jewish festivals, they did not mean anything to them. And Paul makes it clear that they did not have to keep those festivals. He is not referring to the Christian Sabbath, he is talking about specific festivals that were on the Jewish calendar. The Gentile Christians were not required to keep those festivals. Some people did so religiously; other people avoided them religiously. Paul says we have to respect each other at this point. As the Scriptures illumine our minds and inform our consciences, so we must live in accordance to these dictates. Therefore the weak should not bind the conscience of the strong, nor vice versa.

He elaborates in verses 6-12: **He who regards one day as special, does so to the Lord. He who eats meat, eats to the Lord, for he gives thanks to God; and he who abstains, does so to the Lord, and gives thanks to God. For none of us lives to himself alone and none of us dies to himself alone. If we live, we live to the Lord; and if we die, we die to the Lord. So, whether we live or die, we belong to the Lord. For this very reason, Christ died and returned to life so that he might be the Lord of both the dead and the living. You, then, why do you judge your brother? Or why do you look down on your brother? For we will all stand before God's judgment seat. It is written: " 'As surely as I live,' says the Lord, 'Every knee will bow before me; every tongue will confess to God.' " So then, each of us will give an account of himself to God.** As Christians, we have the same Master and Lord, and that Lord is Christ. Christ died for us, to purchase my salvation, and to purchase my brother's salvation. We are not to live in judgment on each other in matters of neutrality. We have to at least give the persons with whom we differ the benefit of the doubt that they are trying to do what they are doing to the honour of Christ. We have to respect their convictions and respect the fact that every brother is a person who wants to do the will of the Lord. Sometimes we don't know what the will of the Lord is, and in that situation we have to bend over backwards to accommodate differences of convictions among ourselves. The cause of benevolence must be promoted. We are reminded how little benevolence was shown our Lord when throughout his ministry he was accused of being a wine-bibber, a glutton, a friend of sinners and a Sabbath breaker. Jesus, from the strength of faith, broke with Jewish custom and man-made traditions to live a life he thought pleasing to God. Precisely because we will all have to render an account of our lives to God, we must be free from the binding constraints of others in matters indifferent.

So Paul says in verse 13: **Therefore, let us stop passing judgment on one another. Instead, make up your mind not to put any stumbling-block or obstacle in your brother's way.** Paul states the practical principle that we ought not to make our brother stumble. Does this mean that if my brother has a scruple against eating meat, that I can't eat meat? What if I eat meat and it causes my brother to stumble? Let's take it down to the present day.

Drinking wine is audioferous, that is, we may drink wine or we may not drink wine. What if my brother is convinced that he is never allowed to touch wine? Does that mean I am not allowed to touch wine? Remember that I am not supposed to make my brother stumble or fall into sin. Let's see what that means.

If my brother thinks that drinking wine is a sin, how could I make him sin, how could I make him stumble? I could make him stumble by doing everything in my power to encourage him to drink wine. If I try to get him to drink wine when he thinks it is wrong to drink wine, I am really trying to persuade him to sin. It is one thing for me to try to get him to do something that he believes is evil, it is another for me to have a discussion with him and say, 'I disagree with you and think it is permissible to drink wine.' But it is one thing to talk about it theologically, it is another to actually convince him to drink wine.

As one who is in the Lord Jesus, I am fully convinced that no food is unclean in itself. But if anyone regards something as unclean, then for him it is unclean. If your brother is distressed because of what you eat, you are no longer acting in love. Do not by your eating destroy your brother for whom Christ died (verses 14,15). If a man believes something is unclean then it becomes unclean for him. But only because he believes it to be, not because in and of itself it is unclean.

Paul is not saying that the stronger brother must be bound by the religious scruples of the weaker brother. Though the stronger brother is to bend over backwards not to offend or to hurt the weaker brother, the stronger brother is not to allow the weaker brother to exercise moral tyranny over the church. Take the matter of circumcision. In the early stages of his ministry, Paul saw no great significance in circumcision, and if people wanted to be circumcised out of mere tradition or family custom, he'd circumcise them. Then the Judaizers came into the church and insisted that circumcision was an absolute requirement for every Christian. At that point Paul stood up to the weaker brothers and said that he would refuse to circumcise, because they were trying to take their scruple and make it a binding law upon the whole community. That's what we have to guard jealously against in our community.

Do not allow what you consider good to be spoken of as evil (verse 16). Let me give you an illustration of that. I went out to a restaurant once with a group of Christians who invited me as the speaker for their group. There were about 15 of us and a woman graciously took us out for a meal to a nice restaurant. At the beginning of the meal, the wine steward came around with the wine list and asked if anyone wanted any wine. Our hostess spoke up for the whole group and said, 'No, thank you, none of us wants wine because we are Christians.' I remember feeling totally embarrassed by that remark. I wanted to go after the wine steward and say to her, 'I am sorry that that woman was so rude to you. I want you to understand that it is not a universal law among Christians that no Christian is allowed to drink wine. There are many Christians who drink wine.'

The damage that was done in that scenario was that the wine steward had been informed that a Christian is a person who never drinks wine. That's a distortion of the gospel. There the weaker brother – the weaker sister in this case – had gone too far. However, I just kept my mouth shut. I probably should have said, 'Wait, I'll have a glass of wine.' I think that's what the apostle Paul would have done in that situation.

Paul would respect and bend over backwards to take care of the weaknesses of the weaker brother, but he would not allow the weaker brother to exercise tyranny over the church to the end that the gospel and its message would be distorted. His principle was that **the kingdom of God is not a matter of eating and drinking, but of righteousness, peace and joy in the Holy Spirit, because anyone who serves Christ in this way is pleasing to God and approved by men** (verses 17, 18). This principle was consistent with the teachings of Christ who had likewise said, 'the kingdom of God does not come with outward display ... the kingdom of God is within you' (Luke 17:21). What is most characteristic of the kingdom is not meat and drink but righteousness, peace and joy. Right standing before God, peace resulting from reconciliation, and joy in a heart set free from sin and guilt, are marks of a citizen of God's kingdom.

Let us therefore make every effort to do what leads to peace and to mutual edification. Do not destroy the work of God for the sake of food. All food is clean, but it is wrong for a man to eat anything that causes someone else to stumble. It is better not to eat meat or drink wine or to do anything else that will cause your brother to fall. So whatever you believe about these things keep between yourself and God (verses 19-22). Do you see what he is saying? Don't be running around creating a problem with people who have scruples. It is between you and God. If you want to drink wine, it is between you and God. Drink wine to the glory of God. Eat meat to the glory of God. But don't let that become a matter of injuring other people. It would be wrong for me to exercise my liberty in such a way as to hurt people's feelings.

Blessed is the man who does not condemn himself by what he approves. But the man who has doubts is condemned if he eats, because his eating is not from faith; and everything that does not come from faith is sin (verses 22,23). This is the same principle mentioned earlier, that we ought not to act against our consciences (see comments on verse 2). We should strive to get our consciences in line with the word of God and continually seek to refine our own moral codes to bring them into conformity to the mind of Christ, so that we don't have this problem of not knowing what God approves and what God forbids.

Paul says in 15:1, **We who are strong ought to bear with the** failings of the weak, and not to please ourselves. This is a theme that we find throughout the Bible. We are not isolated individuals, but we live in community, we live in relationships with other Christians in the brotherhood of the church. We are called to weep with those who weep, to laugh with those who laugh, to rejoice with those who rejoice and so on. The characteristic of the Christian life is not one of selfishness. We have to think about other people and be concerned about them. Christians are called, in a spirit of charity, to be longsuffering and patient toward other people.

Each of us should please his neighbour for his good, to build him up (verse 2). Those who are in positions of authority in the body of Christ must be gracious. If you are called to a position of leadership, you must be careful that the style of leadership does not degenerate into tyranny. It is easy to assume, when one is in a position of authority or power, that everyone around you exists for your good pleasure and to please you. That kind of a mentality lacks grace, because you are called as leaders to be leading other people for their welfare and goodness and not for your own self-interest. But all of us, whether leaders or not, are to constantly have in view the spiritual good of our neighbours. Promoting their welfare sets in motion a virtuous cycle that ultimately rebounds to our own spiritual good.

The clincher of Paul's argument is found in verse 3, where he says, For even Christ did not please himself but, as it is written: "The insults of those who insult you have fallen on me." The supreme example for us of godly living, of being concerned for the other person, and of exercising charity towards those with whom we disagree, is Jesus. Jesus stood between hostile parties as a mediator and he absorbed an unbelievable amount of insult, slander and vicious attacks. None of the things that Jesus was accused of were legitimate. He was without sin. Every time that Jesus was criticised, every time that Jesus was attacked, he was attacked unjustly. No-one ever had a right to insult Jesus. But he absorbed all of that hostility, anger and insults, as a Lamb that was led to the slaughter.

Paul goes on to say: For everything that was written in the past was written to teach us, so that through endurance and the

encouragement of the Scriptures we might have hope (verse 4). Sometimes we struggle to be involved seriously in a disciplined way in deep study of the Scriptures. Every Christian knows that a study of the Bible is a duty, an obligation that we have. But sometimes doing things that are duties and obligations is not fun. We like to do things where we can be helped by it. And yet what an unbelievable opportunity it is to be instructed by God himself! God has given us a Bible not to put on the shelf but to teach us.

Notice how endurance, encouragement and hope fit together as attitudes in our lives. When I am discouraged I tend to be impatient and I tend to be threatened and tempted by despair. When I have hope, hope brings with it endurance, and I am encouraged by that hope. When God teaches me, I immediately have my level of hope raised enormously, which then makes it possible for me to be patient, and to be encouraged, in the midst of the defeats and the frustrations and the difficulties that I encounter in my daily life.

In other words, if we are going to be able to imitate Jesus, Paul says that we should be strong to bear the insults. We are to be those who are vessels of grace, mercy and kindness towards other people. But our ability to handle the difficulties of life is undergirded by feeding on the word of God. We can live out our lives in a posture of hope and endurance because of the encouragement that we find in Scripture. If you are deeply discouraged, if you are bordering on the rim of despair, that is a clear indication that you have been neglecting the word of God, because the word of God produces encouragement.

Paul continues by saying: **May the God who gives endurance and encouragement give you a spirit of unity among yourselves as you follow Christ Jesus, so that with one heart and mouth you may glorify the God and Father of our Lord Jesus Christ** (verses 5,6). Paul calls attention to the fact that God is the author of endurance and encouragement. Ultimately our ability to endure and to have courage and to be concerned with other people is found in God himself. He is the author of these things, and the more we know God, the closer we draw to God, the greater the capacity we will have for these things.

The Lord Jesus Christ has come to reconcile us to God the Father and to move us to praise and adore the Father. There is a sense in which Jesus' own ministry points beyond himself to the Father. It was the Father who sent him. His meat and drink was to do the Father's will, and he wants us to look toward the Father with the same spirit and with the same sense of obedience, love and adoration for the Father that he himself manifested.

Paul continues to apply this to relationships when he says in verse 7: **Accept one another, then, just as Christ accepted you, in order to bring praise to God.** My acceptance of my brothers and sisters in the Lord is a matter of worship. I do this not simply for my own benefit, so that I can be popular with the rest of the church. We are called to receive one another, to respect one another, to be accepting towards one another, for the glory of God. When I receive a brother or a sister without condemning them, then I am doing towards my brother and sister what God would have me to do. And in so doing I call attention to the fountainhead of patience and encouragement which is God himself. And so God is glorified in our charitable attitudes towards one another.

Conversely, God is disgraced when we misbehave, when we are vengeful or impatient, and when we seek to discourage one another with a spirit of destructive competition. Similarly, when we are involved in power struggles, jealousies and covetousness and the things that destroy human relationships. This shows a lack of grace, and it is a disgrace to the body of Christ.

Paul calls attention to the role of Jesus in this: **just as Christ accepted you.** Any unwillingness by me to accept other believers shows gross ingratitude on my part towards the acceptance that I have already received in Christ. Forgiven people are forgiving people. If you lack a spirit of forgiveness in your life towards others, that would indicate that you have no understanding of your own forgiveness at the hands of Christ.

PAUL, A SERVANT OF THE GENTILES (15:8-33)

For I tell you that Christ has become a servant of the Jews on behalf of God's truth, to confirm the promises made to the patriarchs so that the Gentiles may glorify God for his mercy, as it is written: "Therefore I will praise you among the Gentiles; I will sing hymns to your name." Christ is our example. He became a servant to the Jews; he did not come in the role of an authoritarian king. This was the style of Jesus who was the Lord of glory. He came to demonstrate that God keeps his promises, that God is trustworthy, loyal, faithful and does what he says he is going to do. Christ became a servant to confirm God's promises to the patriarchs.

Jesus also came to enable the Gentiles to praise God for his mercy. **So that the Gentiles may glorify God for his mercy, as it is written: "Therefore I will praise you among the Gentiles; I will sing hymns to your name." Again, it says: "Rejoice, O Gentiles, with his people." And again, "Praise the Lord, all you Gentiles, and sing praises to him, all you peoples." And again, Isaiah says, "The Root of Jesse will spring up, one who will arise to rule over the nations; the Gentiles will hope in him"** (verses 9-12). Paul musters a series of quotations from the Old Testament which call attention to the fact that the inclusion of the Gentiles in the kingdom of God is not an innovation brought about by Jesus' earthly ministry, but is part of the promises of God made in antiquity. It is even part of the implied promises that God made to the patriarchs, such as those promises made to Abraham that he would be a father of many nations, and that through him and through the Jews all the nations of the world would be blessed.

Then Paul says, **May the God of hope** - he has just said that God was the source of patience and encouragement – **fill you with all joy and peace as you trust in him, so that you may overflow with hope by the power of the Holy Spirit** (verse 13). The means of that filling, the means by which we experience joy and peace is through trusting in God. The more we trust God, the greater our joy, the greater our peace, and the greater we experience this hope that the Bible elsewhere calls 'the anchor of the soul'. But the hope we experience as Christians is not a static thing, it is a hope that increases in its magnitude and in its proportion. As we grow in grace, the Holy Spirit works within us, increasing the depth, the breadth and the intensity of that hope in our souls.

Paul adds a personal word at this juncture and speaks of his own ministry in a way that is very revealing of the character and personality of the apostle himself. **I myself am convinced, my brothers, that you yourselves are full of goodness, complete in knowledge and competent to instruct one another** (verse 14). Is Paul just being political here? I don't think the apostle, under the inspiration of the Holy Spirit, could be. Rather, Paul was confident that the spirit of goodness prevailed among these saints in Rome, and that they were people who were filled with knowledge. They did have a mature ability to teach each other and admonish each other. Paul does not give himself to idle compliments. This is a sincere compliment from the pen of the apostle which tells us something about the community of Christians that was in Rome. This was an extraordinary church. Imagine a minister honestly being able to say to his congregation - I am sure that you are full of goodness, that you are filled with knowledge, and that you are able to teach one another. There are not many congregations that could hear that kind of honest evaluation and compliment.

Paul continues, **I have written to you quite boldly on some points, as if to remind you of them again** (verse 15). Paul is saying that it is because he knew they were mature that he had been so bold. Obviously, when a teacher is in the company of mature Christians who are deeply grounded in the faith and knowledgeable about the word of God, it is much easier to speak candidly without fear of being misunderstood and without fear of offending a weaker brother. But there is a second reason for his boldness: **because of the grace God gave me to be a minister of Christ Jesus to the Gentiles.** Paul is saying, I have been bold because of my authority as an apostle. The servanthood of the apostle Paul was one that carried weighty, enormous authority, which allowed for a certain boldness.

Now Paul makes a strange comment here: **with the priestly duty** of proclaiming the gospel of God (verse 16). We don't normally think of Paul as a priest. We remember that in the Old Testament the function of the priest was to make oblations, to make offerings to God. But there are not any sin-offerings or atonements to be made any more, because the perfect sacrifice has been offered up once and for all by Christ, our great High Priest. But yet Paul calls himself a priest. Well, what is it that the priest offers now? One activity of the priesthood of the New Testament church is the offering of the gospel to the world. Why? **so that the Gentiles might become an offering acceptable to God, sanctified by the Holy Spirit** (verse 16). It was not Paul's act which was to be acceptable and sanctified. Rather the idea presented is that the Gentiles themselves became an offering to God, made acceptable by the sanctifying work of the Spirit. Paul's great ministry was to bring men and women, through the preaching of the gospel and the work of the Spirit, to offer themselves as a living sacrifice to God.

Paul reminds his readers that there has been fruit to his ministry: **Therefore I glory in Christ Jesus in my service to God. I will not venture to speak of anything except what Christ has accomplished through me in leading the Gentiles to obey God by what I have said and done - by the power of signs and miracles, through the power of the Spirit. So from Jerusalem all the way around to Illyricum, I have fully proclaimed the gospel of Christ** (verses 17-19). What great things Paul could have boasted of. He penned more of the New Testament than any other writer; he did more, according to Acts, than any other apostle; he unquestionably had the keenest theological mind of any in the early church, and probably all of church history. We can only speculate how many were converted through his ministry in his own day, far less through the ages because of his writings. How sincerely he writes in Philippians that all these things, including his marvellous heritage, were as rubbish (3:8). When he boasted it was to bring attention to his weakness and the power of God. The saving grace of God and the glory of the cross were the themes upon which Paul rested his case and in which he took pride. Paul is saying that all that was acceptable to God was done by Christ through the Holy Spirit. He is not boasting of himself and of his own accomplishments; he is boasting in the Lord, he is boasting about what Christ has accomplished.

It has always been my ambition to preach the gospel where Christ was not known, so that I would not be building on someone else's foundation. Rather, as it is written: "Those who were not told about him will see, and those who have not heard will understand." This is why I have often been hindered from coming to you (verses 20-22). Here we find the heartbeat of an evangelist, the heartbeat of a missionary, one who wants to go to those people who have never heard the gospel. Paul was a pioneer missionary. He loved to go where no-one had ever laboured, where he had to start from scratch, where he had to announce the gospel of God from the beginning point.

Paul's intention to visit Rome

But now that there is no more place for me to work in these regions, and since I have been longing for many years to see you, I plan to do so when I go to Spain. I hope to visit you while passing through and to have you assist me on my journey there, after I have enjoyed your company for a while (verses 23,24). Notice that Paul's desire to visit Rome was not a new thing, it was something that he had wanted to do for years, but God had not given him the opportunity to do it. This tells us something about how we live out our ministry, and our Christian lives. God doesn't always send us where we want to go. Paul wanted for years to go to Rome, but he had responsibilities elsewhere. It didn't change the fact that he wanted to come. Paul's plan was to go to Spain. But we have no record in history that Paul ever got to Spain. We don't know for sure that he did not, but we have no indication that he ever did.

Now, however, I am on my way to Jerusalem in the service of the saints there. For Macedonia and Achaia were pleased to make a contribution for the poor among the saints in Jerusalem (verses 25,26). There had been a famine in Jerusalem and Paul, wherever he was on his preaching missions, would gather up contributions to take back to Jerusalem to help those who were in need. So before Paul can go to Rome, he has to go back to Jerusalem to distribute the offerings that were given by God's people to help the poor there.

Paul said the believers had offered their gifts freely: **They were pleased to do it.** But do not forget the fact that it was a debt: **and indeed they owe it to them. For if the Gentiles have shared in the Jews' spiritual blessings, they owe it to the Jews to share with them their material blessings** (verse 27). In the early church those of a totally different culture were willing to give of their means to help the Jews who were the source of the salvation that had come to them.

Paul goes on: **So after I have completed this task and have made sure that they have received this fruit, I will go to Spain and visit you on the way** (verse 28). Isn't that interesting? Every penny that had been collected for famine relief went to famine relief. There was no cut for administration, overheads, or anything. That may have been the last time in the history of the church that a collection went one hundred percent to the cause for which it was raised. After performing such a helpful Christian act, Paul would be empowered by God to continue his ministry. **I know that when I come to you, I will come in the full measure of the blessing of Christ** (verse 29). Paul had no way of knowing the future and the condition which would surround his actual visit to this Roman Church. We know, however, from Acts 24:27; 28:11-31, that the 'full measure of the blessing of Christ' evidently included a hazardous journey, arriving bound in chains as a prisoner, and facing the prospect of death. But because the sufferings of this world are not worthy to be compared with the glory yet to be revealed, Paul could see past these trials to the rich ministry opportunities that took place. Christ was indeed pleased with Paul's faithfulness, and because of his grace, crowned Paul's labours with abundant blessing. Paul's extremity in Rome became God's opportunity to pour out his riches. How profound of Paul to know that true blessings are spiritual and not conditioned by earthly circumstances.

Paul finishes the chapter with an admonition and prayer: **I urge** you, brothers, by our Lord Jesus Christ and by the love of the Spirit, to join me in my struggle by praying to God for me. Pray that I may be rescued from the unbelievers in Judaea. Paul here appeals on behalf of all three members of the Holy Trinity that his brothers join him in prayer. His struggles were so considerable that he beseeched God the Father, God the Son and God the Holy Spirit to come to his rescue from those who sought his life. The subtleties of this construction also allow us to see that Paul appeals to the edifying work of the Spirit to bring about this prayer support. 'By the love of the Spirit' can mean 'by that love which the Spirit alone produces in us for one another', and so Paul beseeches them to so love him that they will pray earnestly for his well-being. So often was Paul rescued from moral evil and natural calamity that he knew his dependency upon the efficacious prayer of the saints.

Paul still has hostile enemies in and about Jerusalem. He needed prayer that he be kept safe from the unbelievers in Judaea. Further, Paul was still suspect among the Jews in Jerusalem: and that my service in Jerusalem may be acceptable to the saints there. There were still those among the Christian population of Jerusalem who didn't trust this man who at one time distinguished himself by persecuting the church of Christ.

So that by God's will I may come to you with joy and together with you be refreshed. The God of peace be with you all. Amen (verses 32,33). Notice again how Paul speaks of God as the source of great virtues. He had spoken earlier in this chapter of God being the source of patience and of encouragement. Later in the chapter he spoke of God as being the source of our hope, and now he declares that God is the source of peace.

6
PERSONAL GREETINGS
(16:1-27)

The last chapter of Romans is an important postscript. It includes the personal greetings that the apostle gives to the Christian community in Rome. I for one am very glad that this list of greetings is included in the text, because it reveals much about Paul's personal relationships with people. And it reveals little insights about the kind of people that built the first century Christian church. There is much for our instruction and for our edification, things of great significance I believe for some of the controversies in the church.

The first person who receives a commendation from Paul is a woman: **I commend to you our sister Phoebe, a servant of the church in Cenchrea. I ask you to receive her in the Lord in a way worthy of the saints and to give her any help she may need from you, for she has been a great help to many people, including me** (verses 1,2). Her name *Phoebe* comes from *Phoebus* which is a derivative of the Greek name for the god Apollo. Many Christians retained their names when they were converted to the Faith, even though many of these names were derived from false gods or from pagan deities, because by this time the names had lost their particular religious significance.

What does Paul mean when he writes that she is a servant of the church of Cenchrea? The word that is translated 'servant' is *diakonon*, from which we derive the word 'deacon'. It is rightly translated 'servant', because deacons and deaconesses were involved in a servant ministry. Whether or not Phoebe held a formal office in the church is at the heart of much controversy in certain denominations in the twentieth century. One thing we know is that Phoebe offered a ministry of sorts in the church at Cenchrea, and Paul's command here is that she should be received in the Lord's name. Cenchrea was a section of Corinth; a church had been organised there and Phoebe was very much involved in its work.

Greet Priscilla and Aquila, my fellow-workers in Christ Jesus. They risked their lives for me. Not only I but all the churches of the Gentiles are grateful to them. Greet also the church that meets at their house (verses 3-5). Priscilla and Aquila were a very important part of Paul's entourage. The name Priscilla is the diminutive form of Prisca, her formal name. It is similar to the difference between Frank and Frankie. Priscilla and Aquila were a husband and wife team that are frequently referred to in Scripture. They are mentioned in the eighteenth chapter of Acts as having left Rome for Corinth because of the edict of Claudius that brought persecution to the city. There, they met Paul and then went with him to Ephesus where they stayed after Paul had continued his journey to Jerusalem. Obviously they had returned to Rome and were there as Paul writes this letter. We don't know what Paul is referring to when he says that they risked their lives for him, but whatever that occasion was it provoked profound gratitude in Paul. And not only Paul, but the churches also recognised that Priscilla and Aquila had done some heroic act of bravery.

In the New Testament, churches often met in some individual's home, such as those who assembled in the house of Aquila and Priscilla. This gives us a clue as to the social and economic status of Priscilla and Aquila. They were tent-makers, and had some financial independence. It is probable that Priscilla and Aquila were somewhat prosperous in their business, which enabled them to have a rather large house, and they gave the use of that house as a place of worship for the early Christian community.

Greet my dear friend Epenetus, who was the first convert to Christ in the province of Asia (verse 5). Other versions say that he was the firstfruits of Achaia. This creates a problem because in 1 Corinthians 16:15, Paul refers to the household of Stephanas as being the firstfruits of Achaia. How do we reconcile the fact that two people were given the honour of being the firstfruits of Achaia? The term 'Asia' appears in some manuscripts and if it is the original rendering, there is no contradiction. One was the first convert in Asia, and the other was the first convert in Achaia. But in any case, even if the other rendering is correct, there is still no problem because it is possible that Epenetus was the first individual of the household of Stephanas that is cited in 1 Corinthians.

Greet Mary, who worked very hard for you (verse 6). We do not know who this Mary is, other than that she is one who has worked very hard. There were many in the early church by that name.

Greet Andronicus and Junias, my relatives who have been in prison with me. They are outstanding among the apostles, and they were in Christ before I was (verse 7). He refers to these people as kinsmen and fellow prisoners. There is a big question here about the name *Junias*. Some translate it *Junias*, others *Junia*. It is doubtful that we can know for sure whether it was a man or woman, because the form that Paul uses here, Junion, could be either male or female. If it is a male, the name is Junias, if it is a woman, it is Junia. It usually is taken as the female, and possibly refers to the wife or the sister of Andronicus.

What does 'outstanding among the apostles' mean? Does it mean that Andronicus and Junias were well known apostles or they were well known by the apostles? The significance of that difference is this: if Junias is a woman, and a well known apostle, then that raises questions about whether or not women were elevated to the rank of apostle. This has great consequences for the debate about women's ordination, because if it could be shown that a woman was ordained to the office of apostle, then that would settle the controversy once and for all. I am persuaded that the correct interpretation is that they were noted *by* the apostles. But even if it meant that they were distinguished *among* the apostles, it does not necessarily mean that either of them had the formal role of an apostle, because the New Testament does speak of a ministry of apostleship in a less formal sense than the technical sense that is given to the Twelve.

Greet Ampliatus, whom I love in the Lord. Greet Urbanus, our fellow worker in Christ, and my dear friend Stachys. Greet Apelles, tested and approved in Christ. Greet those who belong to the household of Aristobulus. Greet Herodion, my relative. Greet those in the household of Narcissus who are in the Lord

(verses 8-11). Not much is said about these people except that they are cited for their labour and for their work in Christ.

Greet Tryphena and Tryphosa, those women who work hard in the Lord. Greet my dear friend Persis, another woman who has worked very hard in the Lord. Greet Rufus, chosen in the Lord, and his mother, who has been a mother to me, too. Greet Asyncritus, Phlegon, Hermes, Patrobas, Hermas and the brothers with them. Greet Philologus, Julia, Nereus and his sister, and Olympas and all the saints with them (verses 12-15). We see something of the pastoral heart of the apostle here. He knows some of the believers by name, and he takes the time to send personal greetings to these people who have been so precious to him throughout his ministry.

Greet one another with a holy kiss. All the churches of Christ send greetings (verse 16). The holy kiss is obviously of Eastern origin, a commonplace function in the Orient, and it continued for a very long time in the early church. We know for example that, in the third century, Christians still greeted each other with a holy kiss. It was usually experienced after a time of prayer and before the celebration of the Lord's supper. The brothers kissed the brothers and sisters, and the sisters kissed the sisters and brothers.

I urge you, brothers, to watch out for those who cause divisions and put obstacles in your way that are contrary to the teaching you have learned. Keep away from them (verse 17). There is great emphasis in the New Testament on maintaining the unity of the body of Christ. Many times in church controversies, if somebody protests an action or a teaching of the church, they are immediately silenced with the charge that they are being divisive. But Paul says here that the ones who cause divisions and who upset people's faith, are those who go against the apostolic teaching. When apostolic teaching is attacked within the church, it is our duty to stand up for the truth of the Scriptures, and if a division comes as a result of it, the cause of that division must be laid to rest on the shoulders of those who deviate from the apostolic truth. It is not just a case of deciding who is the majority and who is the minority. Those responsible for dividing the body of Christ will be judged by God, and that judgment will be against those who have departed from the apostolic teaching. If you ever are involved in bringing divisions in any way in the body of Christ, you had better make very sure that you are standing on the side of the Scripture and not against the Scriptures.

For such people are not serving our Lord Christ, but their own appetites. By smooth talk and flattery they deceive the minds of naive people (verse 18). Beware of crafty, clever, false teachers.

Paul knew that the Roman believers had a very credible testimony but he was concerned that Satan would use false teachers to divert them: **Everyone has heard about your obedience, so I am full of joy over you; but I want you to be wise about what is good, and innocent about what is evil** (verse 19). However, if they remained faithful to Christ, he would give them help and grace: **The God of peace will soon crush Satan under your feet. The grace of our Lord Jesus be with you.**

Timothy, my fellow-worker, sends his greetings to you, as do Lucius, Jason and Sosipater, my relatives.

I, Tertius, who wrote down this letter, greet you in the Lord (verses 20-22). Paul seldom wrote his own epistles by hand. He almost always used a secretary. He would dictate his letters and one of his helpers would write them on his behalf.

Gaius, whose hospitality I and the whole church here enjoy, sends you his greetings.

Erastus, who is the city's director of public works, and our brother Quartus send you their greetings (verses 23, 24).

The book of Romans ends appropriately with a doxology: **Now to him who is able to establish you by my gospel and the proclamation of Jesus Christ, according to the revelation of the mystery hidden for long ages past, but now revealed and made known through the prophetic writings by the command of the eternal God, so that all nations might believe and obey him – to the only wise God be glory for ever through Jesus Christ! Amen** (verses 25-27).

Are you alarmed by Paul's use of the phrase 'my gospel'? Was that not an arrogant usurping of Christ's gospel for his own? Of course not. What is here revealed is the incredible identification of 'Paul' with the 'gospel'. So closely united is Paul's mind, heart, will and ministry with that of Christ that he can legitimately call it his gospel. Far from being an offence, this language attests to Paul as an agent of revelation of the gospel of Christ. But even beyond his role as an agent of revelation, it manifests the wholehearted obedience and devotion to the gospel which was characteristic of all of Paul's ministry. Wrongly understood, this phrase would constitute a stealing of glory from Christ. But God will share his glory with no man - not even the apostle Paul. To God alone be the glory because of *his* gospel is what Paul stresses here in the closing doxology.

The theme of the Protestant Reformation which was born through a study of the book of Romans was the theme *sola deo gloria* - to God alone the glory. God alone is worthy of our honour and all the glory, dominion and power. It is God who is glorified in this epistle, and Paul concludes the epistle with this final admonition: 'Give glory to God'. We glorify God the Father through our obedience and devotion to God the Son who has redeemed us from the curse of the law.